My Glory I WILL NOT GIVE TO ANOTHER

My Glory I WILL NOT GIVE TO ANOTHER

A STUDY IN THE ABSOLUTE SOVEREIGNTY OF GOD

AUGUSTINE VS. PELAGIUS | REFORMATION VS. ROMAN CATHOLICISM
CALVINISM VS. ARMINIANISM

PAVEL STEIGER

Published by Calvary Press Publishing

ISBN: 978-187-973-7990

All Bible quotes are from the English Standard Version 2001 ESV except where stated otherwise.

www.calvarypress.com

PRINTED IN USA

THEME

"Behold, I have refined you, but not as silver; I have tried [bachar = to choose, elect, decide for] *you in the furnace of affliction. For my own sake, for my own sake, I do it, for how should my name be profaned?*

My glory I will not give to another.

"Listen to me, O Jacob, and Israel, whom I called! I am he;I am the first, and I am the last ..." (Isa. 48:10-12)

The Bible does not present the world with yet another of the world's many religions. Its message is unique, God-centered, and focused exclusively on the glorification of God. According to Scripture:

GOD IS THE CAUSE AND PURPOSE OF SALVATION—GOD CHOOSES MAN

"You did not choose me, but I chose you and appointed you that you should go and bear fruit and that your fruit should abide, ..." *(John 15:16a)*

Then Isaiah is so bold as to say, "I have been found by those who did not seek me; I have shown myself to those who did not ask for me. ..." *(Rom. 10:20)*

In contrast, all the world's religions—including many formally Christian religions—are man-centered. At their most basic level, they are 180 degrees away from the Bible. They share the same common denominator—without exception:

MAN IS THE CAUSE AND PURPOSE OF SALVATION—MAN CHOOSES GOD

CONTENT

PART III | CHRIST'S LIMITED, EFFICACIOUS, PURPOSEFUL REDEMPTION

PART IV | IRRESISTIBLE GRACE, EFFICACIOUS CALLING OF THE SPIRIT

PART V | THE PERSEVERANCE OF THE SAINTS, THE PRESERVATION OF THE SAINTS BY GOD

CONCLUSION

SUPPLEMENTS

ENDORSEMENTS

Before we ever affirm a man's teaching, we should affirm his living. What qualifies Pavel to write on the glory of God? It's that he has lived to the glory of God. He has glorified God by loving his wife for sixty years, loving his family, loving his church, evangelizing his lost neighbors, and most of all, loving the Lord Jesus Christ. Pavel's work *"My Glory I Will Not Give to Another"* is not merely a work of the head but the result of a burning passion to see God exalted above the heavens (Ps. 108:5). If you desire and pray for your vision of the greatness and glory of God to increase, if you want your theology to result in doxology, meditate on the truths in this book. Your prayers will be answered.

MARCUS DENNY, *missionary church planter, Kladno, Czech Republic*

Many Christians struggle with the doctrines of predestination and divine election. Do these doctrines mean that people are just robots? What practical value do these teachings have for my daily life? Why does the Bible even teach them since they're so confusing? In *"My Glory I Will Not Give to Another,"* Pavel Steiger answers these perplexing questions with clarity and depth. Read and chew on this book. Your spiritual life will be richer for it.

STEVE COLE, *Retired Pastor, Flagstaff Christian Fellowship, AZ, USA*

In an age of theological shallowness, it is refreshing to see a work that is theologically accurate and clear. This book is a wonderful resource for both the Czech and Slovak believers but now is also available to the English speaking world. I recommend this book to you as it will give you a solid biblical foundation in how God saves his people.

GEOFF VOLKER, *Director of In-Depth Studies. A pastor at New Covenant Bible Fellowship, Gilbert, AZ*

Looking at biblical truth from a different cultural context can serve to broaden and deepen our understanding and commitment to it. Pavel's book winsomely marshals biblical support for the sovereignty of God in salvation and engages with other Christian concepts from creation to church councils–deftly communicating their implications in an increasingly global Christian community. As so much quality Christian material has been translated and published from English to Czech, let us in turn appreciate and learn from brothers and sisters in the heart of Europe—the epicenter of the Reformation.

PETER SMITH, *Missionary in the Czech Republic for nearly 20 years, now pastor of Hope in Christ Bible Church, Berkley, MI.*

ABOUT THE WRITER

Pavel Steiger was born in 1941 in Prague, then Czechoslovakia. From the age of 8 to 12 he was a Catholic altar boy. After his father was forced to work in the mines of Ostrava in 1952, religion gradually disappeared from the family. Pavel graduated from the Mining University, specializing in geological exploration and deep drilling. In 1969 he left for the USA with his wife Klara and two sons. In 1978 God unconditionally gifted him with "Salvation and faith." Until the age of 49, he worked in the USA and Indonesia as an engineer for one of the largest oil companies, ARCO, now British Petroleum. In 1986, he began recording Christian programs for Trans World Radio in Jakarta, which was broadcast on shortwave from Monte Carlo. When so many listeners began requesting a transcript of these programs that correspondence became overwhelming, in January 1989 Pavel and Klara began mailing a small self-published version entitled "The Struggle for the Soul," which ended up reaching Czechoslovakia in the most bizarre way. In January 1990, Pavel left his professional career to become a radio missionary with his wife, for HCJB World Radio. After two years in Quito, Ecuador, and the USA, the Steigers returned to their native Czechoslovakia in April 1992, having lived as expatriates for 23 years. For the next 22 years they prepared and recorded radio programs for both HCJB and TWR. The Steigers are the founders of "Wrestling for the Soul" magazine, which has been in print since 1989. They continue to write, translate, teach, and speak at conferences.

ACKNOWLEDGEMENTS

First, I thank our God and Savior for drawing me to Christ and teaching me His Scriptures with the help of the Holy Spirit. Without the Scriptures, I could not have written a single comma—neither an iota nor a dot.

I would like to express my gratitude to all those who have given me spiritual support and those who have made grammatical corrections and theological comments on the original and translated manuscripts:

IN ENGLISH VERSION

Wilma Bell
Joseph M. Bianchi
Steve Cole
Becky Johnson
Sonya and Peter Smith
Geoff Volker
Adrian Wheeler
Kaye Woodward

IN CZECH VERSION

Miroslava Čejková
Daniel Heczko
Jaroslav Kernal
Radek Kolařík
Štěpán Rucki
Klara Steiger
Jan Suchý

FOREWORD

The Czech Republic is not known for its theological works of substance. But this particular work by Pavel Steiger is a pleasant exception to the rule. He lays out in very readable form what the Bible has to say regarding how God saves. His subject matter is what is called the "Doctrines of Grace" or the "Five Points of Calvinism." But in clear language he is just describing how God saves those who believe in the Gospel message of the work of Jesus Christ through his death and resurrection.

The current common belief is that salvation is truly left up to the individual and the exercise of his free choice. But Pavel makes a compelling case that biblically this is just not so. Man does indeed choose to believe, but God is the one who causes the man to choose to believe. From beginning to end our salvation through the work of Jesus on the cross is all in the hands of a Sovereign Lord. Pavel is not denying that we have a role to play in our salvation, but he is simply stating that our role is controlled by the God of heaven and earth.

I thoroughly recommend this book to you. It is a unique contribution to the current biblical discussion that is very much needed in our day of shallow religious thinking. It is indeed worth the read!

—Geoff Volker, Director of In-Depth Studies.
A pastor at New Covenant Bible Fellowship,
Gilbert, AZ

HOW TO READ THIS BOOK

1. Do not skip, but carefully read all the Bible verses quoted, as they usually contain comments and explanations in square brackets. Even the "greatest" Bible scholar, after reading a passage for the thousandth time, may suddenly discover a truth he had never seen before. Contemplating very familiar verses can build us up in Christ.

2. Each of the five parts of the book deals with one of the five points of God's absolute sovereignty in salvation. The various verbal stylizations of these five points evolved gradually from conclusions of the Synod of Dort, which countered the five points of the Remonstrance. Thus, these five points of God's absolute sovereignty in salvation appear in much theological literature with numerous modifications, depending upon the author and the time. Note that the variety of their verbal expression has the same essence. Today these points have become known as the five points of Calvinism. My own understanding of these five articles differs in wording, though not in substance, from expressions I have encountered in reformed literature.

Because some points are interwoven in certain verses, the repetition of certain principles and verses is unavoidable. It becomes virtually impossible to delineate each point independently in a precise way for they all build upon each other and, in a larger context, permeate the entire gospel. Repetition is therefore necessary in framing each of the five parts alone and thus in a way that can be read independently of the others. For the greatest clarity, I recommend that this book be read sequentially, page by page—just as we learn to add and subtract first, before moving on to multiplication and division, and then finally, after reaching the highest levels, to extraction of the second and third root.

3. The book ends with three SUPPLEMENTS, which are not referred to as chapters because they are not an essential part of the book. The supplements answer questions that the more thoughtful reader may have after reading all 18 previous chapters.

Thank you for your understanding.

—Pavel Steiger

1

INTRODUCTION

BEFORE WE READ

SCRIPTURE PRECEDES EXPERIENCE

Some readers will find this book too long, too theological, too doctrinal, too scriptural, too rational, too analytical, etc. Those readers would certainly prefer a shorter talk with more feeling, more emotion, less theology, more extra-biblical experience of the Holy Spirit, more meditation, mysticism, etc. I am fully aware that God and His purposes cannot be fully or even systematically categorized, however, all of Scripture and all of God's created visible and invisible universe and history are part of one great system. Where there is no system, there is inevitable confusion—a system is an ordered whole. Man cannot act except either to communicate everything objectively and systematically, as Adam named the animals and birds (Gen. 2:19-20), or to react subjectively according to his feelings. Scripture, inspired in all things by the Holy Spirit, must always be primary; emotional experience must be secondary. Scripture is objective, communicable to others, hence it is the cause. Personal spiritual experience is subjective, not transferable to others, and therefore the effect. This is confirmed by these verses:

"For so the Lord has commanded us, saying, 'I have made you a light for the Gentiles, that you may bring salvation to the ends of the earth' [Scripture, the gospel is the objective cause]. *And when the Gentiles heard this, they began rejoicing and glorifying the word of the Lord, and as many as were appointed to eternal life believed* [subjective, joyful consequence, experience]*"* (Acts 13:47-48).

How I would love to share with the readers all the incommunicable things I have subjectively experienced with my Creator and Savior, God the Holy Spirit, while writing this book. Every new joy, every new inner excitement, every new rest in Him, every new knowledge, all came from the Scriptures. Let the Lord Jesus Christ Himself be our example. When tempted by Satan in the wilderness, He did not delve into some subjective, mysterious mysticism or metaphysics, but He objectively disarmed Satan three times with the Scriptures: *"And Jesus answered him, '**It is written**, Man shall not live by bread alone.'" "And Jesus answered him, '**It is written**, You shall worship the Lord your God, and him only shall you serve.'" "And Jesus answered him, '**It is said**, You shall not put the Lord your God to the test.'"* (Luke 4:4,8,12). In individuals, as in churches, where the opposite is true, where people are led primarily by extra-biblical experiences that are man-centered, biblical doctrines become distorted, and there is blatant doctrinal confusion. But God is not a God of confusion (1 Cor. 14:33). Where Scripture is relegated to the back burner, extra-Biblical, subjective, mystical, metaphysical, personal, self-centered, man-centered philosophies and meditations that serve no one come to the fore. No gift that the Holy Spirit bestows upon His promised ones is meant for the benefit of the recipient alone, but rather that the recipient might use God's gift to serve others. *"As each has received a gift, use it to serve one another, as good stewards of God's varied grace"* (1 Pet. 4:10).

LET US COMMUNICATE WITHOUT EMOTION

Communication is not easy. Two people may use the same words while intending that the words mean different things. People understand words in their own way. Before a speaker can clarify his intended meaning, the emotions of his hearers can get so out of tune that they lose understanding and give up interest. Considering religion, for example, every person without exception holds some religious belief, although the agnostic and atheist might disagree with this statement.

The agnostic believes that since the existence or non-existence of God can be neither empirically/experientially known or proven, nor disproved, he therefore cannot hold to any religious system (as, for example, those listed below). But this line of reasoning would suggest that he also could not hold to an atheistic view that denies God. The theory of evolution cannot be empirically/experientially, known, proven, or disproved. In the view of the agnostic, it would also have to be unknowable, unprovable, or irrefutable. The agnostic defeats himself with his ambivalent logic. How does he know that he cannot know? If he does not know, how does he know that he does not know? Such a position becomes rationally untenable. But one thing the agnostic knows for sure—he does not want to know if there is a God. Agnosticism is a ruse, a quasi-intellectual cloak disguising factual atheism, for the agnostic does not find within himself the social courage to openly declare his atheism. Every "sincere" agnostic—there really is no such thing—should put this book down at this point, because "knowing" the unknowable, unprovable, and unfalsifiable is a waste of time. He should likewise put down any atheistic book that denies the existence of God. A true agnostic should abandon any discussion that deals with the origin of all that exists, whether from a naturalistic, materialistic point of view, in which matter is the primary cause of all, or from a supernaturalistic, idealistic point of view, in which, to the contrary, intelligence, idea, thought, plan, are the primary cause of all. He should not discuss anything that is unknowable, but this would exclude him from society altogether. Therefore, there is no such thing as a true agnostic.

Even atheism is a form of religion because it cannot exist without the existence of false gods. The atheist must create and imagine a deniable god in his own image in order to have something to deny. Matter and time are his god, an idol which he cannot but personify and speak of as an "intelligent being." He does not consider that just as there cannot be many false monies without one true money, or many lies without one truth, so his false gods cannot exist without one true God, for all cannot be false. If there really were no God, man could not even have the concept of God. What does not exist could not even enter his mind. What exists comes to mind either in one true form or, because of sin, in many false deformations.

Following is a list of the seven standard religions, none of which can be empirically, experientially, or experimentally proven or disproved:

1. There is no God—**atheism.**
2. There are multiple gods, so necessarily limited—**polytheism**.
3. God is limited and part of creation—**panentheism**.
4. God is limited and not part of creation—**finite deism**.
5. God is unlimited and part of creation—**pantheism**.
6. God is unlimited, not part of creation, and does not interfere with creation—**deism**.
7. God is unlimited, not part of creation, but intervenes in creation—**theism**.

Theism also includes the "three" basic monotheistic faiths—Judaism, Christianity, and Islam. Judaism and Christianity, in terms of Scripture the Old and New Testaments, are one "creature," in which Judaism represents infancy, immaturity, i.e., a temporary state—the "caterpillar" that pupated into Christ. Out of the "cocoon" came Christianity, the now adult, final state—the "butterfly" capable of reproduction. Islam, six centuries younger, is a distortion of both the Old and New Testaments, mixed with Gnosticism and a plethora of extra-biblical Muhammadan "prophecies."

Consistent with the delineation of the first six standard religions, in this book I will always use the term "religion" to refer to unbiblical belief. I will not identify different interpretations of the Old and New Testaments (number seven, biblical Judaism and Christianity) as "religion" but rather as theology, relating to the Word of God.

Within Christianity itself, there are many theologies that divide rather than unite believers. In order to avoid disagreements, many Christians come to believe that a simple faith in Jesus Christ suits them better than a deeper, theological knowledge of Scripture. However, even an individual's simplest faith is nothing more than his personal theology that defines his understanding of God. Within the ranks of Christians, there are groups of believers who do not wish to articulate or name their own confession of faith. In this case, they are often named by their opponents, seldom in a flattering way. We cannot do without theology any more than we can do without names, words, and the definition of their meanings; otherwise, all understanding ends. Different interpretations of Scripture, different theologies, guide and define our view of God in either positive or negative ways.

One of the pillars of monotheistic Christian, biblical faith is the doctrine of God's sovereignty, especially in matters of election and salvation. The doctrine of God's absolute sovereignty permeates all of Scripture, from Genesis to Revelation. Yet since Adam, many men and even theologians have doubted God's absolute sovereignty and holiness. This book rests firmly on the side of believers in Christ who, based upon Scripture, hold God's sovereignty and holiness above all else. God has unlimited power and the right to do with His creation as He pleases (Isa. 46:10) because His will is holy. His every decision is perfect, irrevocable, and beyond human judgment. This book refutes Christians who believe that they can limit God by their internal, inherent, "free," natural will even though, according to Scripture, the human will is sinful and corrupt.

LET US SEARCH THE SCRIPTURES

A.W. Tozer challenges us to test all the insights, interpretations, and conclusions we hear or read in Christian literature of various denominations. So, ask yourself how a new insight, interpretation, article, book, sermon, teaching, etc., is affecting your current relationship:[1]

1. To God—does it add more glory to Him, is God seen as more sovereign? If not, doubt it!
2. To Christ—is He for you the only way, the truth, and the life? If not, doubt it!
3. To the Holy Scriptures—does it transform you, help you to grow in knowledge, cause you to trust it more and to see more clearly the authorship of the Holy Spirit and His infallibility? If not, doubt it!
4. To yourself—does bowing to this truth make you humbler, more dependent on God, and more aware of your sinfulness? If not, doubt it!
5. To other Christians—do you love them more, even though

1 The concept of the seven following points was taken from *"Man - The Dwelling Place of God - How to Try the Spirits"* by A.W. Tozer; https://bibleportal.com/devotional/morning-evening-aw-tozer/man-the-dwelling-place-of-god-how-to-try-the-spirits-0224

they disagree with you on a certain interpretation of Scripture? If not, doubt it!

6. To the world and to the people of the world—does this new knowledge increase your aversion to the values on which the world is based? Do you desire to share the Gospel with them, do you care more about them, and do you love them more? If not, doubt it!
7. To sin—does this new knowledge increase your aversion to sin? If not—doubt it!

Only the Spirit of God can ensure that your mind, will, and heart remain open to what He teaches you. I pray to God that none of you will be subject to what John G. Reisinger so aptly expressed:

> *When we adopt a comprehensive 'system' of beliefs and are convinced that our system is correct, we automatically close our minds to any enlightenment or change. From that point forward, all of our study will consist of looking for further proof of what we already believe. The Word of God alone will no longer be either our sole guide or our final authority.*[2]

Dialogue, understanding, and communication are the most important elements of personal, social, economic, and religious life. There are many different doctrines and principles in the Church that divide us denominationally. We do not have to agree on everything, but we must not suspect, slander, condemn, or alienate each other. Let us seek God's truth together, reflecting on the understanding of Scripture that comes from within our own ranks as well as that of brethren who have gone before us in Christ. Let us pay attention to what is in the hearts and minds of both sides of a theological divide before we jump to conclusions and pronounce judgment. Otherwise, we may pronounce judgment against something that has not even crossed the mind of the other party.

2 https://crosstocrown.org/books/tablets/front-matter/introduction/

It is my prayer and desire that the following pages will shed light into the darkness that has spread through Christendom over the issue of God's sovereign election to salvation.

HUMANISM IS ALIEN TO GOD

SOCIAL HUMANISM

In brief, humanism is a human-centered philosophy which sees man as the center of everything.

> ***Humanism*** *is a movement in philosophy and ethics that emphasizes the value and actions of human beings; individually, collectively, and generally, it privileges individual thought and evidence* (rationalism, empiricism) *over established dogma or belief (fideism)*[3].

RELIGIOUS HUMANISM

Although the term humanism did not appear until the Renaissance, we can see its origins in the Garden of Eden. Adam and Eve longed to be like God after, Satan offered them that "opportunity." Instead of relying on God to be their God, they wanted to make man the center of existence (Gen. 3:5). Humanism is the deification of man, and Adam succumbed to its lure. In so doing, he willfully and deliberately obeyed Satan, thus bringing all mankind into Satan's sphere of influence. Satan has deceived sin-enslaved mankind to the point of humans exalting their own selfhood and independence from God. Mankind's pursuit is toward human knowledge, human judgment, and human decisions in matters of good and evil.

For two decades now, I have been extremely concerned about the spread of a human-centered, a humanistic-philosophical, man-centered interpretation of Scripture in evangelical and Reformed

3 Wikipedia

churches around the world. I am concerned about how evangelical Christians are moving away from the foundations upon which the Reformation of the 15th and 16th centuries was built. I am concerned as I observe believers moving away from Augustine's, Hus's, Luther's, Calvin's, Owen's, and Spurgeon's interpretation of Scripture. I am concerned about how the Evangelical and Reformed churches are succumbing to a non-violent, creeping anti-Reformation stance as they step back into the theological arms of Roman Catholicism. This is especially true with regard to the doctrine of salvation, i.e., soteriology.

The way we interpret and apply Scripture is based on our answer to the questions of who man is and who is God. We will understand these questions quite differently if we start from a humanistic view of man, that man is flawed but essentially good and redeemable, or if we start from the biblical teaching that man is evil in his fallen nature and irredeemable in himself.

Without exception, all revolutions, secular or religious, inspired by a humanistic ideology of the possible redemption of mankind, have done more harm than good. The saying that the road to hell is paved with good intentions is very apt because the good intentions of natural man do not exist in the realm of spirituality. Bloody wars and revolutions have only one cause—man covets the goods or privileges of another (James 4:1-4). Apologetic ideologies, whether religious or secular, are invented only to obscure the real cause, which is the depraved, lustful, greedy heart.

If the reader reads this book with a humanistic view of imperfect but essentially good and redeemable human beings, he will be fundamentally at odds with its contents. If, on the other hand, he reads this book with a God-centered, God-fearing, biblical view of inherently depraved and irredeemable human beings, then he will find it an ally. Such a reader will see a holy God and sinful man after the fall of Adam through a biblical, antediluvian lens: *"The LORD saw that* ***the wickedness of man was great in the earth, and that every intention of the thoughts of his heart was only evil continually"*** (Gen. 6:5). God never took human depravity and wickedness—humanistic and self-centered—lightly. Therefore, in His holy wrath, God justly wiped out all land creatures in a worldwide flood except for the chosen eight human beings and the few animals who survived in the ark. No other natural or man-made catastrophe has been of such epochal and devastating proportions. Post-flood mankind, and by extension, present-day mankind, is no less self-centered, no less humanistic, than pre-flood mankind: *"And when the LORD smelled the pleasing aroma, the LORD said in his heart, 'I will never again curse the ground because of man,* ***for the intention of man's heart is evil*** *from his youth. Neither will I ever again strike down every living creature as I have done'"* (Gen. 8:21).

Such is a holy God's view of man from the Fall of Adam; such is the reality of the human heart to this day. Though every thought of man's depraved heart is evil from his youth, and though man deserves death by God's holy law, God chose to send His Son, Jesus Christ, to come and seek and save His lost people (Luke 19:10). This is God's unconditional grace, His Glory and goodness at its best (Ex. 33:19). When we understand the reality of the human heart and the absolute holiness of God according to Scripture, we will never again be troubled by the humanistic question of why God allows evil. Rather, on the basis of God's Scriptures, we should ask ourselves: "Why is a holy God so patient with us? Why does He allow so much good to happen? We all deserve to be flooded as in the days of Noah!" This is the right, God-centered, God-focused question, which is as far from religious humanism and man-centeredness as the East is from the West.

FOCUSING ON MAN DISTORTS SCRIPTURE

God hates human self-centeredness (Rom. 8:7). Notice how humanistic, man-centered, quasi-biblical platitudes have deeply infiltrated global Christianity. The idea that God loves all sinners with the same saving love, only hating their sin, is widespread today. Such clichés rob God of His last (and therefore first) word. Scripture clearly declares that anyone who is not in Christ is under the wrath of God: *"Whoever believes in the Son has eternal life; whoever does not obey the Son shall not see life, but the wrath of God remains on him"* (John 3:36).

Let me tentatively illustrate this central issue discussed in this book with a short, wonderful passage from Romans 5:8-11:

> "[8] *but God shows his love* ***for us*** *in that while* ***we were*** *still sinners, Christ died* ***for us.*** [9] *Since, therefore,* ***we have*** *now been justified by his blood, much more* ***shall we be*** *saved by him from the wrath of God.* [10] *For if while* ***we were*** *enemies* ***we were*** *reconciled to God by the death of his Son, much more, now that* ***we are*** *reconciled,* ***shall we be*** *saved by his life.* [11] *More than that,* ***we*** *also rejoice in God through* ***our*** *Lord Jesus Christ, through whom* ***we have*** *now received reconciliation."*

First let us examine this passage through a humanistic Christian lens that applies God's saving love and the Cross of Christ to "all men without exception." So we will replace the personal pronouns "us, we, our" in this biblical text (that is, for the people of God, the Church, those whom Christ has justified by the shedding of His blood, including the writer of this letter, the apostle Paul) with the humanistic phrase "all men without exception:"

- [8] but God shows his love for ~~us~~ **all men without exception** in that while ~~we~~ **all men without exception** were still sinners, Christ died for ~~us~~ **all men without exception**.

- [9] Since, therefore, ~~we~~ **all men without exception** have now been justified by his blood, much more shall ~~we~~ **all men without exception** be saved by him from the wrath of God.
- [10] For if while ~~we~~ **all men without exception** were enemies ~~we~~ **all men without exception** were reconciled to God by the death of his Son, much more, now that ~~we~~ **all men without exception** are reconciled, shall ~~we~~ **all men without exception** be saved by his life.
- [11] More than that, ~~we~~ **all men without exception** also rejoice in God through ~~our~~ **all men without exception's** Lord Jesus Christ, through whom ~~we~~ **all men without exception** have now received reconciliation.

We can clearly see that by simply replacing those who are in Christ through His Cross with "all men without exception," utter folly has set in. Such a passage, based on the assumption that God shows the same saving love through Christ to all men without exception, would have to include absolutely everyone, no matter what they have believed or will believe, no matter how long they have lived or will live. Can all men without exception truly boast in God through Jesus Christ, that He has saved them from the wrath of God by the shedding of His blood? Test this absurdity on many other biblical texts by replacing the personal pronouns "us," and "we,"—referring to born-again Christians—with the phrase "all men without exception."

Biblical Christians, regardless of denomination, are not universalists. Surely Christians would agree that all people without exception, are not and will not be saved. Most people do not boast in God through Christ. Therefore, according to these verses (Rom. 5:8-11), Christ could not have died for them, could not have reconciled them to God, could not have saved them from the wrath of God, because God does not demonstrate His eternal Zionic saving love through Christ (John 12:15; 1 John 4:9) to all men without exception. He demonstrates it only to His own, to anyone who is a promised (not necessarily physical) descendant of Abraham, Isaac, and Jacob, without distinction of ethnicity: *"For the LORD has ransomed Jacob* [paid only for his promised line] *and has redeemed him from hands too strong for him* [Satan]. *They shall come* [Abraham's, hence Isaac's and Jacob's promised seed from among the Jews and Gentiles; Gen. 17:5-7; Ps. 22:24; Jer. 33:26] *and sing aloud on the height of Zion, and they shall be radiant over the goodness of the LORD, over the grain, the wine, and the oil, and over the young of the flock and the herd; their life shall be like a watered garden, and they shall languish no more"* (Jer. 31:11-12).

We will return to Rom. 5:8-11 at the end of this book to show how it contains the essence of the Reformation. These verses and others like them, if we look at them closely, will stir the emotions of many sincere Christians. Let us put aside our emotions, ask the Spirit of God for wisdom, and study the Scriptures without ceasing and without prejudice.

2

HISTORY OF THE DOCTRINE OF SALVATION (SOTERIOLOGY)

CALVINISM VERSUS ARMINIANISM

Let us not fear these "isms"—explaining them is not that difficult. Do not be swept away by cultural negativity concerning the doctrines of Calvinism until you have objectively judged them for yourself. The difference between Calvinism and Arminianism is simple and straightforward. In one sentence: "In Calvinism God chooses man, and in Arminianism man chooses God," with implications that follow from either position.

In Calvinism, rebirth—the resurrection of a spiritually dead person—is a unilateral, creative, sovereign work of God. Christ saved His people unconditionally, in accordance with the Father's will, and He accomplished this salvation on the Cross (John 19:30). God created within the born-again person a new heart and seeing eyes in giving him the gift of faith. He sets this born-again person on the path of doing God's will by sanctifying him through the Holy Spirit from the moment he was saved—all through God's unilateral, merciful power. This is monergism: *monos* = one; *ergon* = deed, work.

In Arminianism, regeneration is caused by the cooperation of God and man. On the Cross Christ made salvation possible for all people without exception, on the condition of their faith. Thus, it is a person's decision to accept or reject Christ's substitutionary sacrifice that causes His sacrifice on the Cross to become either efficacious or inefficacious. Such "salvation" is not complete; it is only potential, (i.e., possible). This is synergism: *syn* = together or simultaneously, *ergon* = act, work.

When this book mentions monergism, it is referring to God's unilateral, unconditional election and salvation (i.e., the doctrine of Calvinism). When synergism is mentioned, the reference is usually (not always) to conditional salvation in which God and man must work together (i.e., the doctrine of Arminianism), or the reference is to synergistic theological systems that preceded it. As you can see, this section could have been titled Monergism versus Synergism or Unconditional versus Conditional Salvation.

Neither Calvin nor Arminius was alive when their advocates borrowed their names to ascribe to these two soteriologies—the dead cannot defend themselves. By beginning Questions of God's Sovereignty with a cursory introduction to Calvinism and Arminianism, I do not intend to impose on others the theological system I hold, monergistic Calvinism. My prayer is that readers will clearly understand these two doctrines of salvation, these two soteriologies. We will examine why these two doctrines are diametrically opposed and cannot be harmonized, even partially. Which position the reader leans toward will be the sovereign work of the Holy Spirit.

Both views, monergistic and synergistic, were held by theological giants seventeen centuries ago. Their inclusion in one or the other theological system of salvation (soteriology) ought not be taken dogmatically. The theology of salvation of these giants went through changes as each man developed his position, shaped by the historical context of the time in which he lived. On the side of the unconditional, monergistic view of God's absolute sovereignty, we see names like Augustine, Thomas Aquinas, Prosper of Aquitaine, John Huss, Martin Luther, Philip Melanchthon (in the beginning), John Calvin, John Owen, Jonathan Edwards, Charles Spurgeon, and Arthur Pink. In recent times, we find Francis Schaeffer, Cornelius Van Til, and many others. On the side of the conditional, synergistic view of "free" human will, again with different theological shades, we find the Council of Trent and names like Pelagius, Cassian, James Arminius, Luis de Molina, Philip Melanchthon (toward the end), John Wesley, and Charles Finney. In more recent times, we find C. S. Lewis, Norman Geisler, Billy Graham, and others.

We ought not define truth by relying solely on human theological greats from one position or the other. Truth is determined by God's Scriptures, not by church councils, schools of thought, councils of elders, denominational founders, or theologically knowledgeable scholars. Even theological giants, men with whom few can compare, can and do err. Human knowledge is always partial—every Christian harbors some cherished "heresy" in his heart, if only we could discern it! How many things have you or I said or written, not about the spiritual realm only, that we later regretted, recanted, and apologized for? Since all humans are tainted by Adam's sin, let us respect one another, listen to each other, and seek answers together. This more gracious approach could ease the tension between advocates of God's absolute sovereign will and advocates of man's "free" natural will. It should be noted that we will find differences within the group that subscribes to monergism as well as the group that subscribes to synergism.

Personally, I share the view of Jonathan Edwards (1703-1758), who wrote:

> *I should not take it at all amiss to be called a Calvinist, for distinction's sake: though I utterly disclaim a dependence on Calvin, or believing the doctrines which I hold, because he believed and taught them, and cannot justly be charged with believing in everything just as he taught*[4].

But if my heart were to belittle brethren who hold the Arminian view, I would be guilty of sinful pride in being intolerant of people with whom I have held the same soteriological view for 18 years.

HISTORICAL CONTINUITIES

THE WIDER CONTEXT

Let us first examine this subject in a broader historical context to gain historical perspective. First, every system of theology must be evaluated with regard to its view of salvation, that is, how much of the salvation effort belongs to God and how much is man's. The faith in which God has the first and last word is God-centered, unique, and exclusive because this faith professes that God alone saves (monergism). All "religions" in which man has the last word are (more or less) man-centered, being mixture of divine and human, cooperating sovereignties in salvation (synergism).

Under the following headings, let us briefly study the historical development of salvation theology (soteriology), not along a time axis—from Christ to today—but along a "qualitative axis"—from man-centered, humanistic to a single God-centered soteriology in which God has the first and last word.

---

4 The Works of Jonathan Edwards, vol. I ed. Edward Hickman, (Edinburgh: The Banner of Truth Trust, 1974), p. clx. All citations from the Works refer to this edition. Works, I, p. 3.

PAGANISM AND MAN-CENTERED PSEUDO-CHRISTIANITY AND ITS SECTS

"Religious" people live in the belief that their behavior can contribute to their salvation, so they therefore perform good deeds and make sacrifices to please not only their deities but also powerful demons. The common denominator of salvation in both pagan and man-centered pseudo-Christian religions is that a person must fulfill certain conditions. Man's conditional cooperation with a god (or gods) will then lead to "salvation." Thus, without exception, in all "religious" systems, man seeks "divine" favor by wooing his god(s), expecting to be rewarded for his efforts with salvation. All these systems require the words "if I" or "when I"—if I do this or that, then my god(s) will reward me. There can be as many variations to this pattern as there are unsaved people.

Pantheists repay their karmic debt with good deeds. By their exemplary, divinely acceptable behavior, they redeem themselves to be born into a better existence in the next life. The woman may become a man, the poor a rich man, the sick a healthy man, the stupid a wise man, and so on. But if the pantheist increases his karmic debt by living irresponsibly, he may be born in the next life as a mosquito or a tree, for example. We see that the world is full of innumerable "ifs" and "whens," and the same can be true of any personal religion.

In man-centered religions, the condition of salvation is this: If through his inner, natural, fallen, Adamic will, a person opens his heart to a god (or to gods), then his god(s) will forgive. In other words:

1. god's forgiveness is possible when...
2. god's forgiveness is possible when you personally...
3. god's forgiveness is possible when you personally want it...

Salvation in man-centered pseudo-Christianity, very much like salvation in pagan religions, depends upon the "free" will of natural, fallen, sinful man making the right decision. If you personally accept the offered gift of salvation, you release God's hands, allowing and enabling Him to save you. All man-centered religions rely on man and god(s) working in cooperation with each other in the matter of salvation. Man must first take a fundamental step of faith before God is able to help him. But how is it possible for man to take this first step toward the true God when, ever since Adam, man has lived in the delusion that he is the center of knowledge, supposedly knowing what is good and what is evil (Gen. 3:5)?

Surely you have heard, and perhaps you've even believed, that God cannot impose His will on anyone; that man is not a puppet; that man has a "free" will and a conscience. God certainly has to respect this, doesn't He? So, He must wait to see how you will decide. Such a god is like an "equal" partner, (even like a buddy for the humanistically minded person). How absurd! If God were to give such respect the will of fallen, "free" humans in the matter of salvation, He could only plaintively long for the sinner as He waits to see how man, with his natural will, might handle His most precious gift, the crucified Christ. Such a God would be limited by man, longing to save all the souls of the world while hoping for man's cooperation, having died for all, to be reconciled to all. But sadly, so many people do not care about Him, and many even despise His sacrifice on the Cross. How disappointed such a God would have to be!

PELAGIANISM

The religion of "free" will in human nature first crept into the Church through the influence of corrupting pagan, Hellenistic, and humanistic philosophies. Pelagius (c. 350-418) brought to the Christian scene the most man-centered, humanistic religion of works regarding the doctrine of salvation ever introduced into Christianity. He saddled the Church with belief in the "free" will of natural man and consequently salvation on the condition "if you personally will..." Precursors of the Pelagian view of salvation can be traced back to Clement of Alexandria (c. 150-215). In the 3rd and 4th centuries, many church scholars espoused Pelagianism. A native of the British Isles, Pelagius was a contemporary of Augustine, with whom he completely diverged theologically, as shown below. Let's examine the building blocks of his theology of salvation, his soteriology, by reviewing the following table:

	SIN	GRACE	PREDESTINATION
PELAGIANISM	Adam's sin is not hereditary. If a person wants to, he can live without sin. Adam only set a bad example for mankind.	Grace is the result of human effort. Grace is when one comes to know Christ, when one follows His example.	Chosen by foreknowledge. God sees into the future and chooses those who do good.
IMPLICATIONS OF PELAGIANISM	Man is born innocent, as Adam was created; he is inherently good and redeemable.	Man can attain salvation without God's prevenient grace. Therefore, salvation is not a gift, but a merit.	Election depends on the actions of man.

During our visit to the Blue Mosque of Sultan Ahmed in Istanbul, we were given a beautiful color brochure on coated paper "What is Islam?" The article "Salvation in Islam" begins as follows:

> *In Islam every human being is born without sin; there is no original sin: ... No soul gets except what it is due, and no soul bears the burdens of another. ...* (Qur'an 6:164)

When the "prophet" Muhammad wrote the Qur'an, he was inspired not only by Judaism but also by Christianity, with all its contemporary distortions, such as the would-be Christian but essentially humanist philosophy of Pelagianism. Muhammad (c. 570-632) was born 150 years after Pelagius' death, so the tenets of Pelagianism were likely well known to Muhammad. The booklet continues:

> *Every human being is inspired by the knowledge of Allah and naturally gravitates towards Islam even before birth. Therefore, it is man's responsibility to seek Allah's guidance and keep his heart pure, free from corruption.*

What can I say? Perhaps as Luther said, the natural man is born a Pelagian, entering the world with Pelagian glasses on his nose. All humanity are Adam's offspring and therefore, of necessity, Pelagians. The theology in Islam lines up with the Pelagian theology of salvation regarding natural man.

I remember when I was about six years old, my grandfather's churchgoing neighbor used to tell me on holidays, "If you are good, you will go to heaven, but if you are bad, you will go to hell." This was not a child-rearing scare tactic, but a Pelagian view of salvation from a Catholic perspective, in line with the teachings of the Qur'an, in that "No soul gets except what it is due" (Qur'an 6:164). The idea of Adam's original sin offends people who are convinced that man comes into the world as a blank, uninscribed sheet of paper. Pelagius taught that man is born pure and innocent, with the same moral capacities that Adam had when he was created by God. Disregarding such Scriptures as Psalm 51:5, Pelagians believe that a child is born sinless—how could a tiny baby be filled with evil from conception?

The Church has always struggled with the influence of Pelagianism. Thanks to humanistic Enlightenment philosophy and secular psychology, today's Church is permeated with Pelagian elements. The dominant soteriology in today's churches says that the "free" will of natural man gives him the ability to choose or reject faith in Christ. The implication is that one person finds a kind of spiritual virtue within himself that gives him the ability to believe, while another person lacks this virtue. Grace and salvation are the result of this inner virtue as well as human willingness to follow Christ's example, which some exercise and others do not. If both faith and the ability to follow Christ's example precede salvation, then the Holy Spirit, who circumcises sinners' hearts, is limited by decisions of the fallen human will. All this, in spite of the words of Jesus Christ Himself, after Peter professed that Christ was the Messiah, the Son of the living God: *"And Jesus answered him, 'Blessed are you, Simon Bar-Jonah!* ***For flesh and blood has not revealed*** [your natural virtuous decision] *this to you* [that I am the Messiah, the Son of the living God], *but my Father who is in heaven'"* (Matt. 16:17). Peter believed Jesus Christ was the Messiah, the Son of the living God, because God the Father had revealed it to him, not because of his internal, rational, natural, intellectual reasoning and decision.

According to Pelagianism, saved people are so virtuous that they can mobilize a spiritual instinct for self-preservation through an act of faith. In contrast, the unsaved are so corrupt that they either do not understand or reject the call of the Holy Spirit. If that were the case, salvation would be determined by man. He would have something to boast about, and there could be no talk of God's gracious election.

If man is essentially good, if by his own efforts he can improve himself spiritually and morally, then man's need for Christ as Savior and the Spirit as Sustainer in salvation can recede to the point of vanishing interest. Michael S. Horton wrote:

> *The fact that recent polls indicate that 77% of the evangelicals today believe that human beings are basically good and 84% of these conservative Protestants believe that in salvation "God helps those who help themselves" demonstrates incontrovertibly that contemporary Christianity is in a serious crisis. No longer*

can conservative, "Bible-believing" evangelicals smugly hurl insults at mainline Protestants and Roman Catholics for doctrinal treason[5].

This is a shocking statement. If true, then it's possible that 77% of church-going evangelicals may be Pelagians, and their understanding with regard to the depths of natural man's soul is essentially the same as that of Islam. I witnessed first-hand, having lived in Indonesia for four years, that a significant number of Christians there considered Christianity to be on a par with Islam. At a meeting in Bratislava, Slovakia, I met a practicing, church-going Syrian Orthodox Christian who presented those in attendance with a Qur'an, as the equivalent of a supplement to the Bible. A member of a leading Czech evangelical denomination sent us this thoroughly Pelagian response:

The unbelief for which men are cast away from God is not some condition inherited from Adam, but a total neglect of the ability to believe.

In other words, Pelagians say man did not inherit from Adam the most basic sin of not believing in Christ (John 16:9), but he neglected his own salvation by an inner decision. He had the opportunity, but he rejected God's gift. Belief in man's decisive influence on salvation is not negligible in evangelical churches today, as evidenced by various manipulative and coercive methods of evangelism. If Christians do not pay sufficient attention to the sound teaching of Scripture, Pelagianism will continue to spread in our evangelical churches.

The more self-sufficient, self-confident, and independent humanity becomes, the more terrible will be the history God sovereignly allows. He allows willful men to act according to their "free" natural will. Sowing "good" and suppressing "evil" in the name of God but

5 https://www.onthewing.org/user/Her_Pelagianism_Horton.pdf

in a Pelagian context, will always end in disaster, for it is the ancient, primordial, destructive enslavement by the Devil—of Adam and Eve, and subsequently of all humanity: *"For God knows that when you eat of it* [the tree of the knowledge of good and evil] *your eyes will be opened, and you will be like God, knowing good and evil"* (Gen. 3:5). Man, who is a god unto himself from birth, acts willfully, deciding for himself what is good and what is evil. He has his own opinions, and he creates laws and religious systems that suit his "godly" needs and ideas. The perversity of Pelagian, would-be Christian doctrine and the inadequacy of the religious systems and philosophies it produces was confirmed by the words of our Lord Jesus Christ: *"And when Jesus heard it, he said to them, 'Those who are well* ['good' people] *have no need of a physician, but those who are sick* [sinful people]. *I came not to call the righteous, but sinners'"* (Mark 2:17).

The doctrine of Pelagius was first rejected by the Synod of Carthage in c. 418, then by the Ecumenical Council of Ephesus in c. 431, and then by the Second Synod of Orange in c. 529, which rejected Pelagianism as a heresy. Yet it is still alive and well today, in all denominations around the world.

SEMI-PELAGIANISM

Augustine was so convincing in the controversy between Augustine (c. 354-430) and Pelagius (c. 350-418) over fundamental issues of salvation theology that Pelagianism was challenged by many. Then Cassian (c. 360-435), a contemporary of both Augustine and Pelagius, established a doctrine of a kind of golden mean that is now called Semi-Pelagianism. In Semi-Pelagianism, the "free" will of the natural man is preserved in the spiritual realm, but the inheritance of Adam's sin was taken from the Augustinian teaching. Those who followed Cassian believed that the movement of the will, the need and desire to believe, comes from the nature of the human mind. It is our business to want to believe; it is God's business to make salvation possible. Semi-Pelagianism goes a tiny step further. It makes a slight departure from Pelagian human-centeredness (anthropocentrism) by acknowledging the inheritance of Adam's sin. But Semi-Pelagianism is a poor compromise between Pelagianism and Augustine's doctrine of the total, sovereign grace of God, and in many other ways, it essentially copies Pelagianism. Once again, let us study the following chart:

	SIN	GRACE	PREDESTINATION
SEMI-PELAGIANISM	It recognizes the heredity of sin, but sin is more like a disease. Man is not dead in sin, but sick and in need of healing.	Grace is a human decision for Christ based on a "free" will that is only partially tainted by sin.	Election comes from foreknowledge. God knows from all eternity who will believe, and therefore He will choose him.
CONSEQUENCES OF SEMI-PELAGIANISM	Man is only spiritually sick; as such he is able to cooperate with God in salvation.	God's grace is passive, responding only on the basis of man's decision. Man takes the first step towards salvation. He can attain salvation even without God's prevenient grace. Salvation is not a gift, it is a merit.	Election is conditional. A person's ability to believe comes first.

Semi-Pelagians believe in man's natural, inherent ability to decide by his "free" will whether to accept or reject the sacrifice of Christ on the Cross. Not only Pelagianism, but also Semi-Pelagianism is still alive and well in the Church today. We find it in Catholicism as well as in modern evangelical liberalism. Semi-Pelagianism is not the same as Arminianism, although Semi-Pelagians are often mistaken for Arminians. The Semi-Pelagian controversy was settled at the Second Synod of Orange in c. 529, where the foundations of modern Arminianism were laid.

ARMINIANISM

The teachings of James Arminius (c. 1560-1609) and the Remonstrance (c. 1610) were formulated into their present form by John Wesley (c. 1703-1791), the founder of Methodism. Arminianism is not as man-centered as Pelagianism or Semi-Pelagianism. It allows that man is spiritually incapable of choosing Christ by his fallen will. It admits that initial impulse of God is necessary for salvation, that is, the working of prevenient grace through the Holy Spirit. Only then can a person be converted or not, to ultimately accept or reject Christ. Thus, the prevenient grace of Arminianism makes salvation possible, but it does not guarantee it. Since only some on whom the prevenient grace of the Holy Spirit has been poured out will choose Christ, it is evident that the work of the Holy Spirit is limited and often inefficacious, even though it persuades all with equal force. On this point, Arminianism somewhat builds on the Second Synod of Orange. The following chart tells us more than many words:

	SIN	GRACE	PREDESTINATION
ARMINIANISM	Man is incapable of making a decision for Christ, but the human will is enabled by God's prevenient grace to accept or reject salvation.	God equips man with a prevenient grace that leads to a decision to either accept or reject God.	Election comes from foreknowledge. God knows who will believe because of His prevenient grace, and that is why He elects them.
CONSEQUENCES OF ARMINIANISM	Man is spiritually dead and incapable of responding to God. But through his "free" will, he makes decisions based on the prevenient grace God has bestowed upon him.	God's prevenient grace is an active stimulus to man's salvation. God takes the first step; man takes the second. Salvation is therefore God's offer, which man accepts or not.	Election is conditional. First and foremost is man's ability to believe, that is, how he chooses to deal with God's prevenient grace.

From this table, we see that the "free" will of man is the common denominator of Pelagianism, Semi-Pelagianism, and Arminianism. It does not matter whether man is sinless from birth (Pelagianism) or sinful from birth (Semi-Pelagianism and Arminianism). It does not matter whether his "free" will is innate (Pelagianism and Semi-Pelagianism) or pre-activated by God's prevenient grace (Arminianism). In all of these systems of salvation, these soteriologies, the point is that it is ultimately the "free" will of the individual that determines where the individual will spend eternity. It is a salvific mixture of human and divine merit, a salvific mixture of the synergy of God and man. It does not matter whether human to divine merits are "90:10" in Pelagianism, "50:50" in Semi-Pelagianism, or "10:90" in Arminianism, because it is man's "free" will, whether of natural or divinely inspired origin, that decides. In the end, it is always man who decides his salvation. Whether the prevenient grace of God, which in some vague way mobilizes man's "free" will in matters of salvation, can be defended in Scripture, or whether it is merely a theological concept that has no basis in Scripture, will become clear when we compare the following five articles of the Remonstrance with Calvinism[6].

AUGUSTINE, REFORMATION, CALVINISM

The doctrines of Calvinism in the 16th and 17th centuries did not emerge as a new theology with the arrival of John Calvin (c. 1509-1564). Calvin's predecessor in teaching the monergistic sovereignty of God's will in matters of salvation was Augustine (c. 354-430). The young Augustine lived a turbulent life. His pious mother, Monica, prayed constantly for her son's conversion. Augustine was baptized in c. 387, ordained a priest in c. 391, and became bishop of Hippo Regio (Hippo), now Annaba in Algeria, in c. 393.

6 See chapter 2; section: The Five Articles of Remonstrance and Calvinism.

The basic elements of what we now call Calvinism were vigorously defended by Augustine, a contemporary of both Pelagius (Pelagianism) and Cassian (Semi-Pelagianism). Pelagius was Augustine's chief opponent who, as we have seen, denied Adam's original sin and taught that man could be justified if he believed and kept the law of his own accord.

In accordance with the teaching of Scripture and the Apostle Paul, Augustine preached that the natural man is so afflicted from birth with the consequences of Adam's sin that he cannot and will not accept Christ as his Savior and Lord. He taught that the spiritual side of man's nature had suffered so much from the Fall of Adam that man is enslaved to sin from birth and cannot keep the law or believe the gospel. For man to understand the gospel, rebirth of the Spirit is necessary; man must be irresistibly drawn by God into the Body of Christ, His Church. This unconditional, gracious, creative act of God—God's saving grace—is given only to those whom God has chosen for eternal life before the foundation of the world, through His unconditional and eternal love. The crux of the dispute between Augustine and Pelagius concerned the original sin of Adam, and further, the extent to which the freedom of the human will is affected because of Adam's original sin, in matters of the Spirit of God.

Let us study another table and then compare it with the previous three tables which represented Pelagianism, Semi-Pelagianism, and Arminianism. The difference between this table and the previous three will become very clear. Augustine, the Reformation, and Calvinism represent the one-sided work of God (monergism) in salvation par excellence.

	SIN	GRACE	PREDESTINATION
AUGUSTINE, CALVINISM, AND THE REFORMATION	Total depravity. Every descendant of Adam is under the power of sin, trapped and enslaved by Satan. Therefore, he cannot and will not understand the things of the Spirit of God.	Only the efficacious, unconditional, saving grace of God unilaterally (monergistically) creates a new man in Christ. Man cannot contribute anything to his regeneration and justification.	Election is God's sovereign decision based on His unconditional, eternal love for His people. It is God's choice before the foundation of the world.
CONSEQUENCES OF TEACHING AUGUSTINE, CALVINISM, AND THE REFORMATION	Man is spiritually dead, corrupted and distorted by sin. By himself, he cannot do anything good for the glory of God. He cannot and will not decide for God or salvation on his own or build up faith within himself.	God's unconditional saving grace has efficaciously secured both "salvation and faith" for the sinner. The saved person makes a completely free, joyful, and irresistible decision for God.	A good, loving, and wise God unconditionally chose to save many of the rebels, rather than condemning them all. Election is in God's power alone.

In a sense, Augustine was the "first reformer." Calvin (c. 1509-1564) himself quoted Augustine more than any other theologian. Martin Luther (c. 1483-1546) was an Augustinian monk who agreed with both Augustine and Calvin on the subject of natural human "free" will.

In 1524, Erasmus of Rotterdam (c. 1469-1536) published his book, "De libero arbitrio diatribe sive collation" (On Free Will), which taught that man is capable of choosing or rejecting salvation by his own free will, independent of God's grace. In this work he fully identified himself with both Pelagius (Pelagianism) and Cassian (Semi-Pelagianism). Luther responded to Erasmus the following year (c. 1525) with "De Servo Arbitrio" (On the Enslaved Will) in which he used Scripture to prove that man has an enslaved will, as a result of sin, and is unable to accept salvation apart from God's grace; salvation is entirely dependent on God.

The Reformation, especially the writings of Luther and Calvin, confirmed the biblical truth of Augustine's view of "salvation and faith." The biblical doctrine of God's unconditional grace became the foundational doctrine of the Reformation, differing profoundly from the doctrines of Pelagianism and Semi-Pelagianism. Reformation doctrines came from the Bible, but Pelagianism and Semi-Pelagianism came from the heritage of pagan, Hellenistic, humanistic, and Enlightenment philosophies. As such, Pelagianism and Semi-Pelagianism assert that man's will is completely "free." Reformation doctrines likewise break with the Arminian theology of salvation. The uniqueness of grace in Scripture, affirmed in Augustinianism, the Reformation, and Calvinism—in short, monergism—shares no part in man-centered religion, containing no mixture of human and divine effort in "salvation and faith." The Reformation made clear that "salvation and faith" are entirely in the hands of a sovereign God (monergism), and not in both God's hands and man's hands (synergism).

THE FIVE ARTICLES OF REMONSTRANCE AND CALVINISM

HISTORICAL CONTEXT

The ideas of Pelagianism and Semi-Pelagianism were firmly rooted both in nominal Catholicism and in the thought of Protestant theologians of the 16th and 17th centuries who were influenced by the Renaissance, the Enlightenment, and Humanism. Under this influence, the Dutch theologian Jacob Arminius (c. 1560-1609) formulated a theology of salvation that would be acceptable even for the Reformed Dutch Church of his day, which was based on Augustinian soteriology and rejected the "free" will of sinful, natural man.

In 1610, a year after Arminius' death, his disciples met together to summarize his teachings in five articles, submitting them to the Dutch Reformed Church in the form of a "Remonstrance," or objection. They demanded that the official documents of the Dutch churches, the "Belgic Confession of Faith" and the "Heidelberg Catechism," be changed in accordance with the Remonstrance.

The articles of the Remonstrance (1610) were very carefully worded. At first glance, they seem to be in harmony with Scripture. Unless we read them carefully, we might end each one with an affirmative, "Amen." A more thoughtful reading, however, reveals that they lack unity and integrity and are unbiblical and man-centered. Nine years later, in 1619, the Synod of Dort rejected these articles and affirmed the absolute sovereignty of God in salvation, a monergistic, Augustinian soteriology.

1. CONDITIONAL ELECTION

> *That God, by an eternal and unchangeable purpose in Jesus Christ his Son, before the foundation of the world, hath determined, out of the fallen, sinful race of men, to save in Christ, for Christ's sake, and through Christ, those who, through the grace of the Holy Ghost, shall believe on this his son Jesus, and shall persevere in this faith and obedience of faith, through this grace, even to the end; and, on the other hand, to leave the incorrigible and unbelieving in sin and under wrath, and to condemn them as alienated from Christ, according to the word of the Gospel in John 3:36: "He that believeth on the Son hath everlasting life: and he that believeth not the Son shall not see life; but the wrath of God abideth on him," and according to other passages of Scripture also.*

If we read this first article carefully, we can observe how it differs from Reformed doctrine. God saves those who believe by the grace of the Holy Spirit in His Son, Jesus Christ. This grace is cooperative and is preceded by a preliminary or prevenient revival, as we will see below in Article 4 of the Remonstrance. Here, faith precedes God's salvation and is therefore conditioned by human decision. Furthermore, God rejects those who are incorrigible. The Holy Spirit can thus be resisted and opposed.

2. UNLIMITED REDEMPTION

> *That agreeably thereunto, Jesus Christ the Savior of the world, died for all men and for every man, so that he has obtained for them all, by his death on the cross, redemption and the forgiveness of sins; yet that no one actually enjoys this forgiveness of sins except the believer, according to the word of the Gospel of John 3:16, "For God so loved the world, that he gave his only begotten Son, that whosoever believeth in him should not perish, but have everlasting life." And in the First Epistle of 1 John 2:2: "And he is the propitiation for our sins: and not for ours only, but also for the sins of the whole world."*

According to Article 2 of the Remonstrance, Jesus Christ died for every man without exception, bearing all the sins of the world. Christ has paid the price for all men to be redeemed and all sins to be forgiven, but only believers are saved. Christ's already "completed" redemption of all and forgiveness of sins for all can only take effect in accordance with man's choice, in accordance with his "free" will, which God restores to him by prevenient grace (see below, Article 4 of the Remonstrance). In other words, the efficacy of "universal salvation"—the efficacy of the "universal saving and cleansing work of Jesus Christ on the Cross"—is not 100%, but only partial.

3. SPIRITUAL INCAPACITY

> *That man has not saving grace of himself, nor of the energy of his free will, inasmuch as he, in the state of apostasy and sin, can of and by himself neither think, will, nor do anything that is truly good* (such as saving faith eminently is)*; but that it is needful*

that he be born again of God in Christ, through his Holy Spirit, and renewed in understanding, inclination, or will, and all his powers, in order that he may rightly understand, think, will, and effect what is truly good, according to the Word of Christ, John 15:5, "Without me ye can do nothing."

The third article of the Remonstrance is worded in such a way that if the other four articles did not exist, we would have to affirm its validity in the monergistic, Augustinian, Reformed, Calvinistic sense. As Augustine, Luther, and Calvin believed and taught and as affirmed by the Reformation and the Synod of Dort, man is so spiritually emptied, spiritually incapacitated, and dead that in order to believe in Christ, to understand the will of God, to think, to will, and to do good works, it is necessary that he be born-again of God. All this would be affirmed by the third article of the Remonstrance, if it stood alone. But according to the Remonstrance, one cannot be born of God without a preliminary or helpful awakening and without following and cooperating grace (Article 4), so Article 3 is in complete disharmony with the other four. One cannot equate being born-again of God in the Reformed, one-sided, monergistic sense that Article 3 implies with a prior, helpful awakening and subsequent, prevenient grace, as Article 4 below asserts.

4. PREVENIENT, ASSISTING OR COOPERATIVE RESISTIBLE GRACE

That this grace of God is the beginning, continuance, and accomplishment of all good, even to this extent, that the regenerate man himself, without prevenient or assisting, awakening, following and cooperative grace, can neither think, will, nor do good, nor withstand any temptations to evil; so that all good deeds or movements, that can be conceived, must be ascribed to the grace of God in Christ. But respects the mode of the operation of this grace, it is not irresistible; inasmuch as it is written concerning many, that they have resisted the Holy Ghost. Acts 7, and elsewhere in many places.

We reject that the born-again Christian must first have been enlightened by God through a prior assisting or prevenient awakening. Neither assisted revival nor cooperating grace are biblical, but merely theological concepts. The answer to the question of whether or not assisted revival and cooperating prevenient grace are included in the grace that regenerates the sinner of the Spirit of God is unclear and ambiguous. What is certain, however, is that preliminary or prevenient revival and cooperating grace, whatever they are, can be resisted by the sinner. Helpful revival and cooperating grace are said to influence the "free" will of the spiritually dead man to make his own decisions, much like the created Adam before the Fall.

We have already mentioned that official Roman Catholicism, to its credit, rejects both Pelagianism and Semi-Pelagianism (Synod of Orange, c. 529). However, Roman Catholic soteriology is fundamentally identified with Arminianism on this point. The initial initiative of God and the subsequent "free" action of man coincide in every respect with the prior, prevenient grace of the Arminian Remonstrance:

> *When St. Peter confessed that Jesus is the Christ, the Son of the living God, Jesus declared to him that this revelation did not come "from flesh and blood," but from "my Father who is in heaven." Faith is a gift of God, a supernatural virtue infused by him. "Before this faith can be exercised, man must have the grace of God to move and assist him; he must have the interior helps of the Holy Spirit, who moves the heart and converts it to God, who opens the eyes of the mind and 'makes it easy for all to accept and believe the truth*[7]*.'"*

We see that in Roman Catholic Arminianism, faith is a gift conditioned by the prior and prevenient grace of God and the inward help of the Holy Spirit. A conditional gift is a contradiction in terms;

7 Catechism, paragraph 153.

a conditional gift is not a gift but a reward for a duty done (Rom. 4:4; 11:6). Exactly the same concept of salvation, in the same spirit, is copied by evangelical Arminianism. Some Protestant movements even go beyond both Roman Catholic and evangelical Arminianism to teach that faith is neither a gift nor a work. Furthermore, according to Roman Catholicism, prevenient grace opens one's spiritual sight, faith, but with the knowledge that by no means everyone will agree with the truth. They may reject it, and so "free" will again plays a primacy in salvation:

> *God willed that man should be left in the hand of his own counsel* (cf. Sir 15:14), *so that he might of his own accord seek his creator and freely attain his full and blessed perfection by cleaving to him (GS 17 § 1)*[8].

> *Freedom is the power to act or not to act, and so to perform deliberate acts of one's own. Freedom attains perfection in its acts when directed toward God, the sovereign Good.*[9]

In the sermon of the Evangelical Methodist Church, congregation Pilsen 1, Lochotín, from January 20, 2013, we read:

> *The Lord God is sovereign and omnipotent, but He deliberately limited Himself by creating man with free will. I can imagine how the Lord God entered into this adventurous relationship to have a truly difficult partner in man. How else can we understand the remark about the creation of man, that it was "very good"? But when a person comes to God knowing that he needs a change, he is in a bad, often catastrophic state. But that is not all: The Lord God begins His work of change in a person before that person even understands it. Methodists call this "prevenient grace." We cannot see it at all in the present tense; and when we do catch a glimpse of it, it is usually after the fact. So it was with Moses. The Lord God had a great plan for him*

8 Catechism, paragraph 1743.
9 Catechism, paragraph 1744.

from the beginning. Hence the education, hence Moses' access to the highest levels of Egyptian society[10].

Such statements from evangelical pulpits, that God limits Himself for the sake of man in order to have a truly difficult partner, must raise the eyebrows of any serious student of Scripture, and especially of anyone who dares to believe today that God is the absolute Alpha and Omega. Jesus Christ limited Himself on the Cross, it is true, but not primarily for the sake of man. He limited Himself for His own sake, to glorify Himself, and for His own sake He erases our unfaithfulness (Is. 43:25; 48:11; Dan. 9:19). Certainly, the Lord God did not and does not have His plans only for Moses; therefore, according to His purposes, He places the development of each person in a certain historical context. But this is quite different from a preliminary or helpful awakening, something other than cooperative, prevenient, or preliminary grace, as Arminians use these and other terms to describe the working of the Spirit of God upon the natural man.

Let us conclude this fourth point of the Remonstrance by unifying the nomenclature. Arminianism and Roman Catholicism call the preliminary work of the Holy Spirit, which the natural man can resist and withstand, prevenient grace, cooperating grace, pre-awakening, assisted awakening, and other theological terms. For the sake of clarity, therefore, we will use only the term "prevenient grace," which most accurately captures the essence of the matter.

5. REASSURANCE AND CERTAINTY

That those who are incorporated into Christ by true faith, and have thereby become partakers of his life-giving Spirit, have thereby full power to strive against Satan, sin, the world, and their own flesh, and to win the victory; it being well understood that it is ever through the prevenient grace of the Holy Ghost;

10 http://www.umc.cz/lochotin/index.php?pk21&qk296

> *and that Jesus Christ assists them through his Spirit in all temptations, extends to them his hand, and if only they are ready for the conflict, and desire his help, and are not inactive, keeps them from falling, so that they, by no craft or power of Satan, can be misled nor plucked out of Christ's hands, according to the Word of Christ, John 10:28: "Neither shall any man pluck them out of my hand." But whether they are capable, through negligence, of forsaking again the first beginning of their life in Christ, of again returning to this present evil world, of turning away from the holy doctrine which was delivered them, of losing a good conscience, of becoming devoid of grace, that must be more particularly determined out of the Holy Scripture, before we ourselves can teach it with the full persuasion of our mind.*

If it is truly human, "free" will that accepts Christ, even if it is enlightened by prevenient grace, collaborative grace, a preliminary awakening, or a helpful awakening, then the logic of the matter suggests that this same "free" will can later reject Him. The incoherence of the Five Articles of the Remonstrance is very clear in this article. On the one hand, no one snatches believers out of the hand of Christ, and on the other hand, we have yet to make a separate decision about the assurance of believers.

PHILOSOPHICAL FOUNDATIONS OF ARMINIANISM

Reformed theologian J. I. Packer, in his analysis of the Remonstrant idea, argued that the theology it contained, which we now call synergistic Arminianism, was the synthesis, the union, of two humanistic-philosophical principles:

First, God's sovereignty does not interfere with human freedom and, consequently, human responsibility. Because the Bible in many places views faith as a responsible human decision, Arminians conclude that faith is not caused by God. God reaches out to man, and then man decides for himself whether or not to accept his offer by faith.

Second, the degree of ability defines the degree of obligation. Because the Bible views faith as an obligation for all (who hear the gospel) to take a particular stand, Arminians conclude that everyone has the ability to believe (but not the necessity). Therefore, God's Word is to be interpreted as follows:

1. Man is never so completely corrupted by sin that he cannot savingly believe the gospel when it is put before him, nor
2. is he ever so completely controlled by God that he cannot reject it.
3. God's election of those who shall be saved is prompted by his foreseeing that they will of their own accord believe.
4. Christ's death did not ensure the salvation of anyone, for it did not secure the gift of faith to anyone (there is no such gift): what it did was rather to create a possibility of salvation for everyone if they believe.
5. It rests with believers to keep themselves in a state of grace by keeping up their faith; those who fail here fall away and are lost. Thus, Arminianism made man's salvation depend ultimately on man himself, saving faith being viewed throughout as man's own work and, because his own, not God's in him.

Thus, according to Arminianism, salvation ultimately depends on man himself; saving faith is an act of man, not an act of God in man[11].

THE ORIGIN OF THE FIVE ARTICLES OF CALVINISM

Fifty-four years after Calvin, nine years after the death of Arminius, and eight years after the Remonstrance, the Synod of Dort met in

11 https://www.monergism.com/thethreshold/articles/onsite/packer_intro.html

c. 1618 to examine the teachings of Arminius and the Remonstrance in the light of Scripture. There were 84 members, 18 lay representatives, and 27 delegates from Germany, Switzerland, and England. The first session was held on November 13, 1618. The last, 154th session was held on May 9, 1619. It was not an idle deliberation of scribes; it lasted a full seven months and came to serious conclusions.

Each chapter contains articles of faith and paragraphs that refute the error of the Remonstrance point by point. There are 93 articles and paragraphs in all. The entire Canons of Dort affirmed the pre-Remonstrant view of God's sovereignty. Later, these five chapters of Dort were rearranged, simplified, and gradually refined into the five points now known as the "Five Points of Calvinism." These five points appear in the theological literature in numerous modifications of the same substance and content, depending on the author and the time. They were named after the French reformer John Calvin, who had been dead for more than 55 years. Calvin never saw the sovereignty of God systematized into five points, never knew it, and therefore could not teach it in its present integrity. In its rejection of the Remonstrance and declaration of its five articles incompatible with Scripture, the decision of the Synod of Dort was supported by the vast majority of Protestant theologians of the day. These five points of Calvinism form the backbone of this book, and we will devote a part to each of them. First, let us carefully study the following chart, which compares two completely contradictory soteriological positions regarding salvation. The table does not and cannot contain the five literal chapters of Dort, but only one of their many abbreviated modifications, which fully captures the meaning of the Dort Canon, which is available in English on the Internet[12]:

12 http://www.crcna.org/welcome/beliefs/confessions/canons-dort

FIVE POINTS OF ARMINIANISM AND FIVE POINTS OF CALVINISM	
ARMINIANISM **Shares the Free Will of Natural Man with Pelagius and Cassian** The basic positions of contemporary Arminianism are based on the five articles of the Remonstrance. Although their wording varies according to the source, the essence remains the same:	**CALVINISM** **Satan's Enslavement of the Will of the Natural Man Shared with Augustine** The Synod of Dort also responded to the Remonstrance in five articles that became the core of Calvinism. Although the wording varies according to the source, the substance remains the same:
1. Spiritual Ability is the Result of God's Prevenient Grace Human beings are sinful and incapable of being righteous in themselves without God. But they are not irredeemably sinful. God works through His prevenient grace. He renews the human will to accept or reject salvation.	**1. Total Spiritual Inability is a Result of Adam's Fall** Human beings are so affected by the negative consequences of original sin that they are incapable of being righteous and are always unchangeably sinful. Human freedom is completely enslaved to sin, so that in matters of the Spirit of God, they can only choose evil.
2. Conditional Election God has determined that by His grace all mankind should be justified (have their sins blotted out). However, He calls us to respond to His prevenient grace by exercising our natural will, which He has restored to us to make a choice for Him. Our response conditions the fulfillment of His election.	**2. Unconditional Election** Since men cannot or will not choose God, God chose His people, whom He loves with an everlasting love, to justify them (to have their sins blotted out) for His sake and for His glory. His election is unconditional.
3. Universal Salvation through Christ God's salvation is unlimited in scope but limited by man in its efficacy. Salvation is only a possibility for all. Salvation only becomes efficacious when man believes. Those whom God foreknew would believe, He has also chosen. Man's faith precedes and conditions God's salvation.	**3. Efficacious Redemption through Christ** God's redemption is limited in scope but unlimited in efficacy. Salvation is perfect and complete because it has secured the "salvation and faith" of all whom God unconditionally chose and loved with an everlasting love before the foundation of the world. "salvation and faith" are God's simultaneous and inseparable gifts.
4. Resistible Grace God's grace is offered without merit; however, people have the God-given freedom through prevenient grace to resist and reject His offer.	**4. Irresistible Grace** The grace that God unconditionally gives to His people cannot be refused, cannot be resisted, because it is not a matter of accepting an ordinary offer, but of creating a new inner man who lives his new life in Christ irresistibly.

5. Conditional Guarantee and Assurance In God's grace, there is the assurance that all who choose to accept Jesus Christ are guaranteed salvation. However, this assurance is conditional upon faith to the end. One is free both to accept Jesus Christ and later to reject Him by falling away. (There is no agreement among Arminians on this point.)	**5. The Perseverance of the Saints** The elect cannot lose their salvation or their faith, because "salvation and faith" are the work of the Triune God. The Father chose His elect, the Son redeemed the elect, and the Holy Spirit regenerated the redeemed. God's work cannot be thwarted because it is God who perseveres in faithfulness and causes His elect, redeemed, and regenerated saints to persevere to the end.
According to Arminianism: Salvation is accomplished by the combined efforts of God, who takes the initiative, and man, who must respond. The human response is the crucial factor. God offers salvation to all, but His provision becomes efficacious only for those who, through an aroused, free-will grace, choose to cooperate with Him and accept His prevenient grace. At the critical moment, human will plays a decisive role. Thus, man, not God, determines who will be the recipient of the gift of salvation.	**According to Calvinism:** Salvation is accomplished by the almighty, decreeing, decreed will of the triune God. The Father chose His people; the Son redeemed them by His death; the Holy Spirit guaranteed that Christ's death would be efficacious, i.e., He regenerated the chosen people, brought them to faith and repentance, and caused them to willingly and joyfully submit to the gospel. The whole process of salvation (election, redemption, regeneration) is solely the merit of God, bestowed only by unconditional grace. Thus, God, not man, determines who will be the recipient of the gift of salvation.
Rejected by the Synod of Dort This soteriological system was contained in the Remonstrance. Originally the five articles were in a different order and wording. The Remonstrance was submitted by the Arminians to the Dutch Church for acceptance in 1610. However, it was not rejected as incompatible with Scripture until the Synod of Dort in 1619.	**Confirmed by the Synod of Dort** This soteriological system was confirmed as the biblical doctrine of salvation by the Synod of Dort in 1619. At that time, it was first formulated in five chapters in response to the five articles of the Remonstrance and the Arminians. It later became known as the Five Points of Calvinism.

The five points of Calvinism are sequential. If we accept one, we validate all five; and if we deny one, the remaining four do not hold. Being a one, two, three, four, or four-and-a-half-point Calvinist is a spiritual mirage. Either we are five-point Calvinists or we are not Calvinists at all. How many links in a five-point chain must break before the chain breaks?

Yet there is a theological system that denies the third point of Calvinism. This four-point "Calvinism," called Amyraldism, in line with Arminianism, teaches that Christ died for all and redeemed all, but in line with Calvinism, that God chose only His people to be saved. This compromise seeks to avoid the sacred nature of the atonement, which is limited in its scope, but not in its efficacy. It thereby loses its integrity that Calvinism and to some extent even Arminianism possess. Amyraldism solves nothing; it only makes the problem more problematic.

3

THE REFORMED VIEW OF SALVATION

CHARLES H. SPURGEON—MAXIM

> *And I have my own private opinion, that there is no such thing as preaching Christ and him crucified, unless you preach what now-a-days is called Calvinism. I have my own ideas, and those I always state boldly. It is a nickname to call it Calvinism. Calvinism is the gospel, and nothing else. I do not believe we can preach the gospel, if we do not preach justification by faith without works; nor unless we preach the sovereignty of God in his dispensation of grace; nor unless we exalt the electing, unchangeable, eternal, immutable, conquering love of Jehovah; nor, I think, can we preach the gospel, unless we base it upon the peculiar redemption which Christ made for his elect and chosen people; nor can I comprehend a gospel which lets saints fall away after they are called, and suffers the children of God to be burned in the fires of damnation, after having believed. Such a gospel I abhor. The gospel of the Bible is not such a gospel as that. We preach Christ and him crucified in a different fashion, and to all gainsayers we reply, 'We have not so learned Christ.'*[13]

13 Spurgeon's Sermons, vol. I (Baker Books, reprinted 2007), 88-89.

THE INABILITY OF THE NATURAL MAN

SCRIPTURE DEMANDS WHAT THE NATURAL MAN CANNOT DO

To avoid misunderstanding the Reformed view of salvation[14] in the following section, we must recognize one absolutely crucial point; Scripture requires us to do something that we cannot do in the natural body (Ex. 19:5-6; 1 Pet. 2:9). The Spirit of God in Scripture requires people to personally want to come to God, to personally repent, to personally surrender to Christ, to personally believe. Those who do not willingly turn away from the world and cling to Christ will not have their sins forgiven and be justified by God.

Repentance and faith are as much a free act of the regenerate man through the Spirit of God as the free seeing and hearing of the natural man of Adam. As no one can see or hear for me, so no one can repent or believe for me, not even God Himself. This is an image often used by the Holy Spirit in Scripture (e.g., Isa. 44:18; Jer. 5:21; Ezek. 12:2; Matt. 13:15; Jn. 12:40). Of course, the physically blind, and even deaf-mute, can have spiritual sight and hearing, i.e., faith.

Reformed soteriology, the doctrine of salvation, certainly does not deny the human will; it does not deny the human personality, for Scripture so clearly teaches that man is not without conscience and will. But the question is whether the natural man is capable of doing all that Scripture requires of him in order to be saved. The biblical answer is clear; apart from Christ, man can do nothing (John 15:5). The solution is that just as the natural man, born out of Adam, is the whole creation of God, including the physical organs of the body—eyes, ears, feet, etc.—so also the spiritual, inner man, born of the Spirit of God, is the whole new creation of God (2 Cor. 5:17), including the spiritual "organs" of faith—seeking God, repentance, etc.—from which the whole lifestyle of the

14 See chapter 3; section "Salvation and Faith" According to the Reformation.

Christian flows: *"Know that the LORD, he is God! It is he who made us, and we are his; we are his people, and the sheep of his pasture* [we are his newly created, chosen, spiritual people] "(Ps. 100:3).

Let us look at just two areas under the next two headings: "The question of faith and the search for God." It seems a contradiction in terms, but Scripture demands of all who are invited to hear the gospel a response that the natural man, unless he has been regenerated by God, is incapable of giving on his own.

THE QUESTION OF FAITH

"And they said [to the jailer], *'Believe in the Lord Jesus, and you will be saved, you and your household'"* (Acts 16:31). If Scripture contained such commanding verses as "believe" and the like (Mark 1:15; John 14:11; 20:27), we could argue that faith in Christ is something we bring forth from within ourselves. Furthermore, we might also count on everyone in our household being saved for one simple reason: If we ourselves have believed; and that by our own doing, we might also suppose that we are the final causal link in salvation. But the following verse (Acts 16:32) clearly illustrates the context: Paul and Silas had preached the gospel to all the members of the jailer's household.

The literal interpretation of some verses, taken out of context, often leads to absurdities. None of these verses stands alone; all must be harmonized in the light of the whole of Scripture: ***"All that the Father gives me will come to me****, and whoever comes to me I will never cast out"* (John 6:37). Only those whom God the Father will draw by His Holy Spirit, whom He will empower by the new birth, whom He will create anew with a new spiritual sight, that is, with faith, will come: ***"No one can come to me unless the Father who sent me draws him*** [the first, spiritual resurrection]. *And I will raise him up on the last day* [the second, bodily resurrection into a glorified body] "(John 6:44).

The Lord Jesus Christ did not die on the Cross for all humanity without exception because through His death, He represents and draws only those whom the Father has given to Him: *"And I, when I am lifted up from the earth* [to the Cross], *will draw all people to Myself* [all whom the Father has given and drawn to Me; John 6:37; 6:44]*"* (John 12:32). Neither the jailer nor his family members could believe on their own.

The words of Paul and Silas in Acts 16:31 are true, but the verse contains only part of the truth. It refers to the human manifestation of faith caused by the new birth, but it is silent about God's cause and total merit. Each person's "salvation and faith" is an independent, creative process of the triune, absolutely perfect God, with complete interaction between Father, Son, and Holy Spirit.

THE QUESTION OF SEARCHING FOR GOD

"And he made from one man every nation of mankind to live on all the face of the earth, having determined allotted periods and the boundaries of their dwelling place, ***that they should seek God****, and perhaps feel their way toward him and find him. Yet he is not far from each one of us"* (Acts 17:26-27). There are several similar verses in Scripture that challenge people to seek the Lord, His kingdom, etc. Here is the one most often recalled: *"For what can be known about God* ***is plain to them****, because God has shown it to them. For his invisible attributes, namely, his eternal power and divine nature, have been clearly perceived, ever since the creation of the world, in the things that have been made.* ***So they are without excuse****"* (Rom. 1:19-20). It seems as if God made all of creation so that natural man would seek Him, search for Him, and eventually find Him.

It is true that all of creation proves the existence of God, and only a fool thinks that there is no God (Ps. 14:1; 53:1; Rom. 1:22ff.). All verses such as Acts 17:26-27 and Rom. 1:19-20 prove only that any natural man who is not a fool or a vagabond must conclude, by thinking about nature and the universe, that there is a god. This is confirmed by the fact that there is not now, nor never has been, a single human race or tribe that lacks some idea, however distorted, of a god or gods, that lacks some form of religious profession. But to know that a god exists is one thing, and to know the God of the Bible, to have a personal relationship with Him in salvation, is quite another.

Again, the above and similar verses do not stand alone. They explain only part of the truth; they do not exhaust the whole truth. If they were the only verses in Scripture that spoke on this subject, they would confirm that the natural man is capable of seeking the God of the Bible on his own initiative, by his own inner strength, and that he is ultimately capable of finding God on his own, by his own thinking, logical reasoning, flesh and blood, which the Scriptures reject (Matt. 16:16-17). The Scriptures clearly reveal the complementary part of the truth that the carnal man not only does not seek God, but cannot seek Him because he comes into the world spiritually dead: *"...as it is written: 'None is righteous, no, not one; no one understands;* ***no one seeks for God****. All have turned aside; together they have become worthless; no one does good, not even one'"* (Rom. 3:10-12). What then should we do with the verses that command, "seek Me with all your heart; seek the Lord; seek His kingdom; seek My face; seek Me diligently; find Me" etc.? These are similar to verses that command people to "believe," as explained under the previous heading. The ability to find God, like the ability to believe, is created by God. Only the new creation born of the Holy Spirit can believe and find God. The truth is that the natural man, even if he knows of a divine existence, cannot know the true God; he always wants to bend his god to his own advantage. That is why God makes Himself known to those who, paradoxically, do not seek Him, such as Saul of Tarsus, then the Apostle Paul (Acts 9:1-16): *"Then Isaiah is so bold as to say,* ***'I have been found by***

those who did not seek me*; I have shown myself to those* ***who did not ask for me***'"' (Rom. 10:20).

CONTEXT HARMONIZES SCRIPTURE

Apparent biblical "contradictions" are not limited to the area of faith and the search for God. Arguing isolated verses out of context does not serve the common cause at all, but rather causes confusion among God's people. Without the coherent biblical context of the whole of Scripture, we come to completely contradictory conclusions, as evidenced by the many different denominations that arise and fall away. The point is to see verses *x, y, z* in the context of the whole Bible, in complete harmony with the seemingly contradictory verses *a, b, c*. Arguing only with verses *a, b, c* or only with verses *x, y, z* produces half-truths. The moment a half-truth begins to unconsciously pass for the whole truth, it becomes an untruth; if it does so consciously, it becomes a lie.

"SALVATION AND FAITH" ACCORDING TO THE REFORMATION

The theologians of the 17th century Protestant Reformation rejected both Pelagianism and Semi-Pelagianism as well as Arminianism as unbiblical doctrines. Reformed theology was not born in one day. It has been and continues to be revised and developed. This is sanctification. The Church is to be continually reformed—Ecclesia semper reformanda est. Therefore, it follows that not all Reformed believers could have had—or can have—identical views. But all the Reformed were and are united on the question of God's sovereignty and His monergistic power in salvation, owing to man's total spiritual depravity. The fundamental question of the Reformation was whether Christianity, as far as salvation is concerned, is a doctrine of total dependence on God (monergism), or whether it provides for human effort prior to regeneration (synergism). Do we believe because we are saved (Calvinism) or do we believe in order to be saved (Arminianism)? Salvation is a mystery of God, so we cannot be dogmatic about the details. But what we do insist on is this:

1. The physical birth of man is the sovereign, unconditional decree of God's decreed will: ***"For you formed my inward parts; you knitted me*** *together in my mother's womb"* (Ps. 139:13).
2. The spiritual rebirth, the first resurrection, the creation of the new inner man is also the sovereign, unconditional decree of God's decreed will:[15]: *"...and raised us up with him and seated us with him in the heavenly places in Christ Jesus"* (Eph. 2:6). *"Blessed be the God and Father of our Lord Jesus Christ! According to his great mercy,* ***he has caused us to be born again*** *to a living hope* ***through the resurrection of Jesus Christ from the dead"*** (1 Pet. 1:3).

Both physical birth and spiritual rebirth are decrees of God's will. He sovereignly ordained our physical and spiritual existence. After all, creation cannot participate in its own creation (Rom. 9:21). The sovereign will of God, uninfluenced by man, is without doubt the primary cause that precedes and causes our "salvation and faith." The Reformation excludes the prevenient grace of Arminianism and Roman Catholicism, both of which are efficacious on the condition of the sinner's faith. God's unconditional grace is supreme. The entire Reformed theology of salvation is, in every respect, solely and exclusively God-centered.

The sovereign, saving grace of God unconditionally grants "salvation and faith" to God's elect in one creative moment. Those who believe are saved, but only those who are saved can believe. Faith does not precede salvation, is not superior to it, and does not cause it. "Salvation and faith" are one, like two sides of the same

15 See chapter 10; section: God's Will; heading: Degrees of Will.

coin—one undeserved whole, God-created gift. The only cause of the gift of "salvation and faith" is God's sovereign, unconditional grace, nothing else: *"For by grace you have been saved through faith. And this is not your own doing;* ***it is the gift of God****"* (Eph. 2:8). Scripture also clearly teaches that the unconditional grace of God that monergistically granted salvation to a lost person also monergistically granted faith in Christ: *"For it has been* ***granted to you that for the sake of Christ*** *you should not only believe in Him but also suffer for his sake"* (Phil. 1:29).

Why then does Scripture distinguish between *salvation* and *faith*? What is the difference between them? Let us look at the matter from Adam's perspective. Adam, the created man, had no part in his creation. When he was created from the dust of the ground, he had no consciousness, could not perceive the visible and invisible creation of God around him, and did not know that his body had organs, legs, hands, ears, eyes, and other parts until God breathed into his nostrils the breath of life (Gen. 2:7). Today's natural man is similarly indifferent to the things of the Spirit of God prior to his spiritual rebirth (1 Cor. 2:14). He cannot participate in his rebirth because he is spiritually dead from his birth in Adam. In this dead state, God spiritually baptizes, creates, and begets His own again of the Spirit according to His sovereign will (John 3:8). But how does the suddenly reborn, spiritually born, saved person even know that he has been translated from spiritual death in Satan to spiritual life in Christ? Are the new birth, justification, sanctification, and assurance of a future bodily resurrection visible inwardly and outwardly? How will others recognize this in him?

With our physical eye we see, with our ear we hear, with our feet we walk; but the eye, the ear, the feet, and all the organs with all the senses were created by God for us. They are an integral, created part of our natural being. Likewise, faith is an integral part of the new creation, the newborn, Spirit-raised man. Faith is spiritual sight and hearing. It empowers the child of God to spiritually see, understand, and receive the fullness of God's purposes that are invisible to physical sight and inapprehensible to the senses. Just as we see physical things with the eye that God created, so we see the things of God's Spirit with the faith that God also created. Jesus said: *"Blessed are those who have not seen* [with physical sight] *and yet have believed* [have seen Him with spiritual sight, by faith]" (John 20:29b). Faith is not an incantation that saves a person. Everyone has some faith. Jews, Muslims, Buddhists, Hindus, and communists, fascists, humanists, and everyone else has a faith. Everyone believes in something or someone. Everyone sees or wants to see something that is not visible to the physical eye. But the content of the belief is very important. Faith is only as good as the object of faith. The object of biblical faith is contained in the gospel. The Son of God came into this world in human flesh like sinful man (Rom. 8:3), was conceived by the Holy Spirit, born of a virgin (Luke 1:35), sacrificed Himself on the Cross, and redeemed His people from their sins (Matthew 1:21); therefore, the Holy Spirit will regenerate, justify, sanctify, and glorify His people in new bodies at the resurrection on the last day (Rom. 8:23).

Not only does God grant faith to His children, but He also grants varying degrees of faith: *"For by the grace given to me I say to everyone among you not to think of himself more highly than he ought to think, but to think with sober judgment, each according to the measure of faith* ***that God has assigned***" (Rom. 12:3). The measure of faith that God gave to the apostle Paul, for example, was incomparably greater than ours. Few have seen so deeply into the things of the Spirit of God. The born-again person is sanctified by faith, receives new knowledge, gradually penetrates the mysteries of the gospel with spiritual insight, grows in faith, and bears the fruit of faith. I ask the reader, when he encounters the word "faith" in Scripture, to expand it in his mind to include the terms "to see," "to receive," "to understand." To give an example: *"For I am not ashamed of the gospel, for it is the power of God for salvation to everyone who believes* [receives, sees, understands the gospel], *to the Jew first and also to the Greek. For in it the righteousness of God is revealed from faith for faith, as it is written, 'The righteous shall live by faith* [by the continuous reception, seeing, understanding of the gospel]'"(Rom. 1:16-17).

The Spirit of God expressed it in Scripture as follows: *"For those whom He* [1] ***foreknew*** *He also* [2] ***predestined*** *to be conformed to the image of his Son, in order that He might be the firstborn among many brothers. And those whom He predestined He also* [3] ***called***, *and those whom He called He also* [4] ***justified***, *and those whom He justified He also* [5] ***glorified***" (Rom. 8:29-30).

1. Those who were ***foreknown***, those whom God loved with an everlasting love, were written in the Lamb's Book of Life from the foundation of the world.

2. Those who are written in the Book of Life of the slain Lamb are ***predestined*** to eternal life, that is, to the eternal knowledge of God, even before their natural, physical birth.

3. Those who are predestined to eternal life, eternal knowledge of God, are ***called*** to "salvation and faith" after their natural birth, in the course of their carnal, sinful lives.

4. Those who were "saved and believed" were also ***justified***; they were acquitted of sin.

5. Those who have been acquitted of sin are a new creation, spiritually raised to life with Christ, growing in faith, brought out of Satan's darkness into God's Glory, into Christ's marvelous light, culminating in the second resurrection into a ***glorified*** body.

Let us study the following chart to get a good understanding of everything that will accompany us to the last page of this book. Let us call it "The Integrity of Salvation:"

THE UNCONDITIONAL GRACE OF GOD (SINGLE CAUSE: EX. 33:19; ROM. 9:15)			
FIRST RESURRECTION IS SPIRITUAL	JUSTIFICATION	SANCTIFICATION FOR LIFE	SECOND RESURRECTION IS BODILY
BORN-AGAIN OF THE SPIRIT	THE BLOTTING OUT OF SIN	PROCESS OF BEING SET APART AS VESSELS OF GOD	REDEMPTION OF THE BODY
It takes place at the time of the bestowal of God's unconditional grace upon His elect.	It takes place at the time of the bestowal of God's unconditional grace upon His elect.	It begins at the moment of the bestowal of God's unconditional grace upon His elect.	It is guaranteed at the moment of the bestowal of God's unconditional grace upon His elect.
It causes us to be born-again of the Spirit.	It causes us to be recognized as being righteous.	It causes us to be separated for the sake of God.	It causes resurrection of our bodies.
It delivers us from the power of sin.	It delivers us from the guilt of sin.	It delivers us from participating in sinning.	It delivers us from bodies that are subject to decay.
It is made within us.	It is made for us.	It is made for us, and within us.	It is made for us, and within us.
It is a creative feat.	It is a judicial decree.	It is our growth in Christ.	It is a creative feat.
It changes our spiritual nature.	It changes the status of our life.	It changes the way we live our lives.	It changes our bodies so that we can see Christ and be with Him forever.

All fields in the table must be valid at the same time. "Salvation and Faith" and all it encompasses is a God-created singularity, a uniqueness; it is an indivisible "package." Delete one field and you delete the whole table. The content of each cell of the table always comes from the unconditional, unilateral, monergistic activity of the sovereign God. And yet let us not succumb to the idea that man is a puppet[16]. Man's activity is to truly believe, to be interested in God, to love Him, to repent, to separate himself from the world, to grow in the knowledge of God through knowledge of the gospel (sanctification), to proclaim the mighty works of God, to be a witness for Christ, a royal priest and representative of the heavenly kingdom, to live a righteous life without sin, etc. We know that we are able to do all this only through spiritual sight, through the faith that God has given to us and created within us: *"For **we are his workmanship**, created in Christ Jesus **for good works, which God prepared** beforehand, that we should walk in them"* (Eph. 2:10).

Whenever you encounter the terms regeneration, justification, sanctification, or the redemption of the body, you can use the chart above to better understand the context and concepts in relationship to "salvation and faith" and the unconditional grace of God.

BASIC DIFFERENCES BETWEEN CALVINISM AND ARMINIANISM

The most significant difference is the way the roles of God and man are understood. The Calvinist does not view God's action in the same way as the Arminian. At first glance it appears that the two views differ only in the emphasis they place on the divine or human component of salvation, but they also diverge in their substance. Study the boxes from left to right:

16 See chapter 10; section: Are We God's Puppets?

ARMINIANISM	CALVINISM
God allows all sinners, after giving them prevenient grace, to freely decide whether they want to be saved or not.	God, according to His sovereign holy will, will regenerate elect sinners whose natural fallen wills are incapable of understanding the things of the Spirit of God.
God will choose those whom He foreknew would choose to believe, in spite of their sinful and fallen "free" will.	God gives "salvation and faith" to those whom He has sovereignly chosen according to His will.
The goal of God the Father is the salvation of all mankind; God the Son died on the Cross for all mankind, but did not secure salvation for anyone; the invitation and call of God the Holy Spirit is inefficacious in that man, by his free will, can choose not to cooperate with the Spirit's prevenient grace. The interaction of the three persons of the Triune God is not in harmony, but is thwarted by man. The Father's purpose to save all is not fulfilled.	There are three harmonious, perfect, and completed acts of the triune God: God the Father in eternity sovereignly chose sinners whom He loved with an unconditional, eternal love; God the Son efficaciously redeemed them on the Cross; and God the Holy Spirit irrevocably regenerates them. These sinners are irresistibly drawn, one by one, to Christ, and the Father's purpose to save all the elect is fulfilled.
The sacrifice of Jesus Christ has made salvation possible for every person without exception, but only those who accept it "willingly" will make Christ's sacrifice efficacious.	The efficacious sacrifice of Jesus Christ, apart from man, completed God's perfect and finished salvation within all whom the Father gave to the Son to redeem by His blood on the Cross.
Those who are willing to believe will "freely" allow the Holy Spirit to regenerate them by the Spirit.	God the Holy Spirit will unconditionally regenerate all those who are chosen by God the Father and redeemed by God the Son.
God and the natural man work together before regeneration (synergism). God offers rebirth, and the natural, carnal man accepts it by faith.	God alone is behind regeneration (monergism). He gives grace unconditionally; man does not cooperate in his salvation. He has no faith until he is saved, because faith begins at the same time as salvation.
The glory belongs to God, who made regeneration possible, and to the natural man, who, by his desire for God, made this possibility a reality through faith.	All glory belongs to God alone. He does not consult anyone about His decisions. He gives His glory in salvation to no one; He shares it with no one.
The natural man is indeed spiritually dead, but not to the extent that he cannot cooperate with God's prevenient grace and freely respond to His invitation.	The natural man is spiritually dead in that he is totally incapable of any approach to God. He cannot say yes to God without an unconditional spiritual resurrection.
The heart of the natural man is not so depraved that it cannot cooperate with prevenient grace and choose spiritual good, i.e., to accept Christ, or evil, i.e., to remain in Satan's prison.	The heart of the natural man is a slave to the sinful nature, a captive of the Evil One; it is totally corrupt and therefore can only choose spiritual evil, that is, to flee from God and obey its master, the Devil.
"Free" will is defined by man.	Free will is defined by God.

Let us focus on the differences shown in this table. It presents two basic soteriological interpretations that conflict on every point. These are not meaningless differences in the understanding of "faith and salvation," it is not a matter of finding a needle in a haystack. We will show that these are two completely opposite systems of salvation:

1. Arminianism—if man wants God to be able to...
2. Calvinism—if God wants man to be able to...

In the past, the difference between Arminianism, i.e., the "free" will of natural man in salvation, and Calvinism, i.e., the sovereign will of God, was not primarily a matter of whether or not man could lose his salvation. The main difference, as the Puritans and Reformers understood it, concerned a satisfactory answer to the question of who is the cause of salvation, who is really behind salvation from beginning to end. The advocates of monergistic Calvinism and synergistic Arminianism differed in their answers to these two essential questions:

1. Who put faith in the gospel into the heart of a man who did not yet believe?
2. Who keeps the gospel in the heart of an already saved man to the end?

If one believes that man's free will and faith, prompted by the Spirit's prevenient grace (traditional Arminianism), is the determinant of both questions, then man himself is the finisher of salvation. The possible objection of God's prevenient grace cannot be interpreted as a cause of faith because it is resistible. If a person can decide, by his own "free" will, to stop believing and return to the world, to the realm of the spiritually dead, he bears full responsibility for himself.

But if one believes that God has the first and last word in both matters (Calvinism), then it is the sovereign will of God that saves and creates faith in the heart of man. God has raised him spiritually from the mass grave of the world, of the spiritually dead. And at the same time, through the faith He grants, He testifies to and by His power sustains the salvation of the regenerate to the very end. God's sovereign decree is irrevocable and irresistible. God's grace guarantees that man will not fall away, but will endure to the end.

There are a number of believers in today's churches who are considered "Calminians," but are neither traditional, consistent Arminians nor consistent Calvinists because they believe in a hybrid way. They answer the first question in Arminian terms—it is the person who believes of his own "free" will, but they answer the second question Calvinistically—it is God who keeps faith in man to the end. Although these "Calminians" attempts to harmonize two opposing views of salvation, their soteriology cannot stand in the light of biblical analysis, hermeneutics, and the logical integrity of Scripture. Such a mixture of different systems resolves nothing, but only misleads, confusing the whole matter. Traditional Arminianism is at least logically consistent on the issue of gaining and losing salvation through "free" will.

IMPLICATIONS OF THE THEOLOGY OF THE "FREE" WILL OF THE NATURAL MAN

MAN DISTORTS THE GOSPEL

You may be thinking: "Should we not just preach a simple gospel and stop dealing with doctrinal contradictions that only lead to division?" Why do we even bother with questions about man's "free" will and God's sovereign grace? Isn't this unnecessary?

The Puritans and Reformers believed, preached, and wrote that the spread of the doctrine of man's "free" will in Protestant churches was the root cause of the misinterpretation of Scripture and the preached gospel. They believed that this doctrine led to the debasement, distortion, and overthrow of the gospel as it was unalterably codified in the canons of the Council of Trent (1545-1563), the Roman Catholic response to the Protestant Reformation:

CANON 4 (SESSION 6)

> *If anyone says that man's free will moved and aroused by God, by assenting to God's call and action, in no way cooperates toward disposing and preparing itself to obtain the grace of justification, that it cannot refuse its assent if it wishes, but that, as something inanimate, it does nothing whatever and is merely passive, let him be anathema.*

CANON 5. (SESSION 6)

> *If anyone says that after the sin of Adam man's free will was lost and destroyed, or that it is a thing only in name, indeed a name without a reality, a fiction introduced into the church by Satan, let him be anathema.*

CANON 12 (SESSION 6)

> *If anyone says that justifying faith is nothing else than confidence in divine mercy, which remits sins for Christ's sake, or that it is this confidence alone that justifies us, let him be anathema.*

And so, every Calvinist, every Monergist, is forever and irrevocably damned by the official Roman Catholic Church according to the still-valid Roman Catholic canon. But Scripture clearly teaches that the righteous shall live by faith (Rom. 1:17). Remember the inseparable tandem of "salvation and faith," due solely to God's unconditional grace. Missionaries of the Roman Catholic Church were sent to Protestant lands to counter all "diabolical" doctrines of God's sovereign grace and to restore the doctrine of man's "free" will. The Jesuits in particular saw the sovereign grace of God as the arch-enemy of their religious system of "free" human will and good works. Paradoxically, the Ottomans of Turkey, with God's permission, exhausted the Roman Catholic Church to such an extent that it did not have enough strength left to fight the Reformation completely.

> *In December 1525, in response to Erasmus of Rotterdam, Luther published "On the Unfree Will." He accused the humanist prince of a cold and distant attitude toward fundamental questions of faith. According to Luther, man has free will only in temporal matters. Even if he were given free will in the matter of justification, he would not want it because he could not resist the power of the Devil. Luther takes the position that it is only a merciful God who secures man's salvation. In agreement with Augustine, he emphasized the writings of the church father Jerome. Luther's clash with Erasmus meant a painful choice for many humanists. Some remained in obedience to the Catholic Church, others joined the Reformation*[17].

Many "free" will advocates among Roman Catholics, Protestant Arminians, Semi-Pelagian, and Pelagians will object: "We cannot appeal to the history of the Church, to the creeds of the Puritans or the Reformers. Augustine, Luther, Calvin, Owen, Spurgeon, and others were only men. They were as subject to sin as any other man. We believe only the Bible; we cannot take the beliefs of men 'at face value.'" All we can say is, Amen. Such objections can be summed up as follows: "We believe in our convictions, our interpretation, not the archaic, Reformed, historical ideas which have long since become obsolete in modern times. Although we know nothing about them in principle, we refuse to consider them or even to read anything about them."

17 http://www.luther.cz/martin-luther/dilo

MAN BECOMES THE JUDGE OF GOD HIMSELF

In the Arminian system of "free" will, the supreme act of God, the sacrifice of the Son of God, the second person of the holy triune God, for the sins of His people, is at the mercy of natural man. He judges by his fallen, Adamic, enslaved will whether the Cross of Christ is worthy of acceptance or rejection. Nothing, as far as we know from Scripture, surpasses the greatness and holiness of God's sacrifice. And this supreme act of God is to be judged by the fallen, sinful nature of man, to be dealt with by sinful man at his own discretion? I cannot think of a greater absurdity. I cannot imagine God the Father handing over the sacrifice of His Son to fallen mankind to be disposed of according to their Devil-enslaved and Devil-controlled "free" will—that is, sheer willfulness! This is in direct contradiction to all of Scripture and common sense.

First, mankind has already "judged" God the Son, condemning Him to die on the Cross. This was the greatest crime man ever committed in Adam, even though God foreknew the crucifixion of His Son in eternity. Natural man in his humanistic self-centeredness is not fit for judging God's saving act on the Cross of Calvary: *"For the mind that is set on the flesh is hostile to God, for* ***it does not submit to God's law; indeed, it cannot****. Those who are in the flesh cannot please God"* (Rom. 8:7-8).

Second, according to Scripture, it is not we who evaluate and judge His actions; it is He who judges our motives and actions: ***"For the LORD is our judge*** [judicial power]*; the LORD is our lawgiver* [legislative power]*; the LORD is our king* [executive power]*; he will save us"* (Isa. 33:22).

He, not we, will judge righteously. He has absolute, unlimited power over all that exists, including all mankind: *"...because he has fixed a day on which* ***he will judge the world in righteousness*** *by a man whom he has appointed; and of this he has given assurance to all by raising him from the dead"* (Acts 17:31).

Only God, the Lord Jesus Christ, has the absolute and sovereign power to reveal Himself to His people and to save them (Matt. 11:27). We are not the masters of our lives; it is not in our natural, sinful power to accept the sacrifice of the Lord Jesus Christ. On the contrary, He is Lord over us. He decides whom in His creation He will raise from the spiritual grave and whom He will leave in it (Ex. 33:19). He owes nothing to anyone, and His decisions are holy and good. He alone has the keys to death and hell (Rev. 1:17b-18). So, the question is not what we are going to do with Jesus, whether we may try to "date" Him, how we are going to get along with Him, whether we are going to stay in the relationship or break it off. What can bend the knee to supplication and humility will stand or fall with the question of how God will sovereignly deal with us!

MAN, OFTEN WRONGLY TAKES "CREDIT" FOR SALVATION

When someone "accepts" Jesus, in contrast to being accepted by Jesus (Gal. 4:9a), he is usually surrounded by people who congratulate him on his courageous decision. Going forward will require some courage and overcoming. The popular preacher or evangelist will be praised and admired for his powerful sermon. Those present may feel touched and happy that their intercessory prayers were effective. The focus tends to be on the person, while the most important thing is often overlooked—God's efficacious drawing of the sinner to Himself (John 6:44).

God's goodness, love, mercy and sacrifice on the Cross become overshadowed by man's victory over himself. Who is being glorified in such a case? God or man? As in the Enlightenment, the spirit of the world invades the Church, and man becomes the center of the universe. No wonder our churches today are largely humanistic, Arminian, semi-Pelagian to Pelagian. So many Christians favor "free" will in matters of salvation, believing in their own reason, and placing emphasis on their personal responsibility in matters of the Spirit. It is not in vogue to remind them of God's sovereignty. But a holy God will not share His 100% merit and Glory in matters of salvation and the creation of the new man.

One day as Charles H. Spurgeon was coming down from the pulpit, a man came up to him and said, "You preached a very good sermon today." Spurgeon replied, "You are not the first to praise me; the Devil has praised me during sermons." Preachers must be careful not to take credit for what God the Holy Spirit is doing in and through them. Salvation is not a reward, nor is it made efficacious by human virtue, which we mistakenly call "free" will. May we never forget that everything good in us is through God's merit, including "salvation and faith", while everything bad in us is our fault and responsibility: *"For who sees anything different in you? What do you have that you did not receive? If then you received it, why do you boast as if you did not receive it?"* (1 Cor. 4:7).

MAN DOES NOT REALIZE THE WEIGHT OF GUILT AND THE IMPACT OF SIN

Evangelism motivated by the "free" will of man necessarily obscures the true, holy nature of God the Creator and His authority over life and death. Evangelism motived by "free" will shelters the object of evangelism from the fear of God. The work of the "free" will evangelist is essentially limited to cajoling and comparing what the sinner gains by accepting or loses by rejecting the salvation offered. Christ's salvation thus unwittingly becomes a bargain, a commodity to be purchased or not purchased through an act of "faith."

In contrast, the evangelist of God's sovereign grace makes the sinner aware of God's holy nature. He will emphasize God's fatherhood, uniqueness and sovereignty, the complete, unlimited, absolute exaltation of God in every aspect of the visible and invisible world. He will explain to the sinner the infinite gulf that exists between a holy God and himself. The evangelist will deal with the holiness of God and the fallenness of man. He must explain that his greatest sin is not the greatest abomination he has committed, but the crime he has committed against a holy God—unbelief in Christ (John 16:9). It will not be the eloquence of the evangelist that causes the sinner to see and realize how infinitely fallen and separated he is from a holy God, but the creative power of the Holy Spirit. In new birth of the Spirit of God, the fallen sinner will believe that Christ in the flesh bore his sins on the Cross. From that moment, he will be saved and enabled by the Spirit to repent, that is, to turn away from the sin of the world and, for the first time, to truly and freely follow Christ, for freedom is in Him alone. Outside of Christ there is only slavery to evil. Every new birth, every spiritual birth, is dramatic and painful. The new birth is God's sovereign deliverance of the spiritual corpse from the mire of the sinful nature; it is the redemption of the slave of Satan through the blood of Christ on the Cross: *"He drew me up from the pit of destruction, out of the miry bog* [Satan's prison], *and set my feet upon a rock* [Christ], *making my steps secure"* (Ps. 40:2).

A MAN RELIES ON HIMSELF AT A CRITICAL MOMENT

According to Arminianism, the Holy Spirit works upon the sinner through prevenient grace so that he may (or may not) accept Christ's sacrifice for his sins. According to Arminianism, God can do no more for the sinner as far as salvation is concerned. The sinner is dogmatically encouraged to rely on his own judgment and to make up his own mind. But fallen "free" will is utterly incapable of leading the sinner to God. The phantom of "free" will relegates God to a passive role and elevates man to the position of ultimately choosing his salvation and redemption with his last word. What does Charles H. Spurgeon have to say about this?[18]

> *When you say, 'Can God make me become a Christian?' I tell you yes, for herein rests the power of the gospel. It does not ask your consent; but it gets it. It does not say, 'Will you have it?' but it makes you willing in the day of God's power ... The gospel wants not your consent, it gets it. It knocks the enmity out of your heart. You say, 'I do not want to be saved;' Christ says you shall be. He makes our will turn round, and then you cry, 'Lord save, or I perish!'*

In the Arminian soteriological system, the distinction between a condemned sinner far from God, in Hell, and a saved sinner in the arms of God is due to the decision of the sinner's "free" will. The difference between the saved and the unsaved, then, does not lie in the absolute efficacy of the Cross of Christ, but in the final decision of the "free" will of sinful man, which alone is able to make the Cross of Christ efficacious or inefficacious.

18 Ch. H. Spurgeon: "Total Depravity"; https://amazinggracebibledevotionals.wordpress.com/2015/02/21/can-god-make-me-become-a-christian-spurgeon/

PART I
THE TOTAL SPIRITUAL INABILITY, THE CORRUPTION OF MAN

4

THE TOTAL SPIRITUAL INABILITY, THE CORRUPTION OF MAN

DEFINITION OF THE TERM

The first point of Calvinism, that is, of the Synod of Dort, responds to the third article of the Remonstrance. It concerns the total spiritual corruption and enslavement of man's natural will.

1. ***The natural man, the offspring of Adam, is spiritually dead*** *as a result of original sin, separated from God, unable to understand the things of God. Everything man does in this state takes place on the stage of sin. He is a vassal of Satan, a slave to sin, and because of his corrupt nature is unable of his own accord to desire to follow God.*

For clarity, let us recall both views in the table to see the difference, which again is not in emphasis but in substance:

ARMINIANISM Remonstration	CALVINISM Synod of Dort
1. Spiritual Ability is the Result of God's Prevenient Grace Human beings are sinful and incapable of being righteous in themselves without God. But they are not irredeemably sinful. God works through His prevenient grace. He renews the human will to accept or reject salvation.	**1. Total Spiritual Inability is a Result of Adam's Fall** Human beings are so affected by the negative consequences of original sin that they are incapable of being righteous and are always unchangeably sinful. Human freedom is completely enslaved to sin, so that in matters of the Spirit of God, they can only choose evil.

Although total depravity, the spiritual inability of the natural man to choose God, is the most experientially demonstrable, it is also the most intellectually repugnant because the natural man is self-centered. This is evidenced by a degree of residual "contagion" in the regenerate man of God, in whom the Holy Spirit already dwells. The apostle Paul, perhaps the most spiritually mature born-again follower of Jesus Christ, declared of himself that he does not do what he wants to do, but what he hates to do (Rom. 7:15-25).[19] If this is Paul's condition after being born-again, what was his spiritual condition before being born-again of the Spirit? Completely corrupt, persecuting those who loved Christ! Could he have made a free choice for Christ in such a condition? He could not; he had to be drawn to Christ by the Father in a very dramatic way (John 6:44) on the road to Damascus (Acts 9:4-22). Clearly Paul was not cooperating with God or His "prevenient grace" when he was persecuting Christians. Arminianism does not pay much attention to Paul's experience because Arminianism is man-centered, synergistic, and believes in God's prevenient, cooperating grace.

With regard to regeneration of the sinner, Calvinism is monergistic; it believes in the one-sided, exclusive, sovereign work of God; it is totally God-centered; it believes that the natural man would be

19 Prominent theologians disagree about this passage. Some teach that Paul is describing himself, and therefore all believers; others teach that he is describing an unsaved man.

incapable, unfit, to make a decision for Christ in the way that Paul did on the road to Damascus. Glory to God alone through Jesus Christ our Lord!

THE ESSENCE OF TOTAL PHYSICAL AND SPIRITUAL DEPRAVITY

TOTAL PHYSICAL DEPRAVITY

The corruption of the visible, physical creation, the world, and the universe is not only visible, but verifiable by the laws of physics. As a result of Adam's Fall, not a single material particle of creation remains in its original, perfect, created form. Everything visible has been affected by the second law of thermodynamics, the permanent increase of entropy, or the permanent increase of disorder, i.e., chaos, leading to extinction. The world and the universe are not evolving, they are devolving. The Lord created the earth and man, he stretched out the universe, he subjected everything to his laws, and everything obeys him (Isa. 45:12); the Lord also will roll them up like a book, like a scroll: *"All the host of heaven shall rot away, and the skies roll up like a scroll. All their host shall fall, as leaves fall from the vine, like leaves falling from the fig tree"* (Isa. 34:4). Man is not in a state of development; on the contrary, he is in a state of decline. Our eye, for example, is affected to the last receptor and nerve connection because of Adam's Fall, but only to a certain extent, because we can still see. From birth to death, our bodies are continuously functionally degraded, aging, and prone to decay. The defining adjective "total" (corruption) refers to the extent of the destruction, that is, the destruction in its entirety, the destruction of everything physical, or the entire universe. But the intensity of corruption of physical man and all physical, visible creation cannot be total; if it were, nothing would function, everything would cease to exist.

TOTAL SPIRITUAL DEPRAVITY

When we speak of total spiritual incompetence and corruption, we are referring primarily to the condition of the inner man. Adam's sin created an evil that cannot be controlled by his own will because it is enslaved by the Evil One. We are born sinful; rebellion is within us. We serve sin willingly, without compulsion, in accordance with our nature. The connection between the natural, human spirit and the Spirit of God was completely severed by the fall of Adam. God's Holy Spirit cannot dwell in the presence of a fallen, sinful human spirit. The scope and intensity, the extent and degree of spiritual destruction is total. Man is spiritually dead from birth, separated from God, unable to understand the things of the Spirit of God (1 Cor. 2:14). The spiritually dead man does not and cannot seek the true God (Rom. 3:11); he is not interested in who God is, but only in what He can do for him. He seeks only the idol he has carved out in his mind, the genie in the bottle that will help him solve the problems of life and then get back in the bottle. That is why there is so much idolatry in the world, fondly called religion.

We are all born as bound serfs of Satan. We can only choose what is within the reach of our sinful hearts. The natural man has no liberty, no contact with God, no outreach to God, imprisoned in the Devil's household, therefore there is no opportunity for the natural man to fill his heart with the Spirit of God. Adam made the bed of death for all mankind on Satan's bunk where we are all born to sleep. Everything is caused by man's desire to be like God, the desire to judge for himself what is good and what is evil (Gen. 3:5). The Devil assured the woman that neither she nor her husband would die if they tasted the forbidden fruit of the knowledge of good and evil. Eve obeyed the serpent, Adam chose Eve over God, and a catastrophe of cosmic proportions became a reality: *"And to Adam he said, 'Because you have listened to the voice of your wife and have eaten of the tree of which I commanded you,*

'You shall not eat of it,' cursed is the ground because of you; in pain you shall eat of it all the days of your life; thorns and thistles it shall bring forth for you; and you shall eat the plants of the field. By the sweat of your face you shall eat bread, till you return to the ground, for out of it you were taken; for you are dust, and to dust you shall return'" (Gen. 3:17-19). In Adam's sin, we lost not only eternal spiritual life, which is the "vertical" union of our spirit with the Spirit of God, but also eternal physical life, which is the eternal, "horizontal" union of our spirit with our body. As a result of the Fall, in the spiritual realm, mankind has acquired freedom from righteousness, i.e., bondage to unrighteousness (Rom. 6:20). In the physical realm, sickness, suffering, and death accompany mankind and all living things (Rom. 6:23).

The natural man, then, is unable to choose Christ because his will has no liberty, no contact with the things of the Spirit of God, because it is imprisoned, enslaved, and possessed by evil. Christ is absent from his ballot; no such ballot is printed in Satan's dungeon. The Devil's prisoner has no idea who Christ is, nor can he vote for Him, for he prefers and votes for himself (Rom. 8:7). As Satan's vassal and slave, he cannot do otherwise because his heart is deceitful: *"The heart is deceitful above all things, and desperately sick; who can understand it?"* (Jer. 17:9a).

Allow me to have an imperfect parable. Let us imagine that an imprisoned woman gives birth to a child. The child is raised only within the confines of the dungeon. With no information from the outside, he has no idea what the world outside the prison walls is like. Therefore, he cannot long for freedom as he does not know what freedom means. Escape is an unknown concept to him. He has a certain amount of "free" will in this limited space. He can "freely" decide in his cell to walk from right to left or from left to right, to sit on a bunk or to eat out of a tin can with his left or right hand, but he cannot decide to go on vacation to Croatia. He does not know what a vacation is, he does not know what Croatia is. He has no liberty, no contact with anything that happens outside the walls of the dungeon, which are invincibly guarded by the jailer. Where there is no freedom, knowledge is limited; people are "free" to choose only what they know, what they can reach.

So, it is with all the natural seed of Adam. From birth we are all serfs, vassals, captives, imprisoned in the dungeon of evil, whose ruler is Satan, the serpent, the Devil, the dragon, in short, the Evil One, to whom we are slaves by nature and by choice through sin. Even King David knew that he was fallen, born in the underworld: *"O LORD, you have brought up my soul from Sheol;* ***you restored me*** *to life from among those who go down to the pit* [the final destiny of the reprobate is the lake of fire]*"* (Ps. 30:3). Our natural will has no liberty, no contact with anything or anyone outside the walls of Satan's prison. It has no contact with the things of the Spirit of God; it cannot know who God the Father and the Son are, and therefore, it cannot accept Jesus Christ. The natural man does not and cannot face such a choice. He is "free" to act only in the prison of evil. In the quicksand of the world under Satan's rule (John 14:30), he is "free" only to choose the place and depth of his drowning: *"For when you were slaves of sin, you were free in regard to righteousness* [were imprisoned in unrighteousness]*"* (Rom. 6:20).

Natural people often think that the Devil is the ruler of the lake of fire, hell. This is fatal ignorance with far-reaching consequences. The Devil is not a little goat-man with horns and hooves. The Devil is the father of lies and the evil father of all natural men (John 8:44; 1 John 3:10). His lies have been attractive since Adam. The deceived natural man is lured by the pleasing, humanistic, man-centered, philosophical, pseudo-scientific, and religious "isms" that distort the biblical truth about both God and the Devil. The Devil became the ruler of the world and the father of the spirit of all natural men after the fall of Adam. We are all born under his dominion. He once even ruled over those who are now in Christ (Eph. 2:1-2). But God controls everything, even the Devil's world dominion. The true ruler over death, hell, and the lake of fire is God, not the Devil: *"Fear not, I am the first and the last, and the living one. I died, and behold I am alive forevermore, and* ***I have the keys of Death and Hades****"* (Rev. 1:17b-18).

THE CONSEQUENCES OF TOTAL DEPRAVITY

An understanding of the doctrine of the total depravity of all creation, visible and invisible, will necessarily affect our view not only of the universe, inanimate and animate nature, but especially of God's unconditional grace—"salvation and faith," rebirth, justification, sanctification, and resurrection to a glorified body. We begin to see ourselves, our neighbors, and Christians in a new way. There are only two basic perspectives:

1. ANTHROPOCENTRIC

Man-centered. If we believe that we are born sinless (Pelagianism), or that our spiritual corruption is only partial (Semi-Pelagianism), or that we are spiritually dead but that God revives our spiritual understanding by His prevenient grace, then we must also believe that our salvation through Christ is the result of our own agency, cooperation, synergy, for it is only efficacious when we choose to accept the salvation offered. Those who reject the offer of salvation make Christ's saving sacrifice on the Cross incomplete. He bore the punishment for their sins in vain; He redeemed them with His blood, but He did not win their hearts. He paid the ransom for them, but they did not become His possession. It was as if He did not know that He was dying for them in vain. He painfully longs for all, and yet many reject Him.

If Almighty God has done all He can for the sinner, including the gift of His prevenient "grace", and now the sinner is to decide by his "free" will, independent of God, then God's purpose to save all would be left to natural, sinful man. God's purpose or desire to save all would be thwarted because Satan's slave—not God—would be pulling the longer end of the rope. The lost man would have the final say as to whether God would be pleased or grieved by his decision. If faith and subsequent regeneration were dependent upon the sovereign decision of the "free" will of the natural man, we would lose any incentive to pray for anyone. In a situation where the fallen person had the upper hand, it would be far more efficacious to appeal directly to the person than to intercede to God in prayer. It would suffice to gather enough reasons for Christ, and to persuade him even more urgently to make a "free" and right decision for himself.

All Christians pray, asking God to have mercy on those they love, to move in their minds and hearts, to intervene in their lives. Why is this? Because all Christians, including sincere Arminian brethren, believe in their hearts that ultimately only God can change the hearts of unbelievers. If a truly Arminian prayer for lost loved ones existed, it might be something like this—a caricature, not a prayer:

> *God, I know that my beloved, whom I care about so much, is not Your puppet; preserve his freedom of choice, do not interfere with his free will, allow him to decide according to his conscience. Nevertheless, I ask You to persuade him as best You can with Your prevenient grace. Show him the blessings of heaven and the horrors of hell. I care so much for him. I hope you will succeed.*

Every Christ-loving Arminian proves by prayer that his heart hopes in an almighty and sovereign God. Therefore, every sincere Arminian prays in a Calvinistic spirit. This inconsistency in the thinking of Arminians is because they believe that human "free" will protects God from the charge of injustice. But in His sovereignty, God needs no such protection (Rom. 9:18-21).

2. THEOCENTRIC

God-centered. If we believe that our spiritual depravity and inability is total (Calvinism), then we must also believe that our salvation is by His grace alone, by the will and sacrifice of the One—a monergistic, unconditional decision of God in which we have no merit.

Just as no one can decide by his own will whether, when, and to whom he will be born bodily, so no one can decide by his own will whether and when he will be spiritually born-again of God. Both physical birth and spiritual rebirth are the unilateral creative work of God alone. Both physical birth and spiritual rebirth are by the sovereign decree of God.

The spirit of a spiritually dead person is not connected to the Spirit of God. But just as God created all natural humanity, so He creates His own people spiritually alive—already connected to the Spirit of God. Spirit-born Christians are His adopted children. He is their Father, and He loves them unconditionally with an everlasting love. In all those who are baptized into Christ, the Spirit of God takes up permanent residence. Then, all who are born-again can truly believe freely because they have been spiritually recreated in newfound freedom, i.e., deliverance from the Devil's prison. They are able to see and hear Christ with all their newly created spiritual senses: *"I will run in the way of your commandments when you enlarge* [circumcise] *my heart* [therefore I see You already, I believe in You already]*!"* (Ps. 119:32). Their liberated soul and will are now connected to God the Holy Spirit, therefore can now bear fruit. True free will, love, truth, and "the only way" exist exclusively and singularly in Christ. Outside of Christ, the potential of free will, love, truth, and "the way" languish in the distortions of Satan's implanted lie (Rom. 3:4; John 8:44). There is no doubt that God has the last word.

EVIDENCE OF TOTAL DEPRAVITY

CHRISTIANS USED TO BE SATAN'S SLAVES

Those who know Christ today were spiritually dead at birth, living according to the will of the Evil One, according to the sinful nature they inherited from Adam: *"But God, being rich in mercy, because of the great love* [eternal saving love] *with which he loved us, even when we* [who belong to him from eternity, before the foundation of the world] *were dead in our trespasses* [imprisoned in Satan's prison], ***made us alive together with Christ****—by grace you have been saved—and raised us up with him and* ***seated us with him in the heavenly places*** *in Christ Jesus* [the first resurrection, 'salvation and faith'] "(Eph. 2:4-6).

God's unconditional grace alone circumcises the heart. All who are born-again of the Spirit once walked in darkness; they were evil: *"...for at one time you were darkness* [you belonged to Satan], *but now you are light in the Lord* [you belong to Christ]. *Walk as children of light"* (Eph. 5:8). Those who have not been born-again of the Spirit of God, to whom Christ has not sent the Helper within (John 15:26), remain prisoners of the Evil One. God accomplished spiritual resurrection while we were still separated from God, spiritually uncircumcised and dead: *"**And you, who were dead in your trespasses** and the uncircumcision of your flesh, **God made alive together with him*** [i.e. the first spiritual resurrection], *having forgiven us all our trespasses* [only those who have been spiritually baptized, immersed into Christ through the Spirit] "(Col. 2:13).

All born only naturally, carnally, without God's eternal redeeming love, still obey the ruler of this world, Satan. Isaiah describes such ones as straying sheep: *"**All we like sheep*** [sheep are the image of God's children] ***have gone astray****; we have turned—every one—to his own way; and the LORD has laid on him* [Jesus] *the iniquity of* *us all* [all who are or will be in Him]*"* (Isa. 53:6). The Lord Jesus Christ suffered according to the will of the Father for His beloved people. There is no other way than the way of the Cross that leads people to "salvation and faith." Salvation or damnation is solely in the hands of the Triune God. He reveals His face to some and hides it from others. He is the Creator of the natural, outward, physical man, and He is the Creator of the supernatural, inward, spiritual man: *"We have all* [without exception] *become like one who is unclean, and all our righteous deeds are like a polluted garment. We all fade like a leaf, and our iniquities, like the wind, take us away. There is no one who calls upon your name, who rouses himself to take hold of you; for you have hidden your face from us, and have made us melt in the hand of our iniquities. But now, O LORD, you are our Father; we are the clay, and you are our potter* [You make us into a new, inner, spiritual man]*; we are all the work of your hand"* (Isa. 64:6-8).

MAN IS SINFUL FROM BIRTH

Human lostness is inherent from conception. In the following verse, David is not saying the act of conception is sinful, as if the marriage bed were sinful, for God's Word says that it is holy. David is not referring to the sinfulness of his mother. He is saying that from the moment of conception he was sinful: *"Behold, I was brought forth in iniquity, and* ***in sin did my mother conceive me****"* (Ps. 51:5). The natural man lives in anxiety and fear his entire life and dies before he wants to. Fear of death and restlessness in the soul are consequences of man's sinful nature. Man is not evil because he sins; man sins because he is born evil. Man's sinful nature is the cause; his evil deeds are merely the effect. People are inherently evildoers, that is, children of Satan: *"The wicked are estranged from the womb;* ***they go astray from birth****, speaking lies"* (Ps. 58:3).

People have fallen under the illusion that they can deal with evil, as with poverty and wealth, on their own. For since Adam's Fall, people have "known" what evil is and how to defeat it, and what good is and how to establish it. The Devil's instruction through Adam was to get rid of God (Gen. 3:5). Let us look at just one Czech song by Voskovec and Werich (1935). Ježek's great jazz music accompanies the humanistic, revolutionary lyrics which suggest that humanity will be much better off if the political and economic climate changes. There are countless similar songs that incite even deeper wickedness. Read carefully:

> *Hey, Mr. King, don't be lazy, take some rags and go among the people, you'll know what it is to live by toil, you'll see so much dirt in a day, you'll never have peace until death. And all in all, mighty lords, come and see us,* ***you lords who are guilty that misery makes robbers of men****, that hunger drives the wolves from the woods. Think that we are but a rabble, that you need not fear us. But one day you'll be afraid when we scream under your windows. Hey, hoarders and gluttons, it's time for you to pay,* ***lords, you are guilty that misery has turned men into scoundrels****, that hunger drives us against you.*

But neither lords nor poverty make men robbers. No lord, no hoarder, no glutton, neither riches nor poverty, make men into scoundrels. We are all born sinners—no one can blame another. No one is wicked because he is a victim of the wickedness of others. How many people who are educated, wealthy, and powerful are vicious wolves? D. L. Moody said: "Give an education to a robber who steals nuts and bolts on the railroad, and he will steal your locomotive."

I will never forget a visit to the Genocide Museum, formerly the French Lyceum, S21 Prison in Phnom Penh, Cambodia. The Khmer Rouge officially killed two million people between 1975 and 1979, 25% of the Cambodian population. The locals told me it was a third. God only knows how many it really was. Neither Stalin nor Mao Zedong, who were imperfect models for the French-educated Pol Pot in building a classless society, managed to wipe out at least a quarter of their own population. Those who wore glasses were considered intellectuals and mercilessly executed. What is most striking is the fact that the executive lever of murder was primarily an army of children, around age 16 and under. This made a deeper impression on me than my visit to Auschwitz. Child soldiers are still used today in many Third World countries because of their diabolical, murderous, ruthless capacity and efficiency. Indeed, man is not born as spotless as a sheet of white paper: *"How then can man be in the right before God? How can he who is born of woman be pure?"* (Job 25:4). Today I disagree with my grandfather, who fought in World War I. He used to say: "People are good, but these governments, they are evil." Without our Savior, the Lord Jesus Christ, without His enlightenment, all people remain trapped in the darkness of evil: *"And this is the judgment: the light has come into the world* [the first Advent of Christ], *and people loved the darkness* [the Devil] *rather than the light* [Christ] *because their works were evil"* (John 3:19).

PRIDE, SELF-CENTEREDNESS, AND SEEKING EQUALITY WITH GOD

If we were born as clean as a sheet of white paper (Pelagianism and Islam) or if only partially soiled (Semi-Pelagianism), then God could have addressed our total cleanness or our partial spiritual uncleanness by simply offering us the benefit of being in His company. He would not have had to send His Son to die for us. As Luther noted, we come into the world as Pelagians, filled with pride and self-centeredness. We think we are decent, only corrupted by our environment or by people. But in truth, we are spiritually dead. We live in the illusion that we know what is good for us and what is bad for us (Gen. 3:5), that we are in fact divine: *"For the mind that is set on the flesh* [pride, would-be God-equality] *is hostile to God, for it does not submit to God's law; indeed, it cannot. Those who are in the flesh cannot please God"* (Rom. 8:7-8). The devil has cunningly led us all to believe that we can live in our own strength, that we can be spiritually autonomous. But our nature emanates the spiritual disfigurement of an enslaved, selfish, prideful self-will. No natural descendant of Adam has an innate ability to understand, much less to accept, God's view of his utter spiritual deadness, depravity, and inability: *"The natural person does not accept the things of the Spirit of God, for they are folly to him, and he is not able to understand them because they are spiritually discerned* [the Spirit of God, with whom the spiritually dead, natural man is not connected]*"* (1 Cor. 2:14).

No will, not even Satan's, can rule outside the "boundaries" of God's sovereign will. Only God has no boundaries; in His attributes, God is undefinable. The belief that man has an independent, natural "free" will, capable of ruling outside of God's unlimited sovereignty, testifies of proud self-centeredness, the boorish belief that one's "free" will can "circumscribe" God. It is impossible for man to draw a line that limits God, a line beyond which God cannot go. It is impossible for man to create a zone in which God is powerless. God would be god with a small "g" if he had boundaries. The area beyond this god's boundaries would be the realm of another god, one with "independent" free will—namely sinful, fallen man. As we well know, the Devil hung this particular lie on the noses of the first two people. Pride and self-sovereignty have been with man since Adam. In helpful repetition: *"For God knows that when you eat of it* [the tree of the knowledge of good and evil] *your eyes will be opened, and you will be like God* [you will seek to restrain Him], *knowing good and evil"* (Gen. 3:5).

The Pelagian, Semi-Pelagian, and Arminian lives under the false belief that he has "free" will in the spiritual realm. He believes that from birth he is able (Pelagian and Semi-Pelagian), or from sometime after birth he is empowered by the Holy Spirit (Arminian), to "freely" choose between good (God—light) and evil (the Devil—darkness). Because he is in darkness, sinful, natural man can only choose evil in the spiritual realm, i.e., he cannot choose God. He cannot offer God his "faith," that God might give him salvation in return, because "salvation and faith" is created and given by God: *"Or who has given a gift to Him that he might be repaid? For from Him and through Him and to Him are all things. To Him be glory forever. Amen"* (Rom. 11:35-36).

CHILDREN OF GOD AND THE DEVIL

Paul urged Christians not to live in darkness, in the service of evil, as the pagans do. The Gentile cannot know the measure of his destruction and hardness, because his mind is darkened by the Devil: *"Now this I say and testify in the Lord, that you must no longer walk as the Gentiles do, in the futility of their minds. They are darkened in their understanding, alienated from the life of God because of the ignorance that is in them, due to their hardness of heart. They have become callous and have given themselves up to sensuality, greedy to practice every kind of impurity"* (Eph. 4:17-19). Everyone who is not in Jesus Christ is in the world, and the whole world is under the power of the Evil One (2 Cor. 4:4). The spiritual father of the natural man is none other than the Evil One (1 John 3:10). When speaking to the Pharisees, the religious elite of Israel, the Lord Jesus said: *"If God were your Father, you would love me, for I came from God and I am here. I came not of my own accord, but He sent me. Why do you not understand what I say? It is because you cannot bear to hear my word.* ***You are of your father the devil****, and your will is to do your father's desires. He was a murderer from the beginning, and does not stand in the truth, because there is no truth in him.*

When he lies, he speaks out of his own character, for he is a liar and the father of lies" (John 8:42-44).

The apostle Paul confirmed this state of natural humanity in a letter to his disciple Timothy: *"...correcting* [the servant of Christ] *his opponents* [who do not know Christ] *with gentleness. God may perhaps grant them repentance* [not their "free" will] *leading to a knowledge of the truth, and* ***they may come to their senses and escape from the snare of the devil, after being captured by him to do his will"*** (2 Tim. 2:25-26).

God is the Creator of all men. But only His promised children (Rom. 9:8), those who are His in Christ, can call Him Father. Those who are not in Christ have another father, the Devil (Acts 13:9-10): *"By this it is evident who are the children of God, and* ***who are the children of the devil****: whoever does not practice righteousness is not of God, nor is the one who does not love his brother"* (1 John 3:10). *"Whoever makes a practice of sinning* ***is of the devil****, for the devil has been sinning from the beginning. The reason the Son of God appeared was to destroy the works of the devil"* (1 John 3:8).

This news is not merely unpleasant; it is unacceptable to the natural, humanistically-minded person. The Devil is satisfied when those who do not know Christ or reject Him think of themselves as "decent", albeit imperfect, people. Scripture will lead us out of this error in the next heading.

THERE IS NO ONE WHO DOES GOOD

Humanists believe that a bad environment produces bad people, so they seek to eliminate evil by correcting the environment and social relationships. God's view is the opposite—the evil human heart within evil persons produces environments and social relationships that are evil. God removes the evil by creating new hearts in humans. Only the one whom God draws to Himself will realize his desperate situation, beat his breast and cry out: *"God, be merciful to me, a sinner!"* (Luke 18:13b). When God changes his heart, he becomes a new creation; he is "saved and believing." There is no other way but the way of the Cross—the way of humility and obedience. Let us remember this: *"Surely there is not a righteous man on earth who does good and never sins"* (Eccles. 7:20). When God leaves man in his iniquities, let us avoid condemning God. Man has been guilty throughout all of history, but God fulfills His purpose in human iniquity lead to God's ultimate holy goal and His glorification. Let us not judge His sovereign purposes and ways, which are infinitely beyond our rational understanding (Deut. 29:29). We stagger under the power of our own iniquity, not because of "the iniquity of God": *"What then? Are we Jews any better off? No, not at all. For we have already charged that* ***all, both Jews and Greeks, are under sin****, as it is written: 'None is righteous, no, not one; no one understands;* ***no one seeks for God****. All have turned aside; together they have become worthless; no one does good,* ***not even one****.' 'Their throat is an open grave; they use their tongues to deceive.' 'The venom of asps is under their lips.' 'Their mouth is full of curses and bitterness.' 'Their feet are swift to shed blood; in their paths are ruin and misery, and the way of peace they have not known.' 'There is no fear of God before their eyes'"* (Rom. 3:9-18).

WAS IT WORSE AFTER THE FLOOD THAN BEFORE THE FLOOD?

Today's natural man in Adam is no better than pre-flood mankind. When the former world was flooded, only eight people were saved in the ark[20]. If natural human beings today are better off than pre-flood human beings—which they are not (Gen. 8:21)—they would not be facing a destruction more dramatic and final than the first flood of the world. The flood was merely an example, a preview, of God's final day of judgment: *"But the day of the Lord will come like a thief* [unexpectedly, like the Flood], *and then the heavens will pass away*

20 The ark is one of the many Old Testament types of Jesus Christ.

with a roar, and the heavenly bodies will be burned up and dissolved [this universe cannot enter holy eternity, God will remake it, reshape it], *and the earth and the works that are done on it will be exposed"* (2 Pet. 3:10). Scripture repeatedly reminds us that the lifestyle of natural mankind before the second coming of the Lord Jesus Christ will be strikingly similar to that of the antediluvian world: *"**For as were the days of Noah**, so will be the coming of the Son of Man. For as in those days before the flood they were eating and drinking, marrying and giving in marriage, until the day when Noah entered the ark, and they were unaware until the flood came and swept them all away, **so will be the coming of the Son of Man**"* (Matt. 24:37-39). In fact, the destruction of the world by the flood, the universal drowning of all things on earth, and the rescue of the eight elect were a merely physical foreshadowing of the final spiritual destruction that awaits many at the second advent of Christ. This will have eternal, far-reaching, and final consequences. Then, like the eight in the ark, God's people, that innumerable multitude in Christ (Rev. 7:9-10), will be saved, caught up in the clouds to meet the Bridegroom, the Lord Jesus Christ (1 Thess. 4:17). They will descend with Him to earth as the New Jerusalem, His bride (Rev. 21:2), who will gaze forever into the face of the Lamb.

The reprobates who are not in Christ will meet a fate parallel to those who were kept outside the ark, who drowned, with the immense difference that reprobates at the time of the flood "only" perished bodily, for a time. At the Second Coming of Christ, these will be raised bodily (Dan. 12:2) to perish once more, to "drown" spiritually in the lake of fire, an eternal second death which is spiritual, i.e., eternal separation from the Lord. (2 Thess. 1:9): *"Then Death and Hades were thrown into the lake of fire. This is the second death, the lake of fire"* (Rev. 20:14). Those who do not know Christ will dwell in the flesh in eternal spiritual perdition, far from the living God—that is, they will be forever separated from the very Meaning of existence. This is the second, eternal, spiritual death (Rev. 2:11; 20:6; 20:14; 21:8): *"...in flaming fire, inflicting vengeance on those who do not know God and on those who do not obey the gospel of our Lord Jesus. They will suffer the punishment of* ***eternal destruction, away from the presence of the Lord and from the glory*** *of his might, when he comes on that day to be glorified in his saints* [those whom He has saved from the power of the Devil], *and to be marveled at among all who have believed, because our testimony to you was believed"* (2 Thess. 1:8-10).

EVIL COMES FROM WITHIN MAN

The natural man in his self-centered lostness views true freedom, that is, service to God, as "bondage." And he calls true slavery, that is, service to Satan and sin, "freedom." Addiction to sin devastates mankind. No one can purify himself through his own efforts and inner strength: *"Who can bring a clean thing out of an unclean? There is not one"* (Job 14:4). All people are under the power of sin, as evidenced by our words and deeds. By them one can discern our heart: *"For from within, out of the heart of man, come evil thoughts, sexual immorality, theft, murder, adultery, coveting, wickedness, deceit, sensuality, envy, slander, pride, foolishness. All these evil things come from within, and they defile a person"* (Mark 7:21-23). If we doubt these accusations apply to us, then perhaps we will see ourselves in this verse: *"...but no human being can tame the tongue. It is a restless evil, full of deadly poison"* (James 3:8).

If you are awakening to the true state of humanity, do not blame the times in which we live, do not blame our environment, and do not blame history. Things only act as catalysts. What is hidden in the human heart is the cause of all crimes, all despotic, cruel, totalitarian regimes that surface. It is never the other way around. A regime will not corrupt man's perfectly "good" or neutral inner nature. In fact, if God did not consistently curb the inner man, this world would be short-lived through human plundering. Those who are deceived by evil, believing they are following a good conscience while harming others in their sin, are blinded to the truth: *"If we say we have no sin, we deceive ourselves, and the truth is not in us."..."If we say we have not sinned, we make him* [God] *a liar, and his word is not in us"* (1 John 1:8,10). To a holy God, the one (humanly speaking) "venial sin," Adam's disobedience in eating the fruit of the tree of the knowledge of good and evil, became the most heinous of all possible sins. What was Adam's motivation? The desire for equality with God! This sin is the lifestyle of the world in which we live.

5

GRACE

THE DIFFERENCE BETWEEN PREVENIENT AND COMMON GRACE

We have been introduced to terms that are synonymous in Arminianism and Roman Catholicism—preliminary awakening, prevenient awakening, cooperating grace, prevenient grace, the prevenient grace of God, and the inward help of the Holy Spirit[21]. For the sake of clarity, I combine all these under the term "prevenient grace." Remember that the monergistic doctrine of the Reformation rejected prevenient grace because it could not be justified by Scripture. On the other hand, the Reformation, introduced the concept of common grace. Let us closely examine the difference between the two.

PREVENIENT GRACE

The Remonstrance, Arminianism, and Catholicism teach that God's prevenient grace restores fallen, natural man's ability to choose God. However, prevenient grace is resistible because a person can remain in condemnation if he so chooses. In this case,

---

21 See chapter 2; section: The Five Articles of Remonstrance and Calvinism; heading: 4. Prevenient, Assisting or Cooperative Resistible Grace.

God is powerless to save the sinner against his own will. In short, the doctrine of prevenient grace empowers the sinner's "free" will to consciously choose God or not choose God, and thus man has the final say in salvation.

COMMON GRACE

God's common grace has nothing to do with the awakened "ability" to choose or reject salvation, as prevenient grace is said to enable. Scripture does not recognize a "free" will in natural, fallen man. Rather, it acknowledges only the will of natural man as being enslaved to the Evil One (Rom. 6:20; Gal. 4:3; 4:8), and true freedom as existing exclusively in Christ (John 8:36).

Our entire being, where, when, and to whom we were born, our environment and the people around us, our genetic makeup, all of our physical and mental talents and abilities—all of these things are part of common grace, which God grants to each person according to His sovereign will. For example, if God has chosen not to endow someone with a musical ear and talent, then practicing the piano 24 hours a day will not help. He may have endowed this person with other abilities that a top musician may desire in vain. If God chose to endow Einstein with extraordinary mathematical abilities and a profound intellect, and if Einstein chose to develop these abilities, through God's common grace, into genius, even then Einstein has nothing to boast about. It was God who created Einstein and endowed him with talents so that his mental and physical abilities could be developed, according God's sovereign design. Einstein could use his talents to his and mankind's benefit or ruin—God alone knows if Einstein's choices are for good or for evil.

Another example of God's common grace can be seen in the conversation between Jesus and Pilate: *"So Pilate said to him* [Jesus], *'You will not speak to me? Do you not know that I have authority to release you and authority to crucify you?' Jesus answered* *him, '**You would have no authority over me at all unless it had been given you from above**'"* (John 19:10-11a). Pilate, this self-centered man who wanted to be equal to God, was carried by God's common grace into a high position of authority. He was focused on his own importance and power; he had power and authority to make life and death decisions; he was undoubtedly convinced that he had reached his position through his own efforts and abilities. What Pilate did not realize was that through God's common grace he had become an instrument of God in the greatest drama in human history.

Yet another very vivid example of God's common grace is seen in the sonship of Ishmael. He was born only of man's "free" will; he was not born according to the promise (Gal. 4:23). At the urging of his wife Sarah, Abraham fathered Ismael with the slave Hagar. Abraham wanted his beloved son Ishmael to live in God's presence, to be one of God's promised, chosen people, so it was painful for him to drive him and his mother Hagar into the desert. Ishmael is the archetype of the natural man, born only physically, not spiritually. Though from eternity he had no part in God's eternal covenant of promise, of saving grace, yet God included him in common grace in a way seen of few others: *"And Abraham said to God, 'Oh that Ishmael might live before you* [to be Your chosen]*!' God said, 'No, but Sarah your wife shall bear you a son, and you shall call his name Isaac. I will establish my covenant with him as an everlasting covenant for his offspring after him* [for all the promised ones, loved by Me in Christ from all eternity]. ***As for Ishmael, I have heard you****; behold, I have blessed him and will make him fruitful and multiply him greatly. He shall father twelve princes, and I will make him into a great nation. But I will establish my covenant* [the new Zionic Law of Christ] *with Isaac, whom Sarah shall bear to you at this time next year'"* (Gen. 17:18-21).

God creates the new man in Christ according to His will, according to His promise, not according to the "free" will of man. We see this in the Biblical account of Abraham, an idol worshipper who was chosen by God, loved with everlasting love, and endowed with "salvation and faith." The Bible tells us that all who are in Christ have become Abraham's spiritual sons: *"Know then that it is those of faith who are the sons of Abraham. And the Scripture, foreseeing that God would justify the Gentiles by faith, preached the gospel beforehand to Abraham, saying, 'In you shall all the nations be blessed.* [saved in Abraham's seed—Jesus Christ (Gal. 3:16)—without distinction, not without exception] '"(Gal. 3:7-8).

The most important evidence of God's common grace is the fact that, on the one hand, He saves fallen man from physical self-destruction, and at the same time, He preserves all of creation in a sustainable state[22], despite the fact that man is only evil from his youth (Gen. 8:21). But common grace alone cannot save anyone from condemnation—common grace saves no one. In fact, often the people well-endowed with common grace, those who are educated, gifted, healthy, and successful, whether in business, science, art, or sports, find it much more difficult to accept God's truth. Their successes in life so distract them that, like Pilate, they are blinded to spiritual truths. It is quite common that successful people never realize that what they have accomplished in life is a gift of God's common grace.

WITHOUT SAVING GRACE THERE WOULD BE NO COMMON GRACE

The panorama of history, past, present and future, is carried by God's common grace. If God were to turn away from His creation (deism), everything would collapse (Heb. 1:3a). God's powerful Word sustains life, though no one deserves God's sustaining

22 See chapter 5; section: Common Grace Keeps the World Moving; heading: God Controls Evil.

common grace: "*...so that you may be sons of your Father who is in heaven. For he makes his sun rise on the evil* [in the world] *and on the good* [in Christ], *and sends rain on the just and on the unjust* [outside of Christ]"(Matt. 5:45). This whole world is a picture of God's common grace; it is only through common grace that people experience the love of relatives (storgé), the brotherly love of friends (filia), and the erotic love (erós) between spouses. It is only through God's common grace that we enjoy family, children, friendship, art, science, sports, work, and that we can live in peace and abundance: "*In past generations he allowed all the nations to walk in their own ways. Yet he did not leave himself without witness, for he did good by giving you rains from heaven and fruitful seasons, satisfying your hearts with food and gladness*" (Acts 14:16-17). However, there is no aspect of common grace which includes or contains God's eternal, unconditional, saving grace.

And yet the events and course of this world within the time-space continuum, this common grace, is fulfilled through the Cross of the Lord Jesus Christ. For if a holy God had decided in eternity, before the foundation of the world, not to exercise His saving grace, if He had allowed Adam and Eve to eat of the tree of life (Gen. 3:22), today none of us would be born into life as we know it on earth. Instead, we would have been born into a hellish existence, far from God, having no hope of salvation, eternally separated from the meaning of existence. That alternative would have been far worse than the worst that can happen in the world of violence we live in today. Our Sovereign God did not choose that option. Before the foundation of the world, He foreordained the salvation of the elect in Christ in whom He is most glorified (John 12:27-28). Through the Cross of Christ, He is drawing to Himself people He has chosen from every generation, people beloved from all eternity.

Through God's saving grace, the chosen ones are baptized by the Spirit into the Son. And so it is that through the Cross of

Christ, on account of His saving grace, by default even those who fall under the wrath of God can enjoy abundant common grace in this life (Rom. 9:22): *"For to this end we toil and strive* [undergo sanctification and strict discipline], *because we have our hope set on the living God, who is the* ***Savior of all people*** [He endows all people with a measure of common grace], ***especially of those who believe*** [He endows His elect people with eternal love and saving grace]*"* (1 Tim. 4:10). This verse contains common grace, which applies to all people without exception, as well as saving grace, which applies only to those who are "saved and believe" because of it. Common grace deals with physical birth, genetic makeup, gifting, environment—simply put, the entire earthly life of the natural man. Saving grace extends far beyond the earthly life of the natural man since it is about spiritual rebirth through the Holy Spirit who creates the new man in Christ. The born-again person has already been endowed with eternal life, which is the highest knowledge of God (John 17:3). It is not a choice of the fallen will of the natural man to know God, just as it is not a choice to be endowed with the aforementioned genius of Einstein. God endows some men with genius at physical birth, through His common grace, but to know and see God by faith occurs only through God's saving grace at spiritual regeneration. The above verse (1 Tim. 4:10) certainly does not teach that all men will be saved, but it does communicate that the natural life of unbelievers is blessed by the Savior through common grace. It further communicates that in addition to receiving common grace, the lives of believers are blessed by the Savior in a special way through saving grace, that is, by the new birth of the Holy Spirit: *"What if God, desiring to show his wrath and to make known his power,* ***has endured with much patience*** *vessels of wrath prepared for destruction* [those in whose lives He manifested only common grace], *in order* ***to make known the riches of his***

glory *for vessels of mercy, which he has prepared beforehand for glory* [to those in whom He manifested saving grace]*"* (Rom. 9:22-23).

That final condemnation of the unsaved is not accomplished immediately but is delayed until the second coming of the Lord Jesus Christ is a manifestation of common grace. Thus the reprobate can realize their ingratitude. It is not infrequently the case that the more generous the common grace an unsaved person enjoys, the more hardened he becomes against God: *"But Abraham said* [to the reprobate though healthy rich man], *'Child, remember that you in your lifetime received your good things, and Lazarus* [the saved and sore-ridden beggar] *in like manner bad things; but now he is comforted here, and you are in anguish'"* (Luke 16:25).

How many gifted, intelligent, powerful, successful, wealthy, generous, healthy, and long-lived individuals are there among natural men who do not know Christ? The war criminals of World War II lived comfortably, untainted by worldly justice, often to the ripe old age of nearly a century. On the other hand, how many of God's chosen children have suffered, been persecuted, and been rejected or condemned by the world. Dietrich Bonhoeffer, the eminent German theologian, was hanged a few days before the end of the war. We do not know why, but even this is part of God's common grace: *"In my vain life I have seen everything. There is a righteous man who perishes in his righteousness, and there is a wicked man who prolongs his life in his evildoing"* (Eccles. 7:15). Even pagan myths and fairy tales know of a kind of "common grace," bestowed not by God, but by the cradle prophetess of the newborn. God bestows common grace on all men at physical birth; He bestows saving grace only on His chosen people at spiritual birth, the first resurrection, when He creates a new man. Both gifts are unconditional, for neither birth into physical existence nor birth into spiritual existence occurs through the will of the creature. The will of the Creator brings forth physical life and spiritual life. Each of us is created as unique as a snowflake, and it is God who has the final say in both the physical and the spiritual.

COMMON GRACE KEEPS THE WORLD MOVING

CONSCIENCE

We have already shown that the scope and intensity, the extent and degree, of spiritual destruction (separation from God) is total. Man is spiritually dead, separated from God, unable to understand the things of the Spirit of God[23]. Yet by God's common grace, we are surrounded by people who possess many virtues if not evaluated from a spiritual point of view. I place my trust in nearly all of them, even though I know they are outside of Christ. I trust my hostess not to put poison in my coffee. I trust the pilot to have a sense of responsibility and to land the plane on the airport runway. Many times, I have entrusted my life into the hands of Muslim, Hindu, or Buddhist drivers in Third World countries, on circuitous and dangerous roads over precipices. I trust unbelieving doctors, placing myself in their care because I do not think they will intentionally harm me. How many unsaved people risk their lives to the utmost to save others? How many dedicated volunteers work for the welfare of the handicapped and vulnerable? The list of human good deeds and moral actions is endless. Many people do good deeds, but the goodness and sacrifice of natural man does not belong in the spiritual realm of saving grace. All human, natural goodness comes about through God's common grace; the conscience implanted by God in every natural man is an integral factor in this: *"For when Gentiles, who do not have the law* [the Scriptures, now the law of Christ], ***by nature do what the law requires****, they are a law to*

23 See chapter 4; section: The Essence of Total Physical and Spiritual Depravity; heading: Total Spiritual Depravity.

themselves, even though they do not have the law. They show that the work of the law is written on their hearts, while their conscience also bears witness, and their conflicting thoughts accuse or even excuse them" (Rom. 2:14-15).

Without common grace, without conscience, without common love and compassion, the world could not exist. It is God's common grace, which includes conscience, that sustains this world until God puts all His enemies under the feet of Christ (Matt. 22:44), that is until He has saved all His elect without losing any of His own. If the Triune God ceased to work by His mighty Word (Heb. 1:3; Col. 1:17), if He did not sustain the human conscience through common grace, all of creation would collapse; humans would destroy each other. All people benefit from common grace, especially believers but unbelievers as well (1 Tim. 4:10).

GOD CONTROLS EVIL

Perhaps the most significant manifestation of God's common grace is the little-known fact that God continually tames man's evil nature so that evil will not flourish unchecked: *"Surely the wrath of man shall praise thee: the remainder of wrath shalt thou restrain* [KJV]*"* (Ps. 76:10). No matter what evil man does, God is always glorified in the end. God was glorified by the angry reaction of the Pharisees and by Pilate's decision to crucify the Son of God. The world will endure until the final judgment day of Jesus Christ simply because God continually tames human wrath, for the natural man is capable of all evil. That is why God established governmental powers, laws, judiciaries, militaries, and police forces that do not bear the sword in vain (Rom. 13:3-4). Even the undue oppression of rulers (for which they will be justly punished) is part of God's common grace. Mankind cannot be left to its own devices. God-ordained governments enforce laws to protect, moderate, and restrain the human willfulness. The further a nation is removed from God's law, which is now Christ (1 Cor. 9:21b), the more totalitarian will be the government God allows. Just compare the history and fruits of nations that have historically had a Catholic and Orthodox majority—the nations of southern and eastern Europe or South America—with the nations of northwestern Europe, the U.S., Canada, and Australia which have historically had a Protestant majority. The rest of the world is still today seeking to emigrate to countries that have had a Protestant history—for how much longer, no one knows.

The question of why God allows evil causes many to struggle. This is actually a false question since it is based on the humanistic assumption that man is inherently good and does not deserve to suffer the effects of evil. The true question should come from the perspective that God is holy and man is totally depraved and absolutely deserving of punishment—see the foreshadowing of the global flood (Gen. 8:21). The question should be asked the other way around—why does God hold back His wrath (Isa. 48:8-9); why does He tame the remnants of wrath in us and grant us so much undeserved happiness? Why does He condescend to those who have already fallen into His wrath? How is it possible that God allows so much good? In this, once again we see that God's thinking is different from man's. He does this for His own sake, to display His Glory in the saved and His power in the damned: *"What if God, desiring to show his wrath and to make known his power, has endured with much patience vessels of wrath prepared for destruction, in order to make known the riches of his glory for vessels of mercy, which he has prepared beforehand for glory—even us whom he has called, not from the Jews only but also from the Gentiles?"* (Rom. 9:22-24).

All of us know many decent people, and we count ourselves among them. Many people believe they are decent because their natural nature, while not perfect, is basically pretty good (Pelagians, Semi-Pelagians, and in a strange way, even Arminians).

Others (Calvinists), of whom there are not so many anymore, believe that they are "decent" only because God is so gracious to all in the general sense that He binds and tames us to the point that we are no longer "free" to pour out of our wayward hearts what is truly hidden within (Ps. 76:10; Jer. 17:9). If we only compare ourselves to others, we will never realize the terrible state of our hearts. After all, all of us are all born free from righteousness (Rom. 6:20). If we are pretty decent people from a human point of view, it is only because God keeps us on a short leash; we are under the protection of God's common grace, which tames and constrains evil. The goodness and decency of natural, sinful people is not their own, but God's. God's common grace can save even the reprobate from utter earthly ruin and immediate destruction. From a biblical perspective, the holiness of God and the sinful falsehood of man are not hidden: *"By no means! Let God be true though every one were a liar* [including us 'decent' people]*"* (Rom. 3:4). This verse points to the total depravity of man, manifested first in relation to God and then in relation to man. Until we apprehend and appreciate the holiness of God, we will never understand the extent of man's total depravity reflected in the entire fallen world.

To summarize: If God loosened the reins just a little bit and gave Satan, demons, and mankind just a little bit "freer" will, life on this earth would be unsustainable. God's restraint on the natural fallen "freedom" in the Evil One does not allow the worst in all of us to bubble to the surface.

GOD WITHDRAWS COMMON GRACE

But God can both tighten and loosen the reins with which He tames natural humanity. If for His Glory He chooses to harden a man's heart, as He did the heart of Pharaoh (Ex. 14:4), all He has to do is loosen the reins and take away some of the common grace, and the "free" will enslaved by sin will have more room to act under the influence of the Evil One. Such a person will be drawn further away from God by the centrifugal, satanic force. The farther he is from God, the more darkness will surround him and the more evil he will do. When God acts in this passive but controlled way to harden a person's heart, He is not limiting his "freedom"; on the contrary, He is giving him greater range of action in the Devil's territory. But such a person is not truly free because he cannot help but carry out the intentions of Satan, his master, in accordance with his spiritually dead heart. God does not create evil in human hearts; He only controls it. The human heart is entirely wicked (Jer. 17:9), so natural men should desire as little natural "freedom" and as much common grace as possible.

6

EVIL

WHERE DID EVIL COME FROM?

Let us go back to the beginning of time when God created man perfect and declared that all He created was very good. Adam dwelt in the presence of God, until his Satan-infected desire for equality with God caused the greatest catastrophe in human history. Unlike fallen natural man today, God created Adam with a degree of freedom that allowed him to choose between the good—God—and evil—Satan.

The Bible does not give us a satisfactory, let alone exhaustive, answer to the question of where evil came from. No one can satisfactorily explain whether or not Adam had the capacity to resist temptation. No one can rationally resolve this question. All we know is that Satan deceived the first man and woman, and as a result Adam and Eve were cast out of the Garden as physically fallen and spiritually dead people. A most difficult theological question is whether God turned away from Adam and Eve at the crucial moment, allowing them to eat the forbidden fruit—here Scripture is silent. Many questions cannot be satisfactorily answered, though there have been many attempts, all quite rational and none sufficiently supported by Scripture. Adam's Fall must simply be taken as Scripture describes it. According to Scripture, God is absolutely sovereign, and nothing—absolutely nothing, not even evil, not even Adam's Fall—could have escaped His hands or occurred behind His back, without His permission: ***"I form light*** [where I am] *and create darkness* [where 'I am not']*; I make well-being and create calamity; I am the Lord, who does all these things"* (Isa. 45:7). The curious reader can become more familiar with this subject in the Supplements[24]. God is the first and the last, and there is nothing that He does not control.

This verse, Isa. 45:7, associates light with peace and tranquility, and darkness with evil. Where there is light—where God is—there is peace and goodness. Where there is darkness—where there is "no God"—there is evil: *"This is the message we have heard from him and proclaim to you, that **God is light, and in him is no darkness at all**"* (1 John 1:5). There is no darkness in God, for He is light (Ps. 27:1; John. 12:35). And we already know that where God "is not," if He withdraws His "presence," there will be darkness. God passively permits evil, leaving man at the "mercy" of his darkened "free" will, as in the case of Saul: *"Now the **Spirit of the Lord departed from Saul**, and a harmful spirit from the Lord tormented him"* (1 Sam. 16:14). "A harmful spirit from the Lord" can only mean that the Lord withdrew and allowed an evil, satanic spirit to work in Saul.

Nothing happens without God's permission. And everything that happens will ultimately be good and holy, in accordance with His holy purpose. He is the Alpha and the Omega, the beginning and the end, and everything in between. Man cannot evaluate, judge, or speculate too much about God's unfathomable, holy purposes because he has no infinite standard with which to measure God. *"The secret things belong to the Lord our God, but the things that are revealed belong to us and to our children forever, that we may do all the words of this law"* (Deut. 29:29).

24 See Supplements; III. How to Explain the Cause of Adam's Fall?

God reigns over all good and evil. Where He is, His good works prevail; where "He is not," where He has "withdrawn," evil prevails (Isa. 45:7; 1 John 1:5). The phrase "He is not" is in quotes because God cannot be absent anywhere in His visible or invisible creation*: "The eyes of the LORD are in every place, keeping watch on the evil and the good"* (Ps. 15:3). The biblical Christian need not be troubled by questions that Scripture does not clearly address. The more difficult question to answer is: "Why does God 'create' evil (Prov. 16:4)?" The only answer we have is that God simply moves the clay to His holy will (Rom. 9:21). God wants to display His power through His holy wrath against those who are evil, whether it be Satan, his demons, or natural fallen humanity (Rom. 9:22); He also wants to display the riches of His love, mercy, and glory to those on whom He has mercy (Rom. 9:23). Let us look at the following verses from a different perspective: *"What* ***if God, desiring to show his wrath and to make known his power****, has endured with much patience vessels of wrath* ***prepared for destruction****, in order to make known the riches of his glory for vessels of mercy, which he has prepared beforehand for glory—even us whom he has called, not from the Jews only but also from the Gentiles* [the elect, the promised ones]*?"* (Rom. 9:22-24).

It is at this point that many rational atheists and agnostics would argue that we are naive about evil. But the atheist has a much bigger problem. Not only does he not know where evil comes from, he also does not know where good comes from. Moreover, like the pantheist, he cannot separate good from evil, because to him, good and evil are relative, merging concepts. He cannot be sure that evil or good even exist, yet he acts as if they do. From the atheist's relativistic point of view, the attributes of evil, such things as aging, suffering, death, the food chain in which one species eats another, are all a part of natural selection, an instrument of evolution. Death is considered one of the tools of species evolution and social progress—a necessary "good." Why does man, even the atheist, care so much about death? Why would he call wars and human cruelty evil? Could not both be seen as a struggle for the survival of a more capable biological species? Why so often does the atheist point to violations of human rights and exhaust himself for animal rights? The atheist rejects God but acts and behaves as if God exists; this is irrational. The atheist lives much of his life in accordance with his conscience, as if God existed, and this too belongs to the category of God's common grace[25], so that even those who deny God can survive and do well on earth.

EVIL AS DEFINED BY ARMINIANISM AND CALVINISM

We have already seen in the previous section that satisfactorily resolving the origin of evil is no easy task. Let us now see how Arminianism and Calvinism deal with this problem.

1. Arminianism thinks as follows: "If everything is predestinated, determined (Calvinism) rather than open (Arminianism), then God must cause everything." The logic of Arminianism goes on: "If God causes everything, and if evil and sin exist, then it is God who is the author of evil and sin." If these things are true, then reason dictates that the blame for all the horrors the world is experiencing falls on God's head. With this logical chain, Arminianism accuses Calvinism of making God the author, the creator of evil and sin.

2. Calvinism answers: Since Arminianism believes in God's omniscience and omnipotence and, in a special way, in God's foreknowledge and election (God chooses those whom He knew would believe), then God must know everything in advance. If God commanded and ordained that something should happen, that a

25 See chapter 5; section: Common Grace Keeps the World Moving; heading: Conscience.

certain event should take place, that man should obey Him, etc., He must have known infallibly from all eternity that His creatures, whether Satan or man, would disobey. This caused the evil that God did not intend to prevent from all eternity. Arminianism has no answer for this.

Which view is more in harmony with Scripture? Which kind of God would be "better" or "worse?" The kind of God who passively creates evil (Isa. 45:7) for mysterious purposes that bring glory to Himself and good to His elect, as Calvinists believe? Or the kind of God who watches evil that Satan and man independently cause, doing nothing to prevent it although He has the power to do so, as Arminians must believe? Those who love God must learn to accept His decrees with humility and fear. God does not grant that we fully understand His secret ways: *"Great is our Lord, and abundant in power;* ***his understanding is beyond measure****"* (Ps. 147:5).

However, the American Reformed theologian Jonathan Edwards (1703-1758), nicknamed the Mount Everest of the Reformation, argued in much the way as we have noted above:

> *If by the Author of Sin, be meant the Sinner, the Agent, or Actor of Sin, or the Doer of a wicked thing; so it would be a reproach and blasphemy, to suppose God to be the Author of Sin. In this sense, I utterly deny God to be the Author of Sin; rejecting such an imputation on the Most High, as what is infinitely to be abhorred; and deny any such thing to be the consequence of what I have laid down. But if, by the Author of Sin, is meant the permitter, or not a hinderer of Sin; and, at the same time, a disposer of the state of events, in such a manner, for wise, holy, and most excellent ends and purposes, that Sin, if it be permitted or not hindered, will most certainly and infallibly follow: I say, if this be all that is meant, by being the Author of Sin, I do not deny that God is the Author of Sin, (though I dislike and reject the phrase, as that which by use and custom is apt to carry*

> *another sense), it is no reproach for the Most High to be thus the Author of Sin. This is not to be the Actor of Sin, but, on the contrary, of holiness*[26].

But skeptics object: "How can a loving God allow evil, and therefore sin, to exist in the world if God himself does no evil?" Jonathan Edwards' answer is as follows:

> *God has two wills*[27]*. God's decretive* (i.e. secret—ordering, decreeing, determining) *and preceptive (i.e. manifest—commanding, disciplining) wills. For example, God's preceptive, manifest will commands people not to kill. But His decretive will can declare and command killing, e.g.: "And he said to them, 'Thus says the Lord God of Israel, 'Put your sword on your side each of you, and go to and fro from gate to gate throughout the camp, and each of you* ***kill his brother and his companion and his neighbor****''" (Ex. 32:27).*

God's decretive will may not seem very holy to the natural man, but in this case, as in all others without exception, a divinely decreed, or direct killing by God, such as in a flood, is most holy. For it serves to accomplish the wisest and holiest of God's purposes, which will most glorify Him. In the Book of Exodus, as we have just read (Ex. 32:27), God used the hand of the Levites to remove those who had set up a golden calf. Holiness and evil are incompatible. The removal of evil, the negation of the negative, including the drowning of the whole sinful world in the flood, is good. God's decretive, secret, ordaining will is absolutely holy.

Arminians would further argue: "How can these two wills of God be so 'contradictory?'" In some cases, even the decretive will provides for an action and the preceptive will disapproves of the same action. But this is what every loving parent does when he chastises and disciplines his child. He must punish with the

26 https://www.ccel.org/ccel/edwards/works1.iii.v.ix.html

27 The reader will find a more detailed discussion of God's will in chapter 10

secret decretive will, even though he finds no pleasure in it with his manifest, preceptive will. Let us remind Arminians, in agreement with Jonathan Edwards, of the crucifixion of the Lord Jesus Christ, as follows:

On the one hand, God's decretive, secret, declarative will was that the Son of God should be crucified for the sins of God's people: "*...this Jesus, delivered up according to the definite plan and foreknowledge of God* [decretive will], *you crucified and killed by the hands of lawless men* [God did not prevent it, leaving you to your own perverse natural desire]" (Acts 2:23). To glorify Himself in His power and in His wisest and holiest purposes, God withdraws from reprobates, leaving them at the mercy of their fallen "free" will, to crucify the Son of God in this case. God uses natural men and their perverted motives to accomplish His holy purpose: *"For the Son of Man goes as it has been determined* [by God's decretive, ordaining will], *but woe to that man by whom he is betrayed!* [Judas did not keep God's preceptive, commanding will—You shall not bear false witness against your neighbor]" (Ex. 20:16; Luke 22:22).

On the other hand, God's preceptive, manifest, commanding, holy will rejects the crime committed against the Son of God: *"You shall not murder"... "You shall not bear false witness against your neighbor"* (Ex. 20:13,16). God will judge all who choose to do evil, even though they are unwittingly fulfilling God's holy plan. They have no idea that their sinful deeds serve a God-given task, their role[28]. Out of all human deeds, good and evil, God weaves a tapestry of history that leads toward a holy goal—the eternal kingdom of Jesus Christ. Thus, God uses even evil deeds for ultimate good, His own glorification. However, those who, through evil and their evil-motivated deeds, have "contributed" to the ultimate good, such as Judas, will be condemned. And yet God created them for this very purpose: *"The Lord has made everything for its purpose, even the*

28 See chapter 9; section: Examples of God's Negative Predestinations.

wicked [passively] *for the day of trouble* [the last day of judgment]" (Prov. 16:4).

At times we all play God, as when the thought creeps into our hearts that God is wrong to leave so many people to their "free" fallen will, yet to condemn them to lose eternal life (Acts 13:46) and to face eternal fire far from the Lord. Surely "good" people would never do such as this! This way of thinking exposes that sin has warped our judgment, when we fail to understand the lofty, absolute holiness of God and to grasp the utter fallenness of man and the deadly seriousness of evil, i.e., sin.

PART II
GOD'S UNCONDITIONAL, SOVEREIGN ELECTION

7

UNCONDITIONAL, SOVEREIGN ELECTION I

DEFINITION OF THE TERM

The second point of Calvinism, and therefore of the Synod of Dort, responds to the first article of the Remonstrance. It refers to the unconditional, sovereign election of God. It is inseparably and continuously connected with the preceding point:

1. ***The natural man, the offspring of Adam, is spiritually dead*** *as a result of original sin, separated from God, unable to understand the things of God. Everything man does in this state takes place on the stage of sin. He is a vassal of Satan, a slave to sin, and because of his corrupt nature is unable of his own accord to desire to follow God.*
2. *Therefore, out of inexpressible, amazing goodness, God had mercy on man.* ***God the Father has chosen*** *for Himself and for His own sake His promised people, His Church, whom He loved with an everlasting love from the whole fallen race of Adam before the foundation of the world, and has set apart for salvation. His election is not based on merit or the "faith" of the natural man; it is based solely on God's sovereign grace.*

For clarity, let us recall both views in the table below to see the difference, which again is not in emphasis but in substance:

ARMINIANISM Remonstration	CALVINISM Synod of Dort
2. Conditional Election God has determined that by His grace all mankind should be justified (have their sins blotted out). However, He calls us to respond to His prevenient grace by exercising our natural will, which He has restored to us to make a choice for Him. Our response conditions the fulfillment of His election.	**2. Unconditional Election** Since men cannot or will not choose God, God chose His people, whom He loves with an everlasting love, to justify them (to have their sins blotted out) for His sake and for His glory. His election is unconditional.

First, let us define the meaning of the word "choose." It means a decision for one or a few options among many, but not for all. If the choice included all possibilities without exception, then we could not speak of election; it would be a contradiction in terms. When Scripture speaks of election, it always means the selection or separation of certain people from all.

As we have said, in the Arminian view, man "limits" the almighty and unlimited God with his "free" will and defiance. The Arminian view is that man may choose or may not choose to allow God the Holy Spirit to regenerate him. In such a scenario, faith precedes salvation and thus necessarily becomes a work. Even though faith is awakened by the prevenient grace of God, it is still man who has the final say. The Spirit of God in this soteriological system must respect the "free" will of the natural man. This is the typical man-centered view of salvation as defined by many denominations.

We have seen that in the Calvinistic view it is the other way around. It is God who sovereignly and unilaterally, monergistically, decides in whom His Holy Spirit will dwell to create from sinners the living stones out of which He builds His spiritual house, the temple of God, the body of Christ. Calvinism is in every way a

God-centered belief system. All the credit and inalienable glory for the election, redemption, and creation of the new man belong to the one God—Father, Son, and Holy Spirit—in accordance with the verse that has become the title of this book: *"Behold, I have refined you, but not as silver; I have tried you* [bachar = to choose, elect, decide for] *in the furnace of affliction. For my own sake, for my own sake, I do it, for how should my name be profaned?* ***My glory I will not give to another****"* (Isa. 48:10-11)

We cannot look at the Book of Life as a signature sheet (Arminianism). The Book of Life[29] is God's eternal list of specific names of sinners (Calvinism) whom God, out of His goodness before the foundation of the world, loved with an unconditional saving love (Jer. 31:3) and therefore chose for salvation (Eph. 1:3-5). For the sake of clarity and memorization, let us recapitulate both perspectives on salvation:

1. CONDITIONAL ELECTION (ARMINIANISM)

God's election is conditioned upon man's "free" decision to accept by faith the substitutionary sacrifice of Jesus Christ. It is essentially conditioned on an act of faith. Man's "free" will to make this decision is activated by God's prevenient grace. This view seeks to protect God from being accused of unjustly choosing sinners—as if God were a natural, sinful man. This Arminian view of election seldom provokes objections or outrage because it is consistent with an inherently human understanding of justice, namely a humanistic, conditional system of reward and punishment.

2. UNCONDITIONAL ELECTION (CALVINISM)

The Calvinistic view is that God cannot be limited by any "external" condition. Nothing "outside" His limitless "boundaries" can or does exist. According to Scripture, He sovereignly has mercy on

29 See chapter 17; section: Does God Erase Sinners from the Book of Life?

whom He wills, and He hardens whom He wills leaving this one to his sin (Rom. 9:18). Assuming that God's sovereign election would arouse the disapproval of many, the Apostle Paul addressed the objection of God's "unrighteousness" in advance, affirming that God has mercy on whom He has mercy, and He has compassion on whom He has compassion (Rom. 9:14-15; Ex. 33:19b). If Paul had taught that God's election was conditioned upon human, humanistic, natural faith, he would not have had to mention human objections at all. In the New Testament, God's sovereign election is nothing new; it was God's only plan of salvation for every historical age, which Jews under the Law understood very well.

GOD'S ELECT ACCORDING TO SCRIPTURE

THE UNIQUENESS OF GOD'S GLORY, GOODNESS AND MERCY

Natural man, in his utter spiritual depravity, does not have a single spiritual sense by which he can communicate with God, thus establishing any connection between God and man is entirely dependent upon God's initiative: *"But now that you* [you of the promise] *have come to know God, or* ***rather to be known*** [the elect] ***by God****, how can you turn back again to the weak and worthless elementary principles of the world, whose slaves you want to be once more?"* (Gal. 4:9). God loves His people with an eternal redeeming love, so He gives them a new heart that enables them to love Him and to be truly free in Christ. The Bible identifies no love or freedom outside of Christ: *"We love* [God and neighbor] *because* ***he first loved us****"* (1 John 4:19). He chose His people, created them to bear fruit and to love Him with all their heart, mind and strength. He kneaded them out of the clay for Himself and for His own sake so that they might come to know Him: *"You did not choose me, but* ***I chose you and appointed you*** [created] *that you should go and bear fruit and that your fruit should abide"* (John 15:16a).

In his utter spiritual incapacity, natural man is unable to choose God, unable to make a decision for Him, because he cannot know Him or recognize Him and is therefore unable to love and obey Him. Natural man chooses those who are like him to be his friends—we naturally choose those who think like us and share similar values with us. Natural man is free from righteousness, living in rebellion (Rom. 6:20), and he therefore hates his Creator. To choose God out of the natural will would be a most unnatural decision for the unsaved man because from birth, humanity belongs to the Evil One. Only God can change this state: *"For if while* ***we were enemies*** *we were reconciled* [past participle] *to God by the death of his Son, much more, now that we are reconciled* [God's elect], *shall we be saved by his life"* (Rom. 5:10).

Independently of us, by His sovereign, unconditional grace, God gives all the gifts necessary for life, including the most precious gift of all, "salvation and faith." The biblical gospel is unique, special, and exclusive. Only the Bible presents a God who sacrificed Himself to save man. Only in biblical faith does God choose man and appoint him an heir: *"Therefore he is the mediator of a new covenant, so that* ***those who are called*** [chosen by God] *may receive the promised eternal inheritance"* (Heb. 9:15a). The opposite is true in all religions, without exception. Even the natural man cannot exist without a sense of being, without religion. Therefore, he religiously chooses false gods, idols, made in his own image which he carves in his mind. He indulges in fantasies, cowering before both matter and time (the idol of evolution) and soulless statues made of any material that cannot see, hear, smell, feel or think. Thus, there are almost as many religions in the world as there are natural people. Modern natural man idolizes the creature instead of the Creator—soulless but personified "Mother Nature," sports, art, entertainment, possessions, and the works of human hands (Ps. 115:4; 135:15).

GOD IS GRACIOUS AND MERCIFUL ACCORDING TO HIS WILL

Let us read the following verses carefully, noting that God's decision is monergistic, unilateral, sovereign, and irrevocable: *"For this is what the promise said: 'About this time next year I will return, and Sarah shall have a son.' And not only so, but also when Rebekah had conceived children by one man, our forefather Isaac, though they were not yet born and had done nothing either good or bad—in order that God's purpose of election might continue, not because of works but because of him who calls—she was told, 'The older will serve the younger.' As it is written, 'Jacob I loved, but Esau I hated.' What shall we say then? Is there injustice on God's part? By no means!* ***For he says to Moses, 'I will have mercy on whom I have mercy, and I will have compassion on whom I have compassion*** [Ex. 33:19b]***.' So then it depends not on human will or exertion, but on God, who has mercy****. For the Scripture says to Pharaoh, 'For this very purpose I have raised you up, that I might show my power in you, and that my name might be proclaimed in all the earth.' So then he has mercy on whomever he wills, and he hardens whomever he wills. You will say to me then, 'Why does he still find fault? For who can resist his will?'* ***But who are you, O man, to answer back to God? Will what is molded say to its molder, 'Why have you made me like this?' Has the potter no right over the clay, to make out of the same lump one vessel for honorable use and another for dishonorable use?*** *What if God, desiring to show his wrath and to make known his power, has endured with much patience vessels of wrath prepared for destruction, in order to make known the riches of his glory for vessels of mercy, which he has prepared beforehand for glory—even us whom he has called, not from the Jews only but also from the Gentiles? As indeed he says in Hosea, 'Those who were not my people I will call 'my people,'* ***and her who was not beloved I will call 'beloved'"*** (Rom. 9:9-25). This is God's unconditional, sovereign, unsurpassed election. The rebuke: *"But who are you, O man, to answer back to God?"* suggests that to even doubt God's sovereign election is a presumptuous offense against the Holy Triune God. His ways are always right and higher than ours. God's people are obligated accept the truth of God's election with humility, on our knees.

In Rom. 9:9-25 the apostle Paul here is not presenting some new, unknown principle of divine election; he is referring to the text of Exodus, interpreting it in light of the New Covenant as it applies to the Church today. Here is the text of Moses: *"And he said* [to Moses], *'I will make all my goodness pass before you and will proclaim before you my name 'The LORD.'* ***And I will be gracious to whom I will be gracious, and will show mercy on whom I will show mercy'"*** (Ex. 33:19). To the natural humanistic and religious person, this statement seems unmerciful and, above all, seems "inhuman." How could a just, loving, good God say such a thing? Let us study the immediate context of this amazing foreshadowing of the New Covenant in Ex. 33:18-23:

"Moses said, 'Please show ***me your glory.'*** *And he said, 'I will make* ***all my goodness pass before you*** [I will bear your sins on the Cross] *and will proclaim before you my name 'The LORD'* [I and the Father are one]. ***And I will be gracious to whom I will be gracious, and will show mercy on whom I will show mercy*** [My death will atone for the sins of only those on whom I have shown grace and mercy]. *But,' he said, 'you cannot see my face, for man shall not see me and live.' And the LORD said, 'Behold, there is a place by me where* ***you shall stand on the rock*** [Jesus Christ], *and* ***while my glory passes by*** [when my Son dies for you] ***I will put you in a cleft of the rock, and I will cover you with my hand*** [My Spirit will baptize, immerse you in Jesus Christ] *until I have passed by* [until I complete your redemption]. *Then I will take away my hand, and* ***you shall see my back****, but my face shall not*

be seen [your salvation is a part of My Glory; no one can ever see My full Glory]'" (Ex. 33:18-23).[30]

Moses longs to see the Glory of God. In response, God the Lord identifies His glory with all His goodness, shown through His mercy to His elect. His mercy and grace to whom He wills (Ex. 33:19b; Rom. 9:18a) and His hardening to whom He wills (Rom. 9:18b) include both mercy and saving love for those on whom He has mercy, and judgment for sinners who have fallen under His wrath (Rom. 9:22-24). To accomplish His will, God gave His only begotten Son to die only for those on whom He had mercy and grace—only for them; this is how God defines His goodness and Glory! In the eyes of the natural, self-righteous and religious man, this is "unjust." But is it really unjust? If God had mercy or pity on no one, it would be perfectly just! God's glory and goodness are revealed in His sovereign decision to save anyone at all. Why did God not destroy mankind after the fall of Adam or after the flood? Why has God been patient with the human race to this day? It displays His amazing goodness that He chose, redeemed and recreated a people for Himself out of the mass of fallen humanity, a people to enjoy, to be glorified through, and to be glorified in. To the religious and humanistic man, such an idea is repulsive. Perhaps most disturbing to his envious eye is that God can do whatever He wants with His creation, yet He is good and generous at all: *"Am I not allowed to do what I choose with what belongs to me?* ***Or do you begrudge my generosity****?" (Matt. 20:15).*

Let us pay attention to the last verses quoted (Ex. 33:21-23), where the Lord says to Moses, "You shall stand on the rock." This rock represents God (Isa. 44:8b). God is the rock on which Moses is to stand. "When My Glory passes by you, when My Son dies on the Cross for you, when He bears your sins, My Spirit will hide you

30 Some of you may argue that I am using an allegorical hermeneutic. But I believe that these verses are no less Proto-Gospel than, say, Genesis 3:15.

in this Rock, in My Son. You will be covered by My Hand; you will be baptized into Christ. When I pass over, when My Son completes your salvation, you will know that you have seen the very back of My goodness and Glory. Neither you nor anyone else will ever see the fullness of My Glory."

God in His Glory, goodness and righteousness is an inexhaustible, bottomless well. In eternity, we will know Him in the person of Jesus Christ for all of eternity, yet we will never see the end of His Glory, goodness, and righteousness. This is our God!

A PRE-FIGURATION OF THE HUMAN AND DIVINE CHOICE

The Old Testament provides an exquisite picture of the enslaved, unfree will of natural man as opposed to the sovereign, divine will. Paul interprets it this way: *"For it is written* [in the book of Genesis] *that Abraham had two sons, one* [Ishmael] *by a slave woman* [Hagar] *and one* [Isaac] *by a free woman* [Sarah]. *But* ***the son of the slave was born according to the flesh*** [according man's will; Sarah induced Abraham to go to Hagar], *while* ***the son of the free woman*** [Isaac] ***was born through promise*** [according to God's will]" (Gal. 4:22-23). Ishmael is a representative, a type of the natural man with the will of a slave of the Evil One. Ishmaelites are all those who are only born once, naturally, bodily from Adam.

On the other hand, Isaac is a type of man born (reborn) by God's will, not merely by man's will. The people of Isaac are the promised ones who, in addition to being born naturally of Adam, have been born-again spiritually by God's will and creative power, that is, through God's election. These new creatures have new eyes that already see and believe; they have a newly created, newly liberated will in Christ that does His will as the Son does the Father's will.

Isaac's birth was not by the will of man, because Sarah was barren and old. The supernatural, creative intervention of God in

Sarah's womb caused her to become pregnant. Isaac is also a type, a type of Jesus Christ. God's intervention in Mary's womb was even more extraordinary because Christ's Father was not a man, but the Holy Spirit (Matthew 1:18). Similarly, but by no means identically, God's miraculous, supernatural, creative intervention caused all those who were loved, promised, and chosen from all eternity to be born-again, not physically, but spiritually of the Spirit of God (John 3:6). This parable has far-reaching implications: *"Now this may be interpreted allegorically: these women are two covenants. One is from Mount Sinai* [the killing, Mosaic covenant; 2 Cor. 3:6-7], *bearing children* [natural, of man's will] *for slavery* [to Satan]*; she is Hagar. Now Hagar is Mount Sinai in Arabia; she corresponds to the present Jerusalem* [the world], *for she is in slavery* [carnal nature] *with her children. But the Jerusalem above* [the promised, elect in Christ] *is free, and she is our mother. For it is written, 'Rejoice, O barren one who does not bear; break forth and cry aloud, you who are not in labor* [Sarah is a type of the barren]*! For the children of the desolate one will be more than those of the one who has a husband.' Now you, brothers, like Isaac* [son of the formerly barren but free Sarah], *are children of promise* [born-again of the Spirit, newly created by the will of God, chosen]. *But just as at that time he who was born according to the flesh* [Ishmael] *persecuted him who was born according to the Spirit* [Isaac], *so also it is now* [those born naturally of the flesh persecute and hate those born-again of God, the Holy Spirit]. *But what does the Scripture say? 'Cast out the slave woman and her son* [natural, carnal man], *for the son of the slave woman* [Hagar] *shall not inherit with the son of the free woman* [Sarah].*' So, brothers, we are not children of the slave but of the free woman. For freedom Christ has set us free; stand firm therefore, and do not submit again to a yoke of slavery"* (Gal. 4:24-5:1)

Our redemption from the bondage of sin, the first resurrection with Christ from spiritual death, that is, the new birth (Eph. 2:6), is an immeasurably greater miracle than if a natural man were to be raised from physical death today. The bodily resurrection, or rather revival, of a natural man would only be temporary; sooner or later he would have to die again. But the born-again person will live even though he dies because he has been born-again and has received eternal life in Christ (John 11:25). This most powerful of God's miracles takes place every day before our very eyes. God is creating His beloved people, according to His will, in accordance with His decision, through the promised rebirth.

ONLY THE ELECT CAN COME TO GOD

Let us consider the unconditional decree of the Lord Jesus Christ, which is received only by those whom God has created with a new heart, from whom He has removed the chains of Satan. This decree rejected many disciples who walked with Christ in the flesh but were not His chosen people: *"And he* [Christ] *said, 'This is why I told you that* ***no one can come to me*** [because he is bound by the Evil One] ***unless it is granted him by the Father*** [unless he is chosen by the Father]. *'* ***After this many of his disciples turned back and no longer walked with him"*** (John 6:65-66). When Jesus Christ spoke this decree of the Father's election, many disciples lost interest and stopped walking with Him. They wanted to come on their own, to the manipulatable God whom they had created in their stony hearts. Their self-centeredness blinded them to God's utter sovereignty in all things, including election. Jesus saw into the hearts of those who had gone away. Peter must have been troubled when only a few disciples remained around Jesus. In this tense situation, Jesus turned to the remaining twelve disciples with these words: *"'Do you want to go away as well?' Simon Peter answered him, 'Lord, to whom shall we go?* ***You have the words of eternal life'"*** (John 6:67b-68).

By God's grace, Peter was given spiritual sight and faith to continue to walk with Christ. He could see that there was no other way but to follow his Lord. His reason for not walking away from Christ was not revealed to him by his Adamic judgment, flesh and blood, the heart of stone enslaved to sin; it was revealed to him by God Himself (Matt. 16:17). He had nothing to boast about. It is only through God's gracious will that we, like Peter, can be set free from ourselves. Let us remain in awe of God, rejoice in His grace, and submit to His sanctifying power. Let us do good works for His Glory, for it is He who keeps those who are His in fear and trembling: *"...work out your own salvation with fear and trembling, for it is God who works in you, both to will and to work for his good pleasure"* (Phil. 2:12b-13). The promised, chosen man whom God translates from spiritual death to spiritual life in an instant is endowed with the gift of "salvation and faith" in that same instant. The spiritually resurrected person in Christ is already free to follow God and grow in sanctification by faith. He has become a child of God.

When Martin Luther was rebuked by theologians for teaching God's sovereignty in election because, in their view, it discouraged potential candidates from coming to faith in Christ, Luther replied: "So be it!" He knew that God's purpose could not be thwarted by human initiative or tactics. The salvation of the natural man can only come from heaven.

THE ELECT ARE LITERALLY DRAWN BY THE FATHER

"No one can come to me [Christ] *unless the Father who sent me draws him* [elkó]. *And I will raise him up* [into the glorified body] *on the last day"* (John 6:44). Notice first the Greek verb *elkó*, which means "to draw, to drag, to pull." The natural human will is utterly useless to God's purpose of creating a new man in Christ because it is dead to spiritual things; it can play no part in His creative purpose. The

dead cannot be moved to rise from the grave, therefore, God literally draws His promised ones out of Satan's pit!

As noted, the verb *elkó* means "to pull, to drag, to draw." It certainly does not take the form of wooing, longing, and persuading. Nor does it take the form of the vague, helping grace of Arminianism and Catholicism. Wooing and persuading anticipate the consent of the persuaded. The Lord would never get the consent of a spiritual corpse, so He cannot count on it. He alone consents; He exercises His triune consent because it pleases Him! Thus, the verb *elkó* does not suggest any kind of persuasion. Let us see what its meaning conveys: *"But you have dishonored the poor man. Are not the rich the ones who oppress you, and the ones who* ***drag*** [elkó] *you into court?"* (James 2:6). Here the verb *elkó* is translated "to drag." This is neither persuasion nor prevenient grace; this is an act of force. In another verse where the action of the verb *elkó* can be seen: *"But when her* [the medium, a slave who advised investors] *owners saw that their hope of gain was gone, they seized Paul and Silas and* ***dragged*** [elkó] *them into the marketplace before the rulers"* (Acts 16:19). Similarly, in this verse: *"Then all the city was stirred up, and the people ran together. They seized Paul and* ***dragged*** [elkó] *him out of the temple, and at once the gates were shut"* (Acts 21:30).

The verb *elkó*, to draw or drag, is also found in John 18:10 and 21:11. Through the Cross of Christ our God in heaven literally dragged His chosen spiritual bodies out of Satan's household, out of the economy of evil, as we will see in the next heading.

JESUS CHRIST SNATCHES HIS ELECT FROM THE DEVIL

Christ's sovereign intervention on the Cross was the most dramatic rescue in the history of heaven and earth. To deliver His people from the morass of Satan's house, Christ had to shed His redeeming blood, which paralyzed Satan to the point that he could not prevent Christ from leading His promised servants and captives to freedom. The Cross of Christ delivered the spiritually dead and ignorant from the darkness of the depths of the world, literally plundering Satan's household, οἰκία; He delivered all His elect from Satan's clutches: *"Or how can someone enter a strong man's* [the Devil's] *house and* ***plunder his goods*** [God's elect], *unless he first binds the strong man* [Rev. 20:3a]*? Then indeed he may plunder his house"* (Matt. 12:29).

Eight centuries before Christ, Isaiah foresaw God's action to rescue His people from the Devil's captivity and Christ's liberating Cross that robbed the Evil One of those chosen and promised captives: *"Can the prey be taken from the mighty* [the Devil], *or* ***the captives of a tyrant be rescued*** [the promised and chosen]*? For thus says the Lord: 'Even the captives of the mighty shall be taken, and* ***the prey of the tyrant*** [the Devil] ***be rescued*** [His Church], ***for I will contend with those who contend with you, and I will save your children****'"* (Isa. 49:24-25). We read a similar principle in the following verse: *"For the Lord has ransomed Jacob* [a type, the head of the elect of all the nations; Jer. 31:7] *and has redeemed him from hands too strong* [the Devil] *for him* [Jacob]*"* (Jer. 31:11).

The redemption of the elect was not a financial transaction, but a fierce spiritual battle waged by the Savior: *"And the Lord said to Satan, '****The Lord rebuke you, O Satan! The Lord who has chosen Jerusalem*** [the holy city, the new Jerusalem, beautiful as a bride adorned for her bridegroom; Rev. 21:2] *rebuke you! Is not this* ***a brand plucked from the*** [Devil's] ***fire****?'"* (Zech. 3:2).

The following comprehensive verse from the Psalms describes Christ's crucifixion, His deliverance, His leading of God's people, even the most rebellious, out of the Devil's prison, and His ascension: *"You ascended on high* [Christ was lifted up on the Cross; John 3:14], *leading a host of captives in your train and receiving gifts among men, even among the rebellious* [Christ led out the Father's chosen, rebellious people, captured by the Devil, with whom the

Father had gifted Him], *that the Lord God may dwell there* [Christ is seated at the right hand of God in heaven today; Col. 3:1]" (Ps. 68:18). To the elect—the promised, the redeemed, the plundered, the snatched, the dragged, those brought forth by God—the household of the strong man—Satan has become a ransacked hut. But for those who continue to dwell in perdition, Satan's household is the worst kind of prison, the unenviable place of the condemned awaiting perdition in the burning lake.

From the heavenly perspective, Christ's redemption, the salvation of His chosen people, has already been accomplished: *"And I heard a loud voice in heaven, saying, 'Now the salvation and the power and the kingdom of our God and the authority of his Christ have come, for* ***the accuser of our brothers*** [God's elect] ***has been thrown down*** [Satan is bound; Rev. 20:3], *who accuses them day and night before our God'"* (Rev. 12:10).

THE ELECT ARE ENDOWED WITH "SALVATION AND FAITH"

In the following biblical couplet, we see not only all three persons of the triune God, but especially the cause—the action of God—and the effect—the reaction of His people. Paul prays to the triune God to place the Spirit of wisdom and revelation in His people so that they may know Him by faith, love Him with their hearts and minds, and recognize their calling, that is, their election to be His holy people:

1. Paul's plea for divine action: "*...that the God* [triune God] *of our* ***Lord Jesus Christ*** [second Person], ***the Father*** *of glory* [first Person], *may give you the* ***Spirit of wisdom*** *and of revelation* [third Person]" (Eph. 1:17a).
2. Paul's plea for the response of His chosen people: "*...in the knowledge* [in love] *of him* [the triune God], *having the eyes of your hearts enlightened* [faith], *that* ***you may know*** *what is the*

hope to which he has called you, what are the riches of his glorious inheritance in the saints" (Eph. 1:17b-18).

God's action is to put the new, quickening Spirit of God of wisdom and revelation into His people, according to His will, as prophesied in the Old Testament by Ezekiel (Ezek. 37:14). Without this transforming creative gift no one can come to God. The response of God's Spirit-empowered people (Phil. 2:13) is a continual learning, maturing, growing in obedience and love for God and neighbor. The newly created spirit of man is manifested by perseverance to the end of the physical existence of the child of God. Faith is the created, enlightened, inner vision through which God's children see His actions, His plan for them, and their role as His chosen people, the Church. To whom and for what reason does God give the gift of "salvation and faith?" To whom will He give a new heart and imbue it with a spirit of wisdom and revelation? Who are these elect ones gifted with the inner, enlightened vision, the faith? I fear that Jesus' answer will dissatisfy many: *"All things have been handed over to me by my Father, and* ***no one knows*** *who the Son is* ***except the Father****, or who the Father is* ***except the Son*** *and* ***anyone to whom the Son chooses to reveal him****"* (Luke 10:22).

Until we shed our self-centeredness and humbly accept that God is indeed absolutely and supremely sovereign in all things, we will be troubled by such divine decrees. To whom, then, and why does God reveal Himself and bestow the gift of "salvation and faith?" Simply to those to whom Christ, in accordance with the Father's will, chooses to reveal and grant it (Luke 10:22). God creates a spirit of wisdom and revelation along with enlightened vision in those whom He has unconditionally loved from all eternity (Jer. 31:3). To some it is given to be born-again of the Holy Spirit, to become a new creation with eyes that see and ears that hear, and to respond to the Gospel; God has given these the ability to believe, to know the Father and the Son and the Spirit, to have a filial relationship with God. Others are not given this: *"Then the disciples came and said to him* [Jesus], *'Why do you speak to them in parables?' And he answered them, '**To you it has been given** to know the secrets of the kingdom of heaven, **but to them it has not been given**'"* (Matt.13:10-11). *"But blessed are your eyes, for they see* [you believe], *and your ears, for they hear* [you believe]*"* (Matt.13:16).

Let us embrace this truth forever: God does what pleases Him, not what pleases man, what pleases the natural man. His holy will has nothing to do with human willfulness. Everything He does is holy. All of Scripture is interwoven with the sovereign, unconditional election of God, an election without human merit, lest men boast (Rom. 9:16; Eph. 2:9). Thus, God unconditionally chose sinful Seth, Noah, Abram, Isaac, Jacob, Joseph, Moses, and the fleeing Jonah (Jonah 1:3). What merit did the young virgin Mary possess that caused God to predestine and choose her to be the mother of the humanity of Jesus? God came into the world in the likeness of sinful flesh to condemn sin in the flesh (Rom. 8:3)? How did Paul, who hated Christ and persecuted His followers, earn his election? How did the entire people of God, the Israel of God, His chosen ecclesia, the Church, earn their election? Did any Jew in any way deserve to be born into the chosen nation? Who among us has freely chosen his gender, his place of birth, his appearance, his genetic makeup? Even the first man, Adam, did nothing to deserve being created—the man whose genetics God used to encode all humanity. Similarly, no one chooses to become a new creation, to be born-again of the Holy Spirit. Only a sovereign God decides and creates such things. We are creatures; we are not the Creator. Let us cry out to God to free us once and for all from the Adamic desire for equality with God into which we are all born. He is first and last in all things. He is infinite and absolute—to Him be glory forever:

"Great is our Lord, and abundant in power; his understanding is beyond measure" (Ps. 147:5).

ELECTION IS UNMISSABLE IN SCRIPTURE

Let us examine just a few of the dozens of biblical occurrences of the principle of election.

EXAMPLE 1

"Remember the wondrous works [your salvation] *that he has done, his miracles, and the judgments he uttered, O offspring of Abraham* [the children of promise from the noisy crowd of the nations; Rom. 9:7-8; Gen. 17:4], *his servant, children of Jacob,* ***his chosen ones****"* (Ps.105:5-6)! Not all the physical descendants of Abraham and the sons of Jacob, the Jews, are "His elect" in the spiritual, redemptive sense. The true, saved, spiritual descendants of Abraham, Isaac, and Jacob are all the promised, i.e., "His elect," both Jew and Gentile. Abraham is the spiritual father of all who are in Christ, regardless of their ethnicity: *"But it is not as though the word of God has failed.* ***For not all who are descended from*** [carnal] ***Israel belong to Israel*** [the chosen Israel of God; Gal. 6:15-16], *and not all are children of Abraham because they are his* [carnal] *offspring, but 'Through Isaac shall your offspring be named.' This means that* ***it is not the children of the flesh*** [neither of the Jews nor of the Gentiles] ***who are the children of God, but the children of the promise*** [all the elect of Jews and Gentiles] *are counted as offspring"* (Rom. 9:6-8). *"What then? Israel failed to obtain what it was seeking* [the salvation of all Jews]. ***The elect obtained it****, but the rest were hardened"* (Rom. 11:7).

EXAMPLE 2

"And if those days [of great tribulation just before the second coming of Christ on judgement day] *had not been cut short, no human being*

would be saved. But for the sake of the elect those days will be cut short" (Matt. 24:22). No matter from which eschatological perspective we interpret the fulfillment of this verse, God's purpose is toward His elect. The Great Tribulation will be shortened for the sake of God's elect; otherwise, at the Second Coming of Jesus Christ, none of God's persecuted people would be left alive.

EXAMPLE 3

"For false christs and false prophets will arise and perform great signs and wonders, so as to lead astray, if possible, ***even the elect****"* (Matt. 24:24). The application here is the same as in the previous example. Whether this verse is describing a future, present, or historical event, those who are chosen by God enjoy God's protection from temptations and pitfalls. If they were to fail, to permanently succumb to false messiahs, then God's election would not be fulfilled. Those who continually succumb to such temptations do not belong to God's people, have never been chosen, have not been known by God, have not been loved with an eternal, redeeming love (Matthew 7:22-23). No one can snatch from Jesus' hand those whom the Father gave to Him, those for whom Christ gave His life on the Cross. The Holy Spirit so powerfully seals the elect saints in Christ that they will endure to the end.[31]

EXAMPLE 4

"Put on then, ***as God's chosen ones****, holy and beloved, compassionate hearts, kindness, humility, meekness, and patience"* (Col. 3:12). God's elect are not destined to fall under God's wrath (1 Thess. 5:9) like those destined for destruction (Rom. 9:22). God's sanctifying Spirit works in them to produce humility, compassion, and mercy toward their neighbors instead of crushing them with their

31 See PART V; THE PERSEVERANCE OF THE SAINTS, THE PRESERVATION OF THE SAINTS BY GOD.

"spiritual superiority." Above all, God's elect are called to build up the Church, the Israel of God, not their own pride. They are to lead an active and unceasing life of prayer, not in front of people, in public but in private, in their own little room (Matt. 6:5-6).

THE ELECTION IS GOD-CENTERED

In the following Bible passage, the verbs that refer to God are all in the active voice, in the 3rd person singular. In contrast, the verbs that refer to us, His chosen people, are all in the passive voice. God is the one acting, and His chosen children are being affected by His action: *"Blessed be the God and Father of our Lord Jesus Christ, who has blessed us in Christ with every spiritual blessing in the heavenly places, even as he chose us in him* [Christ] *before the foundation of the world, that we should be holy and blameless before him. In love* [special, eternal, saving grace and love] *he predestined us for adoption to himself as sons through Jesus Christ, according to the purpose of his will, to the praise of his glorious grace* [All my goodness shall pass before thee—but I will have mercy on whom I will have mercy, and I will have compassion on whom I will have compassion; Ex. 33:19], *with which he has blessed us in the Beloved. In him we have redemption through his blood, the forgiveness of our trespasses* [we are justified], *according to the riches of his grace, which he lavished upon us, in all wisdom and insight making known to us the mystery of his will, according to his purpose, which he set forth in Christ as a plan for the fullness of time, to unite all things in him, things in heaven and things on earth. In him we have obtained an inheritance, having been predestined according to the purpose of him who works all things according to the counsel of his will, so that we who were the first to hope in Christ might be to the praise of his glory"* (Eph. 1:3-12).

It is true that in Scripture our faith is often expressed in the active verb form—we have believed, we have known, etc., or in the imperative form—believe, do, etc. However, we should always remember that God is first and last in all things. We should express ourselves in a God-centered way. Instead of a self-centered "I have believed," we should experience and proclaim to those around us, "He has given me 'salvation and faith.'" Thus, the question of salvation is placed in precise order, in the proper "order of salvation."

DID GOD CHOOSE ONLY THOSE WHOM HE FOREKNEW WOULD BELIEVE?

Arminians argue that God conditionally elects those whom He foreknew would accept the sacrifice of Jesus Christ; after He grants them prevenient grace, people decide whether or not to choose Him. This argument contradicts itself. If God is only choosing those He foreknew would be making their own choice to believe in the sacrifice of Christ, that would make God's choosing subordinate to human choosing. But in Scripture the choice is the Lord's, not the sinner's (John 15:16).

When we carefully examine verses in which Scripture speaks of foreknowledge, we find that the word "foreknowledge" is always with reference to foreknown persons, not with reference to foreknown human actions or decisions. The following texts are just three of many examples of this:

Text 1: Here the word "foreknowledge" refers to the person of Christ crucified according to the ordinance of God's counsel and foreknowledge: *"...this Jesus, delivered up according to the definite plan and **foreknowledge** of God, you crucified and killed by the hands of lawless men"* (Acts 2:23).

Text 2: Again, the word "foreknowledge" does not refer to a divinely predetermined human response or decision, but to a limited circle of divinely predetermined individuals: *"For those whom **he foreknew** he also predestined to be conformed to the image of his Son, in order that he might be the firstborn among many brothers. And those whom he predestined he also called, and those whom he* *called he also justified, and those whom he justified he also glorified"* (Rom. 8:29-30).

Text 3: Once more, the word "foreknowledge" does not refer to the decision of the elect, but directly refers to the ones who are elect according to God's foreknowledge and sanctification: *"Peter, an apostle of Jesus Christ, To those who are elect exiles of the Dispersion in Pontus, Galatia, Cappadocia, Asia, and Bithynia,* ***according to the foreknowledge of God the Father****, in the sanctification of the Spirit, for obedience to Jesus Christ and for sprinkling with his blood: May grace and peace be multiplied to you"* (1 Pet. 1:1-2).

A detailed discussion of the concept of "foreknowledge" would consume a lot of space. But we can affirm, in agreement with many Reformed theologians, that in Scripture the verb "to foreknow," as the verb "to know," in many contexts suggests intimacy, closeness, love. It is not being used with reference to prior knowledge of some human decision or action. Let us see just three confirming examples:

1. *"God has not rejected his people* ***whom he foreknew*** [whom He loved with an everlasting love]*"* (Rom. 11:2a).
2. *"And* ***Adam knew*** *his wife again* [he had a loving, intimate relationship with her], *and she bore a son"* (Gen. 4:25a).
3. *"Indeed, I* [Paul] *count everything as loss because of the surpassing worth of* ***knowing Christ Jesus*** *my Lord* [I love Him because He first loved me; 1 John 4:19]. *For his sake I have suffered the loss of all things and count them as rubbish, in order that I may gain Christ"* (Phil. 3:8)

Having made this brief clarification, we can say that the terms "foreknow" or "foreknowing" often mean "loving beforehand," examined in context. It is not that God chose those whom He foreknew would choose to believe in Himself; rather, He chose and foreknew His own, those whom He loved beforehand with an everlasting love, that through His power they might believe.

AM I OR AM I NOT A CHOSEN ONE?

Especially in view of those saved at a ripe old age with a number of sin-inflicted scars, critics may object, "You enjoyed most of your life in a worldly way, before you called to God, and now in heaven you do whatever you want!" Such objections are man-centered, keeping man in the spotlight. But Scripture gives this response: *"Who shall bring any charge against God's elect? It is God who justifies* [who washes away sins, not man]*"* (Rom. 8:33). In election, God is putting Himself on display! The idea that you can do what you like after He saves you is mindless, similar to this: "Why is it necessary that you eat if God has guaranteed you fifty more years of life?" God has ordained not only the end, but the process that leads to the end also. The born-again Christian, even the one with deep scars from sin, is a totally new creation, created for the good works that God has prepared for him in advance (Eph. 2:10). Christianity is not fatalism. The "god" of fatalism is impersonal, arbitrary fate. The true God is the personal God of the Bible, a God of certainty.

So many people now think: "What can 'poor me' do if God has already decided for me about eternity? What can I do?" You can believe, you can call on Him, which will be evidence that you were chosen (Acts 16:31); you can call out to Him day and night. "Salvation and faith" are inseparable. Cry out to Him, and be assured that your place is in Christ: *"And will not God give justice to his elect, **who cry to him day and night**? Will he delay long over them?"* (Luke 18:7). Is not our philosophizing in vain just to justify to ourselves when we do not really want God? Is this not our natural, self-determined pride? Did not Esau freely choose to sell his birthright, and will he not suffer the consequences[32]?

32 See chapter 9; section: Man is Responsible—Compatibilism.

What's more reassuring? That you are in Christ because you chose Him, and therefore God chose you, even though you could not see Him with your natural, dead, spiritual sight? Or that God sovereignly chose you and recreated you while you were still dead in sin, so that you could live and serve Him irresistibly by faith, with new created sight? What's more convincing? The natural, blind decision of man or the creative, providential decision of God?

There are as many approaches from man to God as there are natural men, but man does not know where God is. There is only one way from God to man, and God knows where man is. Rely completely on God's decision, and it will free you from vainly thinking: "Am I chosen, am I not chosen?" As if plucking the petals of a daisy: "He loves me; He loves me not?" Such a roundabout way of thinking leads to self-centered despair. The more we dwell on ourselves, the more the stench of humanity will hang over us. Let us focus on our Lord Jesus Christ, for it is in Him that we are chosen: *"...even as he* ***chose us*** *in him* [Christ] *before the foundation of the world* [in eternity beyond time], *that we should be holy and blameless before him. In love"* (Eph. 1:4).

Until we accept in complete surrender the absolute, limitless sovereignty of the Creator, our minds will be plagued by fear, uncertainty, and doubt. When we come to terms with the fact that we cannot understand everything with our human, time- and space-bound logic, when we shed our human-centered, humanistic approach to the gospel, only then will we begin to experience true freedom-rest in Christ. It is then that God will be supreme in our thinking. A thimble cannot contain a finite ocean, so how could we contain the infinite ocean of God's glorious and holy sovereignty?

8

UNCONDITIONAL, SOVEREIGN ELECTION II

CHOSEN WEDDING GUESTS

We can see "salvation and faith" illustrated in Jesus' parable of the wedding feast (Matt. 22:1-14). It is not made entirely clear, so we cannot fully read the salvation sequence from it, however, we can safely assume that the chosen (elect) wedding guests in this parable represent the Bride of Christ, the people of God, the Church. We should understand this parable in its context of Jesus speaking to the hardened Pharisees who recognized themselves in the parable. At the same time we must understand that it is universally valid. It applies to all who hear or read the gospel, the good news that Christ came to seek and save people who were lost from birth (Luke 19:10). Let us study more closely the parable of the wedding feast (Matt. 22:1-14):

"And again Jesus spoke to them in parables, saying, 'The kingdom of heaven may be compared to a king ***who gave a wedding feast for his son****'"* (Matt. 22:1-2). God the Father has arranged a wedding for His Son in eternity. The Son, Jesus Christ, is marrying His bride (Rev. 21:2), the Church which the Father gave Him (John 17:11).

"...and sent his servants to call those who were invited to the wedding feast, ***but they would not come****"* (Matt. 22:3). God sent His servants, the witnesses, all in Christ, whom He created for Himself to proclaim His praiseworthy deeds (Isa. 43:21), the first of which is Christ's redeeming Cross. The gospel is an invitation to marry the Lamb, the Son of God. The last thing the natural man wants is to give himself to the Bridegroom Jesus Christ, to submit to the marriage covenant, to say "yes" to Him, and to renounce the bondage of sin. The natural man rejects the wedding feast, preferring to entertain the pleasures of the world. Without God, he is quite "comfortable" with evil (Eph. 2:2) because he does not know or want to know anything else.

"Again, he sent other servants, saying, 'Tell those who are invited, See, I have prepared my dinner, my oxen and my fat calves have been slaughtered, and everything is ready. ***Come to the wedding feast****'"* (Matt. 22:4). God is patient, slow to anger (Isa. 48:9), and always gives people the opportunity to receive the good news of salvation right now, to be spiritually saturated through their marriage to Christ (2 Cor. 6:2):

"But they paid no attention and went off*, one to his farm, another to his business"* (Matt. 22:5). The natural man lives only for this world. Daily business is more important to people; they have no time for Christ (Matt. 19:22):

"...while the rest seized his servants, ***treated them shamefully, and killed them****"* (Matt. 22:6). Not only the Old Testament, religious, would-be spiritual "Jews," but also the New Testament, religious, would-be spiritual "Christians" have persecuted and continue to persecute God's prophets, witnesses, and preachers of the gospel—cruelly to the point of death. The secular and religious world hates Christ and His people (John 15:18). The blood of many martyrs' has been shed in the name of God (Rev. 20:4b). The

Greek word "martys" is a homonym, a consonantal word with two Greek meanings; "martys" means both witness and martyr.

"The king was angry, and he sent his troops and ***destroyed those murderers and burned their city****"* (Matt. 22:7). In Old Testament history, Jerusalem was burned and destroyed, along with the temple. Jews who persecuted and killed the witnesses and prophets were destroyed; survivors were scattered all over the world. In New Testament future terms, at Christ's final Day of Judgment the whole earth will be overthrown, along with all the cities, all the religious systems, the entire household of Satan—the "oikia," the visible/materialistic, and invisible, moral economy of this world (Rev. 16:18-21).

"Then he said to his servants, 'The wedding feast is ready, but ***those invited were not worthy****'"* (Matt. 22:8). The gospel of Jesus Christ was first preached to the Jews, but most rejected it (Acts 13:46a). Though invited to Christ's wedding feast, Gentiles are no better off (Acts 13:46b). To many Jews, the bridegroom, Christ, became a stumbling block; to many Gentiles, He is foolishness (1 Cor. 1:23).

"Go therefore to the main roads and ***invite to the wedding feast as many as you find****"* (Matt. 22:9). God's chosen servants today, through the gospel, invite all people without distinction of race, gender, age, or social status, both near (Jews) and far (Gentiles), to partake in the marriage of Jesus Christ (Eph. 2:16-17; Matthew 24:14).

"And those servants went out into the roads and ***gathered all whom they found****, both bad and good. So the wedding hall was filled with guests"* (Matt. 22:10). Although the servants invited all without distinction, they gathered only those they found. Those "found," good or bad, were no more worthy than those "not found" (Rom. 3:23) because those "found" were not seeking Christ (Rom. 3:11). It was Christ who sought them (Luke 19:10).

"But when the king came in to look at the guests, he saw there a man ***who had no wedding garment****"* (Matt. 22:11). This verse is a general warning against tampering with the gospel (2 Cor. 2:17). There are and have been many in the New Testament Church and in Old Testament Israel of whom God's Word speaks: *"They went out from us, but they were not of us"* (1 John 2:19a). This includes people who prophesied, preached, taught, cast out evil spirits, and did many mighty works "in the name of Christ" (Matt. 7:22-23).

"And he said to him, 'Friend, how did you get in here ***without a wedding garment****?' And he was speechless"* (Matt. 22:12). This "friend" was not clothed in Christ, never having had an intimate relationship with Him. He merely pretended to belong to Him, intruding uninvited among the wedding guests (2 Cor. 2:17). There are many in the Christian community who seek only a social connection for themselves and their families among "respectable" people.

"Then the king said to the attendants, 'Bind him hand and foot and ***cast him into the outer darkness****. In that place there will be weeping and gnashing of teeth'"* (Matt. 22:13). It is better to be ignorant of Christ and His saving work on the Cross, to be an ignorant Gentile, than to know the way of salvation and reject it (2 Pet. 2:21; Matt. 11:23-24). The worst-case scenario is when someone fakes a relationship with Christ or uses it for personal gain. To these Christ will say: *"****I never knew you****; depart from me, you workers of lawlessness"* (Matt. 7:23b); i.e., "I never loved you with an everlasting, saving love" (Matt. 7:22-23).

"For many are called [those who have heard the gospel], ***but few are chosen****"* (Matt. 22:14). There are still many who have never heard the gospel and may never hear it. Therefore, many, not all, are invited to Christ through the gospel, whether that invitation was offered indirectly through the Law in Old Testament times, or directly through the preaching of the gospel in New Testament

times. But all who are invited have one thing in common—all without exception, by nature, from birth, do not seek the Savior (Rom. 3:11; Rom. 10:20). Therefore, out of God's goodness, for His Glory, a few will be chosen (Matt. 22:14). No one can or will accept the invitation out of an inner desire or need, because everyone is spiritually dead in Adam (1 Cor. 15:22a).

In summary: The entire parable of the wedding feast (Matt. 22:1-14) does not in the least suggest that any of the invitees were worthy of the invitation or that they were even inclined to accept the invitation. Some invitees were so self-absorbed that they declined the invitation, but the king's servants did find and gather others, even though they too had same fallen nature. *"For many are called, but few are chosen"* (Matt. 22:14).

ELECTION IS GOD'S DECREE

GOD'S ELECTION OF SAUL

Most remarkable is the example of God's sovereign intervention in the natural, religious life of the Pharisee Saul, later the Apostle Paul. The circumstances of Saul's regeneration are unique and unrepeatable, yet in his salvation we find elements common to all elect unbelievers before their rebirth. Saul did not desire Jesus, nor was he seeking Him—he actually hated Jesus. Paul was saved when he was on his way to Damascus on a mission to persecute the Jews who had believed in Christ. So, what happened on the road to Damascus? Jesus appeared to him without Saul ever seeking Him or longing for Him inwardly. Saul had not a single spiritual virtue that could commend him to God. There was nothing in Saul's nature—as there is nothing in any men—that could attract God. Despite Saul's false spirituality, our good God had mercy on him and gave him a new heart. Saul was unable to resist this sovereign, creative, divine intervention. No one, not even Saul himself, could prevent

God from endowing Saul with "salvation and faith" because God had chosen him before the foundation of the world and had loved him with an everlasting saving love. And God commissioned Saul to do what He was calling him to do: *"But the Lord said to him* [Ananias], *'Go, for he* [Saul, Paul] *is a chosen instrument of mine to carry my name before the Gentiles and kings and the children of Israel. For I will show him how much he must suffer for the sake of my name'"* (Acts 9:15-16).

Saul's heart had harbored many antichristian plans, but the Lord's authority stood (Prov. 19:21; 21:30). God's eternal decree is immutable, and no one can resist it. Paul himself realized the truth of this after he was born-again: *"But when he who had set me apart before I was born, and who called me by his grace, was pleased to reveal his Son to me, in order that I might preach him among the Gentiles, I did not immediately consult with anyone* [I did not reason with anyone, not even myself]*"* (Gal. 1:15-16). As a natural descendant of Adam, Saul was chosen by God's saving grace "before" conception, birth, and rebirth. He had been written in God's Book of Life from all eternity. No spiritual corpse, not even Saul's, can either stand against or choose such a triune divine decree and office. It is established in God' s timetable in history when every promised elect person, within time and space, will be conceived and born, when God will create and awaken "salvation and faith" in him, when he will be born-again, justified, sanctified, and raised into a glorified body by God's grace. God put His quickening Spirit in Saul before Saul himself had even a shred of faith in Jesus' saving work on the Cross. It was only by God's sovereign, creative intervention that he became a new creature in Christ with a new heart—ironically, when he was on his way to Damascus to arrest God's elect: *"Therefore, if anyone is in Christ, he is a new creation. The old has passed away; behold, the new has come"* (2 Cor. 5:17).

THE ELECTION OF ABRAHAM, ISAAC, JACOB AND THEIR DESCENDANTS

Let us recall other scriptural evidence that confirms God's complete control over His elect whose names He wrote in His Book of Life before time began: *"Yet the Lord set his heart* [on Abraham, Isaac, and Jacob—the spiritual fathers of all the elect of all nations; Gen. 17:5-6; Rom. 9:7-8; Jer. 31:7] *in love* [God knew them, foreknew them, and loved them with an everlasting redeeming love] *on your fathers and* ***chose their offspring*** [children of promise; Rom. 9:7-8] *after them, you above all peoples* [without distinction—even English speakers; Gen. 17:5-7], *as you are this day"* (Deut. 10:15).

From eternity the Lord has clung to His chosen people—the Israel of God, the commonwealth of Israel (Gal. 6:16; Eph. 2:12), that is, a people made up of Jews and Gentiles who are Abraham's seed in Christ (Gal. 3:27-29). Old Covenant—ethnic Israel was the chosen, physical antitype, the shadow of the spiritual reality of the New Covenant—the Israel of God (Gal. 6:16), that is, the commonwealth of Israel, the Church that knows Christ: *"...remember that you were at that time separated from Christ* [you Gentiles], ***alienated from the commonwealth of Israel*** *and strangers to the covenants of promise, having no hope and without God in the world* [you were not His body, His Church]*"* (Eph. 2:12). In the carnal antitype, Old Covenant ethnic Israel, most of the people did not know God (Rom. 9:31-33); only a chosen remnant knew Him (1 Kings 19:18; Rom. 11:4). In spiritual reality, in the New Covenant commonwealth of the Israel of God, the true Church, God is known by all without exception (Jer. 31:34): *"And they shall not teach, each one his neighbor and each one his brother, saying, 'Know the Lord,'* ***for they shall all know me****, from the least of them to the greatest"* (Heb. 8:11). It is only this special people whom God has drawn to Himself through Christ's wrestling on the Cross alone, without any human intervention. One meaning of the name Israel is "God strives, God struggles, God perseveres." The chosen Jews, Greeks, males, females, free, and slaves are one holy nation because they are the chosen, redeemed, and reborn brothers and sisters in Christ. Abraham (Gen. 17:5-6), Isaac (Rom. 9:7-8), and Jacob (Jer. 31:7) are their spiritual fathers because they live according to Abrahamic faith (Rom. 4:16-18). These who are in Christ are also heirs of God. One does not become an heir by his own will, but only through the will of the one bequeathing his inheritance following his death: *"...for you are all* ***one in Christ Jesus****. And if you are Christ's,* ***then you are Abraham's offspring, heirs according to promise****"* (Gal. 3:28b-29).

GENERALLY, ABOUT ELECTION

Let us look at other verses that deal with God's sovereign election: *"Blessed is the one you choose* [LORD] *and bring near, to dwell in your courts! We shall be satisfied with* ***the goodness of your house****, the holiness of your temple!"* (Ps. 65:4). To the Old Testament saints, the Israel of God who knew the Lord, the principle of election was obvious: *"Remember me,* ***O Lord****, when you show favor to your people; help me when you save them, that I may look upon* ***the prosperity of your chosen ones****, that I may rejoice in the gladness of your nation, that I may glory with your inheritance"* (Ps. 106:4-5). This Psalm implies that salvation is of God alone. "Help me when you save them" is in no way dependent on a human decision necessary to make the work of the Lord Jesus Christ on the Cross efficacious. The psalmist knew that God embraces His people with favor, with the salvation He longs for them to behold, that they might see by faith the goodness of their God.[33] The redeemed remnant of ethnic Jews, who spiritually belonged to the Israel of God through the

33 See Exodus 33:19-23.

Abrahamic faith, knew well that it was God's decision whom He would accept as a son.

In the New Testament, Jesus told Nicodemus that he had to be born-again: *"Nicodemus said to him, 'How can these things be?' Jesus answered him, 'Are you the teacher of Israel and yet you do not understand these things?'"* (John 3:9-10). Jesus assumed that Nicodemus should have known this. It was more than the Old Testament verses about election should have convinced Nicodemus. The Old Testament addresses God's unilateral, monergistic, creative action as well, in passages such as this one: *"And I* [I the LORD] *will give you a new heart, and a new spirit I* [I the LORD] *will put within you. And I* [I the LORD] *will remove the heart of stone from your flesh and give you a heart of flesh. And I* [I the LORD] *will put my Spirit within you, and* [I the LORD] *cause you to walk in my statutes and be careful to obey my rules"* (Ezek. 36:26-27). Ezekiel was prophesying the creation of God's people, the Church, the true Israel of God from all the nations of the world. He who is created with a new heart (note the passive voice) cannot participate in his own creation. The Creator is the active voice, never the one created. The Jews, the elect of the Old Testament, were not trying to "keep" the Law in order to be saved—only Christ could keep the Law. When they were rushing toward salvation, they were actually rushing to Christ who fulfilled the Law. What the promised coming of the Messiah meant was a spiritual resurrection in Christ: *"...and all* [the Jews in the wilderness] *drank the same spiritual drink. For they drank from the spiritual Rock that followed them, and the Rock was Christ"* (1 Cor. 10:4).

The separation, or sanctification, of the chosen remnant in the Old Testament (believing Jews) and of the New Testament Church (Jews and Gentiles) was then, as it is now, God's work.

THE CONTEXT OF ELECTION

THE ABSURDITY OF A PREVENIENT GRACE

The Arminian idea of reviving a spiritually dead person through what they call God's prevenient grace[34] so that he is "free" to accept or reject the grace offered is as absurd as trying to persuade a corpse to rise from the dead. For example, the dead Lazarus could neither accept nor reject bodily revival because he was totally inert, dead. Only God can raise the dead (John 11:38-46). The same is true of our first resurrection (Eph. 2:6), our new birth through the Spirit (John 3:8). Both physical and spiritual birth occur only under God's sovereign, creative authority.

I used to believe that God the Holy Spirit relentlessly persuades all people who hear the gospel to repent and turn to the saving Cross of Christ. This, in a nutshell, is the essence of the Arminian doctrine of prevenient grace which most evangelicals and all Catholics accept today. Now I know from Scripture that a person who is spiritually dead cannot be persuaded.

Let us take the assumption of Holy Spirit persuasion, of a kind of prevenient grace and its influence, to its absurd conclusions.

Possibility 1: If God the Holy Spirit persuades all awakened souls by prevenient grace with the same persuasive effort, how is it possible that some awakened souls are persuaded, and others are not? Why do some believe while others do not? Is it that some people have an inner spiritual quality that obeys God's persuasion, while others lack this quality and resist the call of the Holy Spirit? If this be the case, then in what or in whom is success found? Is it found in human receptivity? Sensitivity? Intelligence? In the search for meaning in life? Desire? Faith? Covetousness? Choosing any of these answers only buries the satisfying answer ever deeper. If salva-

34 See chapter 5; section: The Difference Between Prevenient and Common Grace.

tion is not caused by the unconditional grace of God but rather by personal choice, then some kind of inner virtue is needed; if the efficacy of Christ's sacrifice must be activated by helpful prevenient grace plus a subsequent act of human choice, then the saved do have something to boast about, despite the clear teaching of Scriptures (Eph. 2:9).

Possibility 2: Also, purely theoretical and even more absurd is the possibility that God the Holy Spirit persuades some souls more and others less. Those on whom He presses more are more likely to capitulate and answer "yes," while those on whom He presses less may resist His wooing. Such an inability of the Holy Spirit to work decisively must be rejected by everyone.

So, what is left for us to conclude? Simply the truth God revealed in the Scriptures, that He pours out His saving grace, choosing His own with 100% efficacy out of Satan's house. God is forming His people for Himself and for His Glory because it pleases Him to do so. God does not need to use prevenient grace, nor does he need to wait for man's consent; He gives saving grace to those who are His own. When God creates, He needs no help from man: *"**For by grace you have been saved** through faith. And **this is not your own doing**; it is the gift of God, **not a result of works**, so that no one may boast"* (Eph. 2:8-9).

If we fail to give full credit to our Creator and Savior for our spiritual sight and hearing, for our "salvation and faith," then we are infected with self-centered pride. We may profess God's love and mercy with our mouths, but if we claim salvation as our own choice, thinking our will was "free" to limit the Sovereign God, then we should conduct a deep examination of our souls (2 Cor. 13:5). No one has the slightest merit in "salvation and faith." We believe because God has chosen us; He spiritually resurrected us and the second death no longer has power over us (Rev. 20:6); we cannot fall into the lake of fire (Rev. 20:14). If we truly understand

and believe that God created us anew, born-again, though He did not have to, then we glorify God with gratitude, obedience, and humility. I do not understand why God made us His people in Christ Jesus—we were not chosen through any merit of our own, but by the decree of His will[35]. All our philosophizing must go. Let us stand firm in the faith, live in obedience, and work out our salvation with trembling (Phil. 2:12), motivated by the Cross of Christ, not by human selfishness.

THE CONTRADICTION BETWEEN ARMINIANISM AND CALVINISM

These two soteriological systems are in complete causal contradiction. Arminians believe (the cause) in order to be saved (the effect). Calvinists are "saved and believe" (the effect) at the moment God creates in them a new heart (the cause):

	CAUSE	EFFECT
ARMINIANISM	**Faith** awakened by the prevenient grace of God. Prevenient grace is resistible.	**God's conditional grace** creates a new inner man; **man's unbelief limits its efficacy**.
CALVINISM	**God's unconditional grace** creates a new inner man; it is not conditioned by "human faith." **God Himself limits its extent**.	**"salvation and faith"**—rebirth, regeneration, justification, sanctification, bodily resurrection.

- In Arminianism, faith is the cause; in Calvinism, it is the effect.
- In Arminianism, the creation of the new inner man is the effect; in Calvinism, the cause.
- God's grace is the effect in Arminianism, the cause in Calvinism.
- In Arminianism, God's conditionality is the effect; in Calvinism, God's unconditionality is the cause.

35 See chapter 10; section: God's Will; heading: Degrees of Will.

- In Arminianism, man's "free" will, i.e., his response to God's helpful prevenient grace, is decisive; in Calvinism, only the sovereign, unconditional will of God is decisive.
- In Arminianism, God's grace is limited in efficacy by man; in Calvinism, it is limited by God in its extent.

It is only unconditional, integral salvation that creates a truly free, Christ-based will within the spiritually-born person. Outside of Christ there is no truly free person. Adam lost that freedom for us in paradise. *"So Jesus said to the Jews who had believed him, 'If you abide in my word, you are truly my disciples, and you will know the truth* [of Me], *and the truth* ***will set you free****'"* (John 8:31-32). "Salvation and faith" are due solely to God's sovereign, unconditional grace. God's chosen people are spiritually resurrected through no merit of their own through the monergistic rebirth of His Spirit alone: *"The wind* [figuratively, the Spirit of God] *blows where it wishes, and you hear its sound, but you do not know where it comes from or where it goes* [no one knows into whom the Spirit will enter]. *So it is with everyone who is born of the Spirit"* (John 3:8).

THE CHURCH, THE ECCLESIA, ARE THE CALLED ONES

Use Biblical terminology to get to the heart of the matter. The Czech word *církev*, the Russian *cerkev*, the Scottish *kirk*, the English *church*, the German *Kirche* are all terms derived from the Greek word *kyrios*, which means *ruler* or *Lord*. Undoubtedly, the Church belongs to the Lord—who among Slavic or Germanic peoples today knows from whom or from what their word for the Church is derived?

The Greek word *ekklēsia* is made up of the prefix *ek* and the verb *kaleo*. When translated as closely as possible to its original meaning, the prefix *ek* means *from* or *out of* (similar to the Latin prefix *ex*) and the verb *kaleo* means *to call, name, invite, appoint, be named*. So, the Greek *ekklesia*, or church, refers to all who have been, are now, and will be called by Christ out of bondage to Satan's economy.

Zechariah prophesies the coming of Jesus Christ to Jerusalem on a colt to save His flock of chosen people on Zion, i.e., on the Cross (Zech. 9:9-17). In the very next chapter, chapter 10, the Holy Spirit put into Zechariah's mouth a much more expressive verb than *to call out*: *"**I will whistle for them*** [for those whom I have saved] *and gather them in, for I have redeemed them, and they shall be as many as they were before"* (Zech. 10:8).

The Greek world "ekklesia," the Church, evokes the sense of "salvation and faith," rather than a sense of church organization. It is through God's call—not through registration on a membership list—that God's people become a part of His true Church: *"And we know that for those who love God all things work together for good, **for those who are called*** [whistled for by God] *according to his purpose"* (Rom. 8:28).

DIVINE ELECTION BRINGS PEACE TO THE FAITHFUL

Unconditional election is wonderfully comforting because it means our salvation is in God's hands. If God's election were conditioned on man's "free" will, then those Christians who truly see the horror of their sin-stained hearts would be the most neurotic. People who seem to have made up their own decision and are able to live "at ease" have not yet realized the terror of their sin-stained hearts.

Let us just look at three assurances that come from election:

1. No sinner is so rebellious that he cannot be saved: *"You ascended on high, leading a host of captives in your train and receiving gifts among men, **even among the rebellious**, that the Lord God may dwell there"* (Ps. 68:18).
2. Those who proclaim the saving Cross of Jesus Christ to a perishing world can rest assured that God has His elect whom He

will surely draw to Himself (John 6:44). Were it not for God's election, preachers of the gospel would be laboring in vain, speaking to the wind, but in election their witness cannot miss its God-ordained target: "*to one* [the reprobate] *a fragrance from death* ***to death****, to the other* [God's elect] *a fragrance from life* ***to life****. Who is sufficient for these things?"* (2 Cor. 2:16).

3. God's people know that they could not come to God on their own because of their natural inability, but that God unconditionally chooses and adopts each one of them. It is for this very reason that they praise and glorify God from the bottom of their hearts: *"And they sang a new song, saying, 'Worthy are you to take the scroll and to open its seals, for you were slain, and* ***by your blood you ransomed people for God*** *from every tribe and language and people and nation* [without distinction, not without exception], *and you have made them a kingdom and priests to our God, and they shall reign on the earth'"* (Rev. 5:9-10).

DIVINE ADOPTION: AN EXAMPLE FROM PERSONAL LIFE

The principle of divine adoption is absolutely central to our salvation. We are not by nature children of God; rather, by nature, our father is the Evil One (John 8:44; 1 Pet. 2:10). When a person adopts a stranger's child, the adopted child has the same rights of inheritance as blood children. This is precisely what God has done for us: *"So then* ***you are no longer strangers and aliens****, but you are fellow citizens with the saints and members of the household of God"* (Eph. 2:19).

Sometime in 2006, our son and daughter-in-law who live in the USA told us that they wanted to adopt a girl. That was the first surprise. The bigger surprise was that they were considering adopting a little girl from Ethiopia. Why were we surprised? Because they already had three children. Then, I asked, why from Ethiopia? Apparently, adopting children from Ethiopia was less demanding administratively and financially because this avenue of adoption had just opened. I thought a Chinese girl would be a better fit with the family. I had all kinds of thoughts running through my head—hidden disapproval, prejudice, suspicion, etc. I wondered how they even came up with this idea. They explained that before they had married, they had promised each other that their last child would be adopted. This blew my mind. My son, who never closed a door until he grew up, seemed to have outgrown me! I had to have a talk with the Lord about my unpleasant response. When our minds accepted their decision, we happily signed a family resolution in favor of the adoption, and through adoption, the child becomes an heir. We just watched the paperwork fall into place. My daughter-in-law bought a folder to file all of it—documents in Czech, birth certificates, marriage certificates, official translations into English from somewhere in Texas, then translations from English into Amharic, naturalization certificates, documents confirming their visits to the Christian intermediary organization, documents from social workers, correspondence with the Ethiopian court and with the orphanage, etc. etc. It was a complete bureaucratic tsunami! I will not even mention the required financial arrangements. In the end the folder contained about 180 certified documents. The preparation and approval process took my son and his wife over a year to complete. When the final notice came that eight-month-old Santayahu was approved for adoption and travel, my son and daughter-in-law flew to Ethiopia, and Grandma Klara and Grandpa Pavel flew to America to take care of our other grandchildren. Little Santayahu received not only a new first name, Jordan, but a new birth certificate as well, which gave the names of our son and daughter-in-law as her parents.

The process of rescuing her from the misery of being an abandoned child had begun four months before her birth. The significance of so much paperwork, so many hurdles, and so much effort made for a child who was not even born yet gradually began to dawn on me. What had this little girl, abandoned by her natural mother and father, contributed to her rescue? Absolutely nothing. Her "election" to a new home and her departure to a new world were totally undeserved and unconditional. The world would say she was lucky, but there is no such thing as luck, only Divine Providence. One child, out of hundreds of thousands of orphans, was called to "salvation." Our son and daughter-in-law showed their unconditional love for a child they did not know and had never seen, a child who had not even been born.

This personal experience gave us a figurative example of what election is all about. In the adoption of our granddaughter, I was able to understand and experience what God had done for His chosen children, those whom He loved unconditionally before they were born. In eternity past God already had the binder for their adoption documents, the Book of Life; He foreknew whom He would redeem—not through a bureaucratic "calvary," but at the real Calvary where His Son paid for His adopted children with His own life (Rom. 8:15, 23; 9:4; Gal. 4:5): *"...he predestined us* ***for adoption*** *to himself as sons through Jesus Christ, according to the purpose of his will"* (Eph. 1:5). I thank God for giving me, by His sovereign, gracious will, a son and daughter-in-law who practically showed me and my wife what it means to be unconditionally adopted as sons and daughters. They have become for us a shadow of God's true adoption, the adoption of His elect.

Our granddaughter's full name is now Jordan Santayahu Steiger. Santayahu commemorates her ancestry. As the locals told us, it means "I have been through a lot." Steiger is a sign of her acceptance, her adoption, of her becoming part of a new, loving family. Jordan refers to the fact that she crossed the "Jordan River," leaving the shores of poverty as an abandoned Ethiopian orphan to the other side where full "sonship" and a loving family and siblings awaited her, just as the Jews left slavery on one bank of the Jordan River and on the other, they entered the Promised Land that the Lord was giving them to enjoy. This pictures all of us, adopted by Christ, crossing from the wretched shores of this fallen world to enter the Promised Land, the homeland of heaven where we will gaze upon the face of our Lord.

9

DOUBLE PREDESTINATION

DOUBLE PREDESTINATION

INTRODUCTION TO THE CONCEPT

As we open an interesting but difficult chapter, we know that it is impossible to exhaust the subject of election, let alone the double predestination that Scripture makes evident. Yet know that even this topic is but a drop from the depths of the infinite ocean of God's sovereignty and wisdom. The question of double predestination is usually the province of theologians, so we must approach this ground with the utmost humility.

If God chooses, predestines, and saves some from condemnation, then He necessarily leaves others in condemnation. If election exists—that is, predestination to salvation—and not everyone is saved, then we must also examine the flip side of the matter. When we speak of the elect Jacob, we must remember the reprobate Esau (Mal. 1:2-3). This fact is the essence of double predestination.

For many years I made all sorts of detours around this difficult dilemma, but in all honesty, I was not looking for an answer. Double predestination sounded sinister, cruel, and unjust to me.

I tried to defend God from being accused of such "injustice." I considered predestination to eternal life acceptable, but to leave someone in perdition and final damnation was unthinkable! Is not God the loving Father of all people? Are we not all finite and imperfect human beings? All people should be given the opportunity to receive the gift of faith through patient persuasion, by the loving and non-violent invocation of the Holy Spirit through prevenient grace! So, I reasoned until I began to think I was so depraved that I could not accept Christ. Is this not the kind of thinking and the real reason why so many Christians prefer Pelagianism, Semi-Pelagianism, or Arminianism? In our man-centered, sinful nature, it does not occur to us that it is the sovereign God who passively creates evil and creates darkness (Isa. 45:7)[36].

Only a turn, or rather a return, to Reformed doctrine would give me a satisfactory, though not exhaustive, answer. It was then that the Spirit of God revealed to me in Scripture that while God is the Creator of all and everything, He is only the Father of His chosen people, beloved from all eternity: *"Now may our Lord Jesus Christ himself, and God our Father,* ***who loved us*** [His chosen and promised people] *and gave us eternal comfort and good hope through grace"* (2 Thess. 2:16). The implication is that God has not loved others, such as Esau, with saving love. Since He has not given them eternal joy and good hope, they remain children of the Evil One from birth (John 8:44; 8:47b; Eph. 2:2; 1 John 3:10). God embraces His children with saving love and grace; He "only" embraces the children of the Evil One with common grace[37]. This is the principle of double predestination. How can we accept this? How are we to understand it?

36 See chapter 6; section: Where Did Evil Come From?

37 See chapter 5; section: The Difference Between Prevenient and Common Grace; heading: Common Grace.

For some (Calvinists), God's work, the plan of predestination and election, is perfect in that it must be unconditionally fulfilled. God's decretive will[38], his oracle, his decree, is always final (Prov. 19:21). For others (Pelagians, Semi-Pelagians, and Arminians), God determines and elects according to His foreknowledge of man's conduct. God's office is thus dependent upon man's decision; thus, predestination and election have two sides:

One side is positive: This concerns those who are chosen by God, i.e., not left in Satan's household at the mercy of their natural "free" will. God is active in the salvation of His elect, both in intention—God chose them before the foundation of the world—and in action—God the Son bore their sins, and the Holy Spirit regenerated them.

The other side is negative: This refers to all those whom God has left to their natural, "free" will, who therefore choose to remain apart from God in Satan's abode. In this case, God is active in intention—everything happens according to His will (everything is His ministry)—but He is passive in action, leaving sinners to their natural, sinful inclinations. He does not actively create evil in them; He merely "departs" from them, leaving them to their natural "free" evil will (1 Sam. 18:12).

DOUBLE PREDESTINATION IS GOD'S SOVEREIGN PURPOSE

Election to eternal life is the sovereign, positive predestination of God, manifested in God's activity, that is, in His saving the sinner from his natural, reprobate state. But leaving the sinner in his natural, reprobate state is also a sovereign predestination of God, manifested by God's passivity, that is, His withdrawal from the sinner. The asymmetry of this consists in God's activity in the case of the elect and His passivity in the case of the reprobate, but in both cases it is God's sovereign purpose, fulfilled by His permis-

38 See chapter 10; section: God's Will; heading: Degrees of Will.

sion, leading to one end: *"So the honor is for you who believe, but for those who do not believe, 'The stone that the builders rejected has become the cornerstone,' and 'A stone of stumbling, and a rock of offense* [Christ]*.' They stumble because they disobey the word, as they were* ***destined*** *to do"* (1 Pet. 2:7-8). The phrase "they disobey the word, as they were destined to do" is interpreted by Arminians to mean that they were destined by God to stumble because of their willful rebellion against the Word. This is true, however every man without exception willfully resists the Word in his natural state, even those whom God has chosen for salvation. This reasoning provides no way out. Providentially, the text does not state "you are not destined to not to stumble because you naturally obey the word." It continues with God's decree: *"But you are a* ***chosen*** *race, a royal priesthood, a holy nation, a people for his own possession, that you may proclaim the excellencies of him who called you out of darkness into his marvelous light"* (1 Pet. 2:9). The contextual contrast between "*destined* reprobates" and "God's *chosen* people" clearly shows God's primacy in double predestination.

A MORE IN-DEPTH ANALYSIS

Whenever God pronounces positive predestination, He is always active in carrying out that predestination; His hands are working for good. Whenever God pronounces negative predestination, He is passive; His hands have never "dipped" in evil. Evil is done by those from whom God withdraws, those whom He leaves to their enslaved will: *"...he reveals deep and hidden things; he knows what is in the darkness* [human sin, which He uses and controls], *and the light dwells with him* [God is never a partaker of sin, He is Holy]*"* (Dan. 2:22).

Even in His negative predestination, whether His withdrawal is temporary or permanent, i.e., leaving certain sinners, fallen angels, and Satan in reprobation, the effect is positive because the reprobation of evil is good (Gen. 6:5; 6:17; Rev. 6:9-10). The difference between positive and negative predestination lies in the way God sovereignly carries out His predestinations, whether He is active, doing good, or passive, allowing others to do evil. God's positive and negative predestinations always and without exception lead to the ultimate goal of bringing all things under the feet of Christ for His Glory (Heb. 2:7-8; Matt. 22:44). Therefore, all of history has been and will be subject to the holy decrees of God. Had history been shaped by the "free" will of natural man, after Adam's Fall all would have been irreversibly consigned to eternal flames, far from God. Were it not for God's sovereign predestination, no one could have been redeemed by God and brought into His eternal kingdom.

EVERY PREDESTINATION GLORIFIES GOD

GOD'S POSITIVE PREDESTINATION GLORIFIES HIM

God is active in fulfilling His positive predestinations. He is actively creating "salvation and faith," regeneration, justification and sanctification in the hearts of His chosen people. He purposes this for the advancement of the kingdom of God. Every good thing a child of God does is through God's own merit, as God actively works in His child's heart. The category of God's positive predestination includes common grace. He actively gives common grace to the saved and the reprobate as well. This world remains only because God continually tames man's destructive wrath: *"Surely the wrath of man shall praise thee:* ***the remainder of wrath shalt thou restrain****"* (Ps. 76:10, KJV)[39]. In the category of God's positive predestination and action, we include God's judgments, such as Adam's expulsion from Eden, the flood, the Last Judgment, and any other judgment in which God actively punishes by His own hand. The removal of evil is a good act; the negation

39 See chapter 5; section: Common Grace Keeps the World Moving; heading: God Controls Evil.

of the negative is a positive, merciful act in which God is always glorified (Ps. 136:15).

GOD'S NEGATIVE PREDESTINATION GLORIFIES HIM

Where God's negative predestination is concerned, God is passive in action. He is never active in the realization of negative predestinations; He does not create evil in the hearts of sinners, but He steps back, leaving natural men at the mercy of their own enslaved, "free" will and sin. From the cradle mankind obeys the Evil One (Eph. 2:2). Whenever God withdraws (more or less) from sinners by loosening the reins, He gives more vent to human wrath (Ps. 76:10); the more "freedom" He gives, the more sinners' self-will is manifested. This will manifest in increased self-slavery and increased dependence on evil desires that are controlled by Satan (1 Sam. 16:14-15). All evil that man does is his own fault and responsibility and to his own shame. Yet even in God's negative predestination, when He opens the floodgates to man's sin, God glorifies Himself—see Judas, Pharaoh, Joseph's brothers, and others[40]. In all revealed history, God cannot fail to glorify Himself.

If we have difficulty accepting God's holy negative predestination, which includes leaving some people in their sinful, natural depravity, then we do not yet understand that in Adam man is totally depraved[41]. God's Glory and goodness is in saving anyone at all (Ex. 33:19).

SYMMETRICAL, UNBIBLICAL DOUBLE PREDESTINATION

There is an unbiblical view of double predestination in which God works symmetrically, actively working in the case of both the saved and the reprobate. Symmetry in predestination necessarily presup-

40 See chapter 9; section: Examples of God's Negative Predestination
41 See PART I

poses that the natural man is morally neutral from birth, that from birth he is not a vassal of Satan but a blank, unwritten sheet of white paper. This is what most religions, including Islam, teach. In this system, according to God's will, God's hand actively raises His elect from a neutral state to heavenly heights, and in symmetry He actively, by His own hand, takes those He has destined to damnation from a neutral state down to the depths of hell.

This is the way all Pelagians and many Semi-Pelagians and Arminians misunderstand double predestination—no wonder they reject it! But even the Reformation and Calvinism rejected this view. The principle of an erroneous, symmetrical understanding of double predestination arose from verses in which God (as if actively acting) hardened Pharaoh's heart with His hand (Ex. 4:21), created the self-willed for His purpose (Prov. 16:4), or created darkness and evil (Isa. 45:7), and so on.

Symmetrical double predestination has never been and is not now a doctrine of the Reformation, even though Pelagians, Semi-Pelagians, and Arminians erroneously assume that it was and is now. If symmetrical predestination were true, then God would also be the active author of sin, but there is no darkness in God. It is, in fact, anti-Calvinism to think that God predestines both salvation and reprobation through His own symmetrical, equal, and active acts. This wrong understanding is a major reason why so many Christians reject or distort the biblical doctrines of predestination and election and espouse Pelagian, Semi-Pelagian, or Arminian thinking to "protect" God from the charge of being the author of evil and sin.

HYPER-CALVINISM

To examine the topic more completely, the heresy of hyper-Calvinism with only a small number of adherents, is defined as the gospel being preached and salvation being offered only to the elect. Martyn Lloyd-Jones (1899-1981) recorded an interesting experience related to hyper-Calvinism. A Calvinist himself, Lloyd-Jones was once challenged as to why he preached the gospel to all men. This was his response:

> *If you were asked to define the difference between a Calvinist and a hyper-Calvinist, how would you do it? It is a question worth asking for this reason; I know large numbers of people who, when they use the term 'hyper-Calvinist' generally mean Calvinist [and vice-versa]. In other words, they do not know what a hyper-Calvinist is. A hyper-Calvinist is one who says that the offer of salvation is only made to the redeemed, and that no preacher of the Gospel should preach Christ and offer to all and sundry. A hyper-Calvinist regards anyone who offers, or who proclaims salvation to all as a dangerous person. For what it is worth, there is a society in London at the moment that has described me as a dangerous Arminian because I preach Christ and offer salvation to all!*[42]

ASYMMETRICAL, BIBLICAL DOUBLE PREDESTINATION

The asymmetrical view of the dual predestination of the saved and the reprobate is the doctrine of both Calvinism and the Reformation. God deals with the elect and the reprobate asymmetrically. In the case of the elect, the same is true as in symmetrical double predestination—God is active, exercising His positive predestination, redeeming and delivering His own by His own hand from the bondage of Satan. But in the case of the reprobate, He exercises His negative predestination, leaving sinners in their natural state in the bondage of Satan. In other words, God does not actively work in negative predestination; He is passive, withdrawing from the reprobate, leaving them to themselves. He does not actively participate in their evil, nor does He create it with His own hand as He does

42 Dr. Martyn Lloyd-Jones (Great Doctrines of the Bible).

with good. The reprobate, by their evil motives, fulfill the history of this sinful, fallen world which God sovereignly predestined to be negative for His ultimate Glory. This table speaks more than a thousand words:

	DOUBLE PREDESTINATION			
	Calvinists understand double predestination asymmetrically, which is why they accept it		Arminians understand double predestination symmetrically which is why they reject it	
	IN SALVATION	IN REPROBATION	IN SALVATION	IN REPROBATION
God's will is always accomplished:	By His decree	By His decree	By His decree	By His decree
God's predestination is:	Positive	Negative	Positive	Positive
God's action is:	Active: He creates faith and causes good works	Passive: He leaves sinners to their own willfulness; He does not actively create unbelief or cause evil deeds	Active: He creates faith and causes good works	Active: He creates unbelief and causes evil works

OVERVIEW OF DOUBLE PREDESTINATION

- God's predestination is twofold—some are saved from the Adamic destruction; others remain in it.
- God's predestination is not symmetrical.
- The bestowal of saving grace is God's positive predestination in accordance with His holy will (Ex. 33:19). God is active in purpose—He chose some for His Glory, out of His goodness, and God is active in action—He died for the elect and keeps them in the faith.

- To be left in a state far from the Lord, in the power of Satan, is God's action as well, but in negative predestination (Rom. 9:22; 1 Peter 2:8). God is active here in purpose—justly, according to His holy will, passing over those whom He wills—but God is passive in action, never producing sin in the human heart. Man, himself, is the one actively sinning, serving his master Satan with his enslaved will.
- God creates a new man out of all whom He redeemed on the Cross, leading them out of Satan's household.
- God does not create sin in the natural hearts of sinners. Sinfulness is human nature inherited from Adam.
- The elect receives a grace that conforms with righteousness, because the Son of God was punished in the flesh in their place as sinful man (Rom. 8:3).
- The wicked will receive punishment that is entirely just.
- God will not deal unjustly with anyone.
- God's predestination is absolutely sovereign, unconditioned by any virtue pleasing to God, merit, or act of faith on the part of a spiritually dead person.
- Neither of God's predestinations is arbitrary—it is conditioned by God's holy nature, the decision of His triune counsel: It is what pleases Him, and He will bring to pass (Isa. 46:10).
- All the good we do is based on God's merit. He actively builds, creates, and plants the born-again on the mountain of His goodness. Any goodness done by man requires God's activity.
- All the evil we do in Adam, in bondage to the Evil One, is our fault.

- God, by His common grace, tames natural, spiritually dead people, keeping them from falling into the depths of evil, from total self-destruction (Ps. 76:10).
- Do not let this thought enter your mind: "If all cannot receive saving grace, then let no one receive it; let all be condemned (Matt. 20:15-16)."

I pray for those of you who struggle spiritually with God's sovereign negative predestination. It is one thing to proclaim God's sovereignty, and it is another thing to bring it to consequences that magnify God infinitely. The greater He is, the smaller we will be: *"He must increase, but I must decrease"* (John 3:30).

EXAMPLES OF GOD'S NEGATIVE PREDESTINATION

The following examples will show how God's negative predestinations take place in the lives of those whom God has given over to their will, and how God's temporary, educational, negative predestinations take place in the lives of His elect.

PHARAOH AND THE EGYPTIANS

The Bible clearly teaches that God hardens the heart. Such negative predestination can grow in strength over time. A typical example is the gradual hardening of the heart of Pharaoh and the Egyptians: *"And **I will harden Pharaoh's heart**, and he will pursue them* [Jews], *and I will get glory over Pharaoh and all his host, and the Egyptians shall know that I am the LORD"* (Ex. 14:4) *"And I will harden the hearts of the Egyptians so that they shall go in after them* [Jews], *and **I will get glory over Pharaoh** and all his host, his chariots, and his horsemen"* (Ex. 14:17). The hardening was a sign to both Egypt and Israel. From God's perspective, it was a saving action that was ultimately just another link in the chain of events leading to the glorification of God and God's eternal kingdom. But how do we satisfactorily answer the question of why God punished Pharaoh? Was it not God Himself who used Pharaoh for His purposes? Is not He who hardens the heart the author of evil? Paul wrote the following to the humanistic Christians in Rome who understood God's negative predestination symmetrically: *"But if our unrighteousness serves to show the righteousness of God, what shall we say? **That God is unrighteous to inflict wrath on us?** (I speak in a human way.) By no means! For then how could God judge the world?"* (Rom. 3:5-6).

It all depends on how we understand the concept of hardening. Generally speaking, there are only two ways to achieve any intention—actively or passively. This is also true in everyday life. Either we achieve our goal actively, by getting involved in the matter, or, as the popular saying goes, we let it "burn out," we remain passive, assuming that others will work things out according to our intention.

God's active hardening of Pharaoh's heart, according to the symmetrical, erroneous view, would mean that God would have to work in the deep chambers of Pharaoh's heart, forming evil plans which Pharaoh's will would of necessity have to carry out, for the will is always the executor of the heart's desires. If this were true, then the author of Pharaoh's evil deeds would undoubtedly have been God Himself.

God's passive hardening, according to the asymmetrical view, is something else entirely. God foreknew—not predicted—the course of events. He knew in detail the ardent desires of Pharaoh's heart. All He had to do, within the framework of His negative predestination, was to withdraw to just the right "distance" from Pharaoh, allowing him to exercise "freer" will, giving him more room for his willfulness. Pharaoh and his people were doing all the dirty work themselves. Therefore, they bore full responsibility for their evil, even though their evil actions fulfilled God's holy purpose. The

Bible gives many examples of God exercising His negative predestination in similar cases where the deceitful human heart overflows with evil activity (Jer. 17:9).

JUDAS

Neither Satan, nor the Pharisees, nor Pilate, nor the crowd, nor Judas, of their own volition, purposed that in a particular time and place in history they would crucify the Son of God, the second, eternal Person of the Holy Triune God. How could God's creatures, earthly locusts (Isa. 40:22), come up with a plan so unprecedented? Can a creature overpower God? The crucifixion on Calvary of God's Son, Jesus Christ in human flesh (Heb. 1:2), was ordained by God Himself: *"He* [Jesus Christ] *was foreknown* [by the Father] *before the foundation of the world but was made manifest in the last times* [between His two advents] *for the sake of you* [the elect, not for all men without exception] "(1 Pet. 1:20). He came to save His chosen people, whom He foreknew, knew, and loved with an everlasting, redeeming love, just as He did Jeremiah (Jer. 31:3). Through the Cross He spiritually recreated the people He foreknew and loved, regenerating them for His Glory and pleasure, that He might rejoice in them: *"For as a young man marries a young woman, so shall your sons marry you, and as the bridegroom rejoices over the bride,* ***so shall your God rejoice over you****"* (Isa. 62:5).

The crucifixion of the Lord Jesus Christ was not man's plan, but God's alone. His triune office established everything in eternity. None of it was outside of His will and being. Satan, the Pharisees, Pilate, the crowd, Judas, and all the rest were placed by God's negative predestination in position to exercise their "free" will voluntarily, willingly, without any divine compulsion to accomplish their task. The moment God withdrew from Judas, the moment He withheld from him a portion of His common grace, Satan rushed into his God-empty heart. When God passively hardens the heart, He often, if not always, uses the work of Satan, the god (2 Cor. 4:4) and father (John 8:44; 1 John 3:10) of all natural men, to accomplish His purpose: *"Then* ***Satan entered into Judas*** *called Iscariot, who was of the number of the twelve. He went away and conferred with the chief priests and officers how he might betray him to them"* (Luke 22:3-4). The Devil controlled his slave Judas, who naturally obeyed the ruler of this world (Eph. 2:2). God did not free Judas from the Evil One; rather, He stepped back, allowing Judas to be controlled by the Evil One. Thus, Judas' "free" will could only operate under the tutelage of the Devil—that is, God's passive hardening of the heart (Isa. 63:17). Thus, both Satan and Judas as well as all the active participants in the crucifixion, according to God's eternal office and in accordance with their own evil nature and action, without knowing it, contributed to God's work of salvation for His elect. Each one performed that which is hidden within him: *"We know that we are from God, and* ***the whole world lies in the power of the evil one****"* (1 John 5:19).

Judas will take full responsibility for his betrayal, with all the consequences. He was overcome by his own greed, and as such he became a suitable candidate to show us how easy it is to betray. He had no idea what he was capable of, whom he was working under. God did not put his betrayal in his heart. Judas did what he wanted to do—he fled from Christ in accordance with his own "free" decision, to gain thirty pieces of silver. God withdrew from both Satan and Judas, allowing both to demonstrate their freedom from righteousness (Rom. 6:20), to turn their evil motives into His victory: *"Jesus said to him* [Judas], ***'Friend, do what you came to do.'*** *Then they came up and laid hands on Jesus and seized him"* (Matt. 26:50). God held up a mirror for Judas to see how enslaved to sin his heart was (Matt. 27:4). Judas was only one of the countless links that led to the culmination of the perfect work of redemption, the climax of God's history, the crucifixion of the Son of God which gave salvation of God's people.

If Judas' passive hardening and rejection by God had failed, if God had "miscalculated" in granting "freedom" in the heart of Satan, Judas, and thousands of others involved, the unique plan of salvation would have collapsed. Judas' mission and purpose were fully known to God: *"'But there are some of you who do not believe.' (For Jesus knew from the beginning* [in eternity] *who those were who did not believe* [they never believed, though they walked with Jesus], *and who it was who would betray him)"* (John 6:64). Judas' evil deeds, like the deeds of any natural man, unwittingly and unintentionally bring to light God's righteousness (Rom. 3:5). God accomplished His purpose—Judas' betrayal and the crucifixion of His Son in the flesh as a sinful man (Rom. 8:3)—for His Glory: *"The Lord has made everything for its purpose* [for his Glory], *even the wicked* [negative predestination] *for the day of trouble"* (Prov. 16:4).

Judas is the prototype of the natural man who seems to walk with Christ, but whom Christ never knew (Matt. 7:22-23). Any natural man could have been in Judas' place had God backed away from him a little, if He had withheld a little of His common grace, if He had loosened a little the bridle that tames the evil dwelling within him (Ps. 76:10).

You who do not believe in the gospel and are quite satisfied with yourselves, considering yourselves to be quite decent, humanly speaking, good people, you should thank God for His common grace. Despite your lack of merit, common grace keeps you high above the abyss, not because you are quite decent people, but because God wills it so. His triune counsel has decreed this for you from eternity.

We who believe in the gospel, who are children of God, should realize how often we have behaved worse than those who still reject

Christ. We do not belong to God because we were better, because we sought God, because we made a "free" choice to follow Him, but because God chose us and created us for His Glory. Even more should we rejoice, in fear and trembling (Phil. 2:12). On the last day of judgment, God will command: *"I will say to the north, Give up, and to the south, Do not withhold; bring my sons from afar and my daughters from the end of the earth, everyone who is called by my name,* ***whom I created for my glory, whom I formed and made****"* (Isa. 43:6-7).

KINGS OF THE WORLD, ISRAEL, ASSYRIA

As we have seen, for His Glory, for His holy purpose, God uses the evil motives of those who belong temporarily or permanently to the Evil One. No evil, whether it is within Satan, demons or human beings, can thwart God's holy purpose: *"And the ten horns that you saw, they and the beast will hate the prostitute. They will make her desolate and naked, and devour her flesh and burn her up with fire, for* ***God has put it into their hearts*** [withdrawn from them, controllably releasing their willfulness] *to carry out his purpose by being of one mind and handing over their royal power to the beast, until the words of God are fulfilled"* (Rev. 17:16-17).

Good is where God is present, where there is light, where He is actively working toward His holy purposes. Evil is where God is "not present" when He has withdrawn,[43] where there is darkness (Isa. 45:7), where He is passive in action yet still sovereignly controlling the activity of the forces of evil—Satan, demons, and natural man: *"Woe to Assyria, the rod of my anger;* ***the staff in their hands is my fury*** [passively]*! Against a godless nation* [Israel] *I send him, and against the people of my wrath I command him* [negative predestination], *to take spoil and seize plunder, and to tread them* [Israel] *down like the mire of the streets* [according

43 However, God is omnipresent: (Ps. 139:7-10; Jer. 23:23-24)

to her perverse lust]" (Isa. 10:5-6). God took away the measure of common grace from both Israel and Assyria and gave vent to their wickedness. The Assyrians of their own accord rushed upon the Israelites to rob and murder. Although the Assyrians had fulfilled God's holy purpose, no reward was or will be due them. Their motive was robbery and murder. Woe to them! *"Shall the axe* [Satan, demons, natural men, Assyria] *boast over him who hews with it* [passively God], *or the saw* [Satan, demons, natural men, Assyria] *magnify itself against him who wields it* [passively God]*? As if a rod* [Satan, demons, natural men, Assyria] *should wield him who lifts it* [passively God], *or as if a staff* [Satan, demons, natural men, Assyria] *should lift him who is not wood* [passively God]*! Therefore the Lord God of hosts will send wasting sickness among his stout warriors* [Assyria], *and under his glory a burning will be kindled, like the burning of fire"* (Isa. 10:15-16).

God knows what is hidden in every natural man; therefore, He can passively chop, cut, swing, or lift the rod with His hand to bring all things to His predestined, holy purpose, bringing all things under the feet of Christ. Satan, demons, and reprobate men are God's instruments, the vessels He created for reproach (Rom. 9:21). Driven by their evil, self-centered motivation, they actively, willingly, carry out God's purposes.

PUNISHMENT OF WILLFUL PERSONS BY OTHER WILLFUL PERSONS

The prophet Habakkuk laments and cries out to God to help, to intervene, because of lawlessness, violence, wickedness, destruction, strife, contention, dissension, the law being perverted and paralyzed, the law not being upheld, the wicked besieging the righteous, etc. (Hab. 1:1-4).

In response, the Lord says the wicked Chaldeans are the instrument of His wrath against a wicked nation. He says it is a cruel, fierce nation, it seizes everything not its own, it is fearful and terrible, proclaiming its own right with horses as swift as leopards, it is more ravenous than wolves, like an eagle that swoops down on its prey, it pursues violence slaughtering multitudes of people, it mocks kings and dignitaries, it takes its own strength for a god. We note that the "cure" for wickedness seems more terrible than the wickedness itself (Hab. 1:5-11).

Habakkuk affirms that God is active in His purposes and passive in the actual punishment of the wicked. He entrusts this dirty work to other wicked people, and He will eventually punish them because their motives are evil. The self-willed punish the self-willed without knowing that they are fulfilling God's will (Rev. 17:17). God removes the negative lifestyle of some with the negative intentions of others; and so, the result (even mathematically) is always positive: *"Are you not from everlasting, O Lord my God, my Holy One? We shall not die.* ***O Lord, you have ordained them*** [the Chaldeans] *as a judgment, and you,* ***O Rock, have established them*** [the Chaldeans] ***for reproof****"* (Hab. 1:12).

JOB

The following passage shows how God sovereignly deals with Satan. No one else can increase or decrease the scope of his rampage. God pronounced negative predestination, allowing Satan to touch Job's health, but He did not allow Job to be killed. God alone is the Lord of life and death: *"'But stretch out your hand and touch his* [Job's] *bone and his flesh, and he will curse you to your face.' And the Lord said to Satan, '****Behold, he is in your hand; only spare his life****'"* (Job 2:5-6). Satan has only as much "freedom" to tempt, harm, and kill as God allows him. Every natural man is subject to Satan in proportion to how much common grace God gives him and how much Satan is allowed to work in him. Job persevered to the end only because of God's saving grace, which God irrevocably secured on the Cross for His people, His children. Saving grace did not forsake Job; he went through a very painful experience with God's help. He endured the Father's strict discipline, which every child of God goes through to some degree (Phil. 1:29), and through His discipline, God radically changed Job's life. God limited His common grace in essential areas of Job's life. He lost property, family, servants, health, friends, but he did not and could not lose eternal, special, saving grace. In the end, God again bestowed on Job even more abundant, double, blessed, common grace (Job 42:10-17).

DAVID

The following example is compelling because it is an explicit, sovereign negative predestination of God: *"Again the anger of* ***the Lord was kindled against Israel****, and he incited David against them, saying, 'Go, number Israel and Judah'"* (2 Sam. 24:1). This time He chose His favorite, David, as His instrument. Appropriately, He withdrew from David for a time to give his sinful nature "freedom" to act. God did not for one moment lose control as Satan, together with David, was actively carrying out God's negative predestination. This event, in which God would not fail to be glorified, is described from a different point of view in Chronicles: *"Then* ***Satan stood against Israel*** *and incited David to number Israel"* (1 Chron. 21:1).

So, who incited David against Israel? Was it God (2 Sam. 24:1) or Satan (1 Chron. 21:1)? God always has the first place in all things. Motivated by evil, Satan was actively carrying out God's plan, His holy negative predestination, like the case of Job. And what about David? Had David been a humanist, a Pelagian, a Semi-Pelagian, or an Arminian, he surely would have believed that what happened was according to his own "free" will, since he was the one who numbered Israel.

JOSEPH

Perhaps you know the story of Joseph, who was Jacob's favorite son before the birth of Benjamin. Jacob favored Joseph because he was born of his beloved wife Rachel, and this caused Joseph's brothers to be jealous. His brothers sold him into slavery, telling Jacob that Joseph had been torn apart by wild animals. After he was taken to Egypt, Joseph became the servant of Potiphar. He had to flee from Potiphar's wife, who falsely accused him of wanting to sleep with her. In truth it was Potiphar's wife who had lusted after Joseph. His subsequent imprisonment and his interpretation of Pharaoh's dream of seven fruitful and seven unfruitful years led to him becoming the second most powerful man in Egypt. He had granaries built and filled them. When the dry years came, Jacob sent his sons to Egypt to buy grain so that the family would not starve, and his brothers once again met Joseph. After some exciting twists and turns, Joseph finally identified himself to his brothers with these words: *"...I am your brother, Joseph, whom you sold into Egypt. And now do not be distressed or angry with yourselves because you sold me here* [first to kill him, then to let him die in a dry pool; Gen. 37:20], *for* ***God sent me before you to preserve life****. For the famine has been in the land these two years, and there are yet five years in which there will be neither plowing nor harvest. And* ***God sent me before you to preserve for you a remnant on earth, and to keep alive for you many survivors. So it was not you who sent me here, but God****. He has made me a father to Pharaoh, and lord of all his house and ruler over all the land of Egypt"* (Gen. 45:4b-8).

To Joseph, it was clear that God's temporary negative predestination of both himself and his brothers was for God's ultimate Glory. We do not know if Joseph knew of the future Savior, but he did understand that the salvation of God's people, God's Israel, was through the Jews (John 4:22): *"Do not fear, for am I in the place of God? As for you, you meant evil against me, but God meant it for good,* ***to bring it about that many people should be kept alive****, as they are today"* (Gen. 50:19b-20). Joseph knew that God was working in his life. He knew that in doing their dirty work, his brothers had nonetheless been directed by God's sovereignty, without God getting His hands dirty through their sin. God withdrew from Joseph's brothers to passively accomplish His holy purpose through His negative predestination. He kept the nation of Israel alive for the sake of the ultimate coming deliverance of both Jews and Gentiles, through the most prominent Israelite—Jesus Christ.

MAN IS RESPONSIBLE—COMPATIBILISM

INTRODUCTION TO COMPATIBILISM

It is not within man's power to fully understand the principle of God's positive and negative predestination. The one thing we can know for certain about this subject is that all of God's predestinations are always holy; there is not an ounce of evil in them. They all serve the ultimate purpose of glorifying God in the highest (Rev. 4:8-11). No one escapes responsibility. On the last day of judgment, no one will say to God: "This is Your fault; I failed and was forced to do evil because You withdrew from me." On the contrary, on the last day every knee will bow before the judgment seat of Jesus Christ: *"Therefore God has highly exalted him and bestowed on him the name that is above every name, so that at the name of Jesus every knee should bow, in heaven and on earth and under the earth,* ***and every tongue confess that Jesus Christ is Lord, to the glory of God the Father****"* (Phil. 2:9-11).

Let us approach the issue of God's sovereign positive and negative predestinations with the principle of compatibility, i.e., the mutual compatibility or tolerance of two different elements, things, components, principles, doctrines, propositions, etc. Similarly, the theological term compatibilism means that the "free" will of sinful, natural man and God's sovereign predestination, His election, are mutually compatible propositions, i.e., one does not exclude the other. In a radical liberal, earthly, space-time context, these two propositions seem logically incompatible, not compatible. It seems that one excludes the other, and therefore compatibilism is logically unacceptable to Arminians. However, if we consider that the "free" will of sinful, natural man operates in an earthly, space-time context, but God's election operates in an eternal context outside of time and space, then compatibilism no longer has logically inconsistency, i.e., it can make logical sense. Decisions of "free" will then do not then preclude God's predestination, and nor does God's predestination preclude man's responsibility for sinful decisions made according to his own "free" will. Each person is responsible for his or her actions without excuse.

The theological term compatibilism defines "free" will as the freedom to act within a predetermined context without being constrained in any way by other persons or institutions. In light of Scripture, human choices are made voluntarily, but the circumstances under which man makes "free" choices are determined by God (Acts 2:23) and/or: *"...for truly in this city there were gathered together against your holy servant Jesus, whom you anointed, both Herod and Pontius Pilate, along with the Gentiles and the peoples of Israel,* ***to do whatever your hand*** [God] ***and your plan had predestined to take place****"* (Acts 4:27-28).

D. A. CARSON WROTE

> *I shall begin by articulating two truths, both of which are demonstrably taught or exemplified again and again in the Bible:*
>
> ***1.*** *God is absolutely sovereign, but his sovereignty never functions in Scripture to reduce human responsibility.*
>
> ***2.*** *Human beings are responsible creatures—that is, they choose,*

they believe, they disobey, they respond, and there is moral significance in their choices; but human responsibility never functions in Scripture to diminish God's sovereignty or to make God absolutely contingent.

My argument is that both propositions are taught and exemplified in the Bible. Part of our problem is believing that both are true. We tend to use one to diminish the other; we tend to emphasize one at the expense of the other. But responsible reading of the Scripture prohibits such reductionism.

*We might begin by glancing at the large picture. Proverbs 16 pictures God as so utterly sovereign that when you or I throw a die, which side comes up is determined by God (*16:33*). "The LORD works out everything for his own ends—even the wicked for a day of disaster" (16:4). "In his heart a man plans his course, but the LORD determines his steps" (16:9). "Why do the nations say, 'Where is their God?' Our God is in heaven; he does whatever pleases him" (Ps. 115:2-3).*

According to Jesus, if the birds are fed it is because the Father feeds them (Matt. 6:26*); if wild flowers grow, it is because God clothes the grass (6:30). Thus God stands behind the so-called natural processes. That is why biblical writers prefer to speak of the Lord sending the rain, rather than to say, simply, "It's raining"—and this despite the fact that they were perfectly aware of the water cycle. The prophets understood the sweep of God's sway: "I know, O LORD, that a man's life is not his own; it is not for man to direct his steps" (Jer. 10:23). "The LORD does whatever pleases him, in the heavens and on the earth, in the seas and all their depths" (Ps. 135:6). The passage (Eph. 1:3-14) is as strong as any: God "works out everything in conformity with the purpose of his will" (Eph. 1:11). In some mysterious way, and without being tainted with evil himself, God stands behind unintentional manslaughter (Ex. 21:13),* *family misfortune (Ruth 1:13), national disaster (Isa. 45:6-7), personal grief (Lam. 3:32-33, 37-38), even sin (2 Sam. 24:1; 1 Kings 22:21ff.). In none of these cases, however, is human responsibility ever diminished. Thus although it is God in his wrath who incites David to take the prohibited census (2 Sam. 24:1), David is nevertheless held accountable for his actions.*

The second of my two statements is no less strongly supported in Scripture. There are countless passages where human beings are commanded to obey, choose, believe, and are held accountable if they fail to do so. God himself offers moving pleas to incite us to repentance, because he finds no pleasure in the death of the wicked (Isa. 30:18*;* 65*:*2*; Lam.* 3*:*31-36*; Ezek.* 18*:*30-32*;* 33*:*11*). In his day, Joshua can challenge Israel in these words: "Now fear the LORD and serve him with all faithfulness ... But if serving the LORD seems undesirable to you, then choose for yourselves this day whom you will serve. ... But as for me and my household, we will serve the LORD" (Josh. 24:14-15). The commanding invitation of the gospel itself assumes profound responsibility: "That if you confess with your mouth, 'Jesus is Lord,' and believe in your heart that God raised him from the dead, you will be saved. ... As the Scripture says, 'Anyone who trusts in him will never be put to shame'" (Rom. 10:9, 11). Of course, none of this jeopardizes God's sovereignty: only a few verses earlier we find the apostle quoting Scripture (Ex. 33:19) to prove that "God has mercy on whom he wants to have mercy, and he hardens whom he wants to harden" (Rom. 9:18).*

Hundreds of passages could be explored to demonstrate that the Bible assumes both that God is sovereign, and that people are responsible for their actions. As hard as it is for many people in the Western world to come to terms with both truths at the same time, it takes a great deal of interpretative ingenuity to argue that the Bible does not support them.

In fact, not only does the Bible support both these truths in a large number of disparate passages, both truths come together in many passages. We have space to mention only seven [Gen. 50:19-20; 2 Sam. 24; Isa. 10:5-19; John 6:37-40; Phil. 2:12-13; Acts 18:9-10; Acts 4:23-30][44].

LET US THINK BIBLICALLY, NOT EARTHLY

It is wise to keep the principle of compatibilism in mind. We should not think in purely earthly terms about God's election, that it absolves man of responsibility for voluntarily choosing to remain in evil, or that man's "free" will in any way limits God's sovereignty to have mercy and compassion on whom He wills. We are wise to think biblically that while God is supreme in all things, even in the election of His people, man remains responsible for his defiance of God. On the day of God's judgment, no one will be judged on the basis of whether or not God chose him, but on the basis of his actions which he did voluntarily, apart from external pressure: *"But because of your hard and impenitent heart you are storing up wrath for yourself on the day of wrath when God's righteous judgment will be revealed. He will render to each one according to his works: to those who by patience in well-doing* [which they have from God] *seek for glory and honor* [of God] *and immortality, he will give eternal life; but for those who are self-seeking and do not obey the truth* [deny the Cross of Christ], *but obey unrighteousness, there will be wrath and fury. There will be tribulation and distress for every human being who does evil, the Jew first and also the Greek, but glory and honor and peace for everyone who does good, the Jew first and also the Greek"* (Rom. 2:5-10).

44 A Sovereign and Personal God—http://www.monergism.com/thethreshold/articles/onsite/prayerchangesthings.html

10

GOD'S VERSUS HUMAN WILL

GOD'S WILL

What Arminians, Semi-Pelagians, and Pelagians do not and cannot agree on is sovereign, unconditional election by the will of God. Most of them believe that it is God's will that all men, without exception, be saved. It would logically follow that every natural man is endowed from the cradle with a "free" will, and thus it is his business and responsibility to decide how to respond to God's invitation. One of the most famous verses used by the Arminian brethren to prove this, while at the same time seeking to deny the Reformed doctrine of salvation, is this: *"The Lord is not slow to fulfill his promise as some count slowness, but is patient toward you, not wishing* [God's will is not] *that any should perish, but* [God's will is] *that all should reach repentance"* (2 Pet. 3:9). When we speak of God's will, we must first clarify what we mean. When two people use the same words, they often do not mean the same thing.

DEGREES OF WILL

We will first consider the degrees of God's will, as understood by the Reformation, to help us understand the nature of the controversy between the Remonstrants and the Reformation[45]. According to R. C. Sproul[46], contemporary Reformed theology recognizes three degrees of God's will: Decretive, Preceptive, and Dispositional. Again, the chart tells us more than many words:

1	God's Decretive Will	God's sovereign, efficacious will; e.g.: "I am God, and there is none like me, declaring the end from the beginning and from ancient times things not yet done, saying, '**My counsel shall stand, and I will accomplish all my purpose**'" (Isa. 46:9b-10).	Men cannot resist the Decretive will
2	God's Preceptive Will	God's commanding will; e.g.: "**For this is the will of God, your sanctification**: that you abstain from sexual immorality; that each one of you know how to control his own body in holiness and honor, not in the passion of lust like the Gentiles who do not know God" (1 Thess. 4:3-5).	Men can resist the Preceptive will
3	God's Dispositional Will	What pleases or displeases God, What is His disposition; e.g.: "And God saw everything that he had made, and behold, **it was very good**. And there was evening and there was morning, the sixth day" (Gen. 1:31).	Men can resist the Dispositional will

In our personal lives, we can identify degrees of human will that are very similar. For example, every parent can well identify these three concepts of human will:

1. Parents, with good reason, decide *by decretive will* and tell their child, "You are not going out with your friends today!" And the child stays at home, no matter what.
2. Parents teach, educate, and command their offspring the rule *by preceptive will*: "Close the door behind you." The child need not, but may, resist. The door is either closed or left wide open.
3. What the parents wish, would like to see, out of their inner desire and nature, expresses their *dispositional will*. For example,

45 See chapter 2; section: The Five Articles of Remonstrance and Calvinism.

46 R. C. Sproul: Grace Unknown, p. 169.

they may want their offspring should study medicine. The child may resist, may decide not to honor their parent's desire. He may choose to become a profitable businessman in the garbage business, or a rock star, or something else.

A THREEFOLD INTERPRETATION OF 2 PETER 3:9

> *"The Lord is not slow to fulfill his promise as some count slowness, but is patient toward you, not wishing* [God's will is not] *that any should perish, but* [God's will is] *that all should reach repentance"* (2 Pet. 3:9).

If God does not want anyone to perish, but wants all to come to repentance, we can interpret His desire in three ways, depending on which of the above degrees of will we use. When there are several interpretations, all cannot be true at the same time. Either only one interpretation can be correct, or none at all.

1. **God does not desire in a decretive sense that cannot be resisted:** *"...that any should perish, but that all should reach repentance."* This would mean that all mankind would be redeemed by God's decree; no one would be condemned. Neither the Calvinist, nor the Arminian, nor the Semi-Pelagian, nor the Pelagian can accept such an interpretation of God's will. The universalist who will gladly accept it believes that all without exception will ultimately be saved.
2. **God does not desire in a preceptive, educating, commanding sense that can be resisted:** *"...that any should perish, but that all should reach repentance."* In the same was that God educates with commandments like do not kill, do not steal, do not commit adultery, do love, etc., He can also give the preceptive command, "Do not perish, but do come to repentance." This interpretation might be acceptable in an extreme case, yet it is highly improbable because it leads us to

a strange conclusion—namely, that God commands natural people not to perish, as if not perishing could be commanded.

3. **God does not desire in a dispositional sense that can be resisted:** *"...that any should perish, but that all should reach repentance."* To perish is not in God's nature, so it displeases Him. On the contrary, coming to repentance is in His nature. One of the many texts that reveal God's dispositional will, His character toward man, is this: *"Have I any pleasure in the death of the wicked, declares the Lord God, and not rather that he should turn from his way and live?"* (Ezek. 18:23). No righteous judge of character rejoices in condemning a criminal, even to death (in some countries). God is the hand of the law, and He therefore must pronounce a just sentence. Likewise, God's holy satisfaction of justice, that is, the satisfaction of His dispositional will, comes not from the condemnation of hardened sinners, but from the fact that nothing unclean can enter His kingdom.

God's dispositional will, the desire of His holy nature, is further summarized in the following verse: *"Yet it was the will of the Lord* [it pleased Him] *to crush him* [His Son]*; he has put him to grief; when his soul makes an offering for guilt, he shall see his offspring* [His redeemed people]*; he shall prolong his days; the will of the Lord shall prosper in his* [Christ's] *hand"* (Isa. 53:10). God did not find satisfaction and joy in pouring out His wrath on His Son for the sins of His chosen people; the Father experienced deep pain at the death of His Beloved Son. His dispositional will contained no hint of pleasure or delight in the crucifixion, suffering, and death of His Son. God's joy and delight flowed from the Son's obedience in taking upon Himself—though He did not have to—the Lord's agony and suffering on the one hand, and the salvation of His elect, His Church, on the other. God's dispositional will was pleased with the consequences of Christ's suffering, not with the suffering itself.

The dispositional interpretation of 2 Peter 3:9 would seem to harmonize with many other Scriptures and is therefore far more acceptable than the previous two interpretations, and all Arminians, Semi-Pelagians, and Pelagians will surely agree with it. However, if this Arminian interpretation were true, then God could not take full pleasure in the result of His Son's atoning death, because all who reject the Cross of Christ by their "free" will would be spoiling His pleasure. This would be especially true after God had granted prevenient grace, and thus the 100% efficacy of Christ's sacrifice would be nullified.

REFORMED INTERPRETATION OF 2 PETER 3:9

There is, however, a fourth, Reformed view. John Owen, an English Puritan theologian (1616-1683), offered a solution using a principle we explored earlier in this book. The verse contains a commonly used defining pronoun—*you*. Peter, who is in Christ, is thus writing a letter to his fellow brothers, who are also in Christ. Peter and those he addresses are a special category of people who have been baptized into Christ, Christians who are members of Christ, the true Church. When Peter uses the pronoun *you*, he is referring to others like himself. We can refer to these in a broader sense as the whole number of God's people. The interpretation of 2 Peter 3:9 is then easy to read: *"The Lord is not slow to fulfill his promise as some count slowness, but is patient toward you* [to us-ward (KJV); with us (WEB); to us (YLT) to us God's chosen people], *not wishing that any* [of us, God's chosen people] *should perish, but that all* [of us, God's chosen people] *should reach repentance"* (2 Pet. 3:9).

God's eternal will, then, is that none of the full number of His separated, chosen people, whom He loves with an everlasting love, should perish, but that all should surely come to repentance, and God grants all this group of people "salvation and faith." This interpretation of the text of 2 Peter 3:9 is consistent with the context of Scripture as a whole (Matt. 18:12-14). Therefore, this is what Reformed theology understands and accepts in terms of God's decretive will. This decree of God's salvation applies only to a particular, limited category, namely, His people, His Church. God's decree of salvation does not apply generically, universally, to every human being without exception. The Triune God has declared His office; by His unchangeable will He has predetermined that He will create a certain, complete number of people to be His people in Christ, His Church. Those whom God has created, either physically or spiritually, cannot resist the One who created them. The clay cannot resist the potter (Rom. 9:20-21).

THE FREE WILL OF MAN

FREE WILL ACCORDING TO SCRIPTURE

Having written much about "free" will, I will now take it a step further. Free will is the ability of a conscious being, under given circumstances and in a given context, to make decisions that are not forced upon us by a third party. In this sense, in natural spacetime all humans have free will. But according to Scripture, the spiritual environment, the spiritual context, in which all natural people exist is Adam (1 Cor. 15:22a); in him, all are spiritually dead from birth. By contrast, the spiritual environment, the spiritual context, of born-again people of God is the living Christ (1 Cor. 15:22b). Therefore, the wills of the natural man and the born-again man function in completely different environments, contexts, and circumstances. It is inevitable that the natural will in Adam—in the Evil One—will make choices opposite to the will of those born-again in Christ. If the choice between God and the Devil, good and evil, were made by "free" will in a general, humanistic sense, then:

1. God would not be free, since He does not want to and cannot, by His holy nature, choose sin.

2. A born-again person would not be free, since he would neither want nor be able to choose sin (evil) as his permanent lifestyle from his new nature of being born-again, i.e., being sustained and sealed in Christ by the Holy Spirit. The Devil is no longer his father or god—God is!
3. Natural man would not be free because he would not and could not choose God (good) out of his natural, Adamic nature, i.e., belonging to the household of Satan. The Devil is his god (2 Cor. 4:4) and father (John 8:44; 1 John 3:10). Therefore, God is not and cannot be on his ballot.

THE "FREE" WILL OF THE NATURAL MAN

The natural man is spiritually dead, trapped in the Devil's territory, surrounded by an impenetrable wall. He has no liberty, nor does he or can he have fellowship with the Spirit of God. Therefore, his "free" will in spiritual decision making is limited only by the space in which he is held by his captor: ***"God may perhaps grant them*** [natural, unlearned men] *repentance leading to a knowledge of the truth, and they may come to their senses and escape from the snare of the devil, after being captured by him to do his will"* (2 Tim. 2:25b-26).

The natural man is free from righteousness (Rom. 6:20). In all things, he makes choices within the bounds of sin, for his greatest sin is to remain outside of Christ (John 16:9). His self-humane and self-serving actions do not glorify God (1 Cor. 10:31); therefore, from the standpoint of Scripture, they are man-centered and glorify fallen man.

THE FREE WILL OF THE BORN-AGAIN MAN

The born-again, redeemed person lives in a holy territory, spiritually defined by God. He has freedom—he has contact with God because he is no longer of this world (John 15:19), no longer a slave to evil (Eph. 2:2). In Christ he has freedom in righteousness. His decisions are good because they glorify God: *"For sin will have no dominion over you, since you are not under law but under grace. What then? Are we to sin because we are not under law but under grace? By no means! Do you not know that if you present yourselves to anyone as obedient slaves, you are slaves of the one* ***whom you obey, either of sin, which leads to death, or of obedience, which leads to righteousness****? But thanks be to God, that you who were once slaves of sin have become obedient from the heart* [newly created heart; Ezek. 11:19; Ezek. 36:26] *to the standard of teaching to which you were committed, and, having been set free from sin, have become slaves of righteousness. I am speaking in human terms, because of your natural limitations. For just as you once presented your members as slaves to impurity and to lawlessness leading to more lawlessness, so now present your members as slaves to righteousness leading to sanctification.* ***For when you were slaves of sin, you were free in regard to righteousness****"* (Rom. 6:14-20).

There is no freedom outside of Christ. Freedom is only in Christ. God's people gained it unconditionally when the Lord Jesus Christ wrested it from the dragon through His redeeming death on the Cross. It is God, not man, who defines true freedom: *"So if the Son sets you free* [from Satan, the dragon, the Devil, the strong man; Mark 3:27; Isa. 49:24-25], ***you will be free indeed*** [you will love Me freely and irresistibly]*"* (John 8:36).

Freedom in Christ is defined by the actions to which God has chosen, predestined, created, and drawn us for His own sake, for Himself and for His Glory (John 6:44). His people are His glory. God's people find freedom in loving God and spreading the Word of their Creator and Savior; that is what they were created to do: *"Behold, I am doing* [creating] *a new thing; now it springs forth, do you not perceive it? I will make a way* [Christ] *in the wilderness and rivers* [my chosen ones] *in the desert* [spiritually dead world] ... ***the people whom I formed for myself*** [my royal priesthood] *that they might declare my praise* [that I have redeemed them by my death]"(Isa. 43:19,21).

Even the natural man feels freest when he does what he likes, when he can exercise the talents with which God has endowed him by common grace. The hockey player is freest on the ice, the scientist in research, the musician in playing, the writer in writing, the builder in building. Forbid them what they enjoy doing, and you will plunge them into despair.

ARE WE GOD'S PUPPETS?

Many Christians object: "If God's election and calling (new creation) is 100% efficacious and irresistible, then the elect are mere puppets without free will." Do you feel like a puppet because you were physically born, because you exist, because you were physically created by God, because God chose your father, mother, skin color, gender, nationality, place of birth, intelligence, talents, abilities, appearance, health, social status, etc.? All these were given to us from above, by God's holy will, under God's common grace. Was the Virgin Mary, the pure girl, a puppet because God created her to bear Jesus in her womb? Was the apostle Paul a puppet because God created in him a new inner man, an efficacious vessel for spreading the gospel to the Gentiles, while he was still possessed by an active hatred for the followers of Christ? Were Abel, Noah, Abram, Isaac, Jacob, Moses, and the apostles puppets? Were any of them seeking God, or did God seek them? As God proved to them, so He continually proves to us that His holy will is infinitely superior to our fallen wills. For the will of the creature, whether fallen or born-again, cannot transcend the infinite, transcendent will of the Creator. The following text refutes any notion that God, in His sovereignty, makes puppets of men: *"And do not presume*

[Pharisees] *to say to yourselves, 'We have Abraham as our father* [biological, carnal],*' for I tell you,* ***God is able from these stones to raise up children for Abraham*** [spiritual, promised, chosen offspring]*"*(Matt. 3:9).

In the Psalms the redemption of God's chosen saints is identified with God's new creation, which already believes, sees its God, and therefore praises Him for His Glory: *"Let this be recorded for a generation to come, so that a people yet to be created* [God's holy, chosen people, the Church in Christ] ***may praise the Lord****: that he looked down from his holy height; from heaven the Lord looked at the earth, to hear the groans of the prisoners* [those on whom he has had compassion and mercy; Ex. 33:19], *to set free those who were doomed to die* [his chosen vassals of Satan]*"*(Ps. 102:18-20).

The controversy is not whether or not we are controlled puppets. The controversy is whether we have God's freedom, contact with God Himself, and association with Christ, or Satan's "freedom" that is contact and association with the Devil—whether our limited place of operation is the City of God (Rev. 21:10*),* or the den of the Evil One; whether we are already in Christ or still in the Evil One. Only freedom in Christ guarantees a truly free will: *"So if the Son sets you free* [delivers you from Satan's grip], ***you will be free indeed*** [your enslaved will be set free]*"*(John 8:36). The One delivering is always the One choosing to deliver; the choice does not belong to the one being delivered. But is the one saved a puppet of the Savior simply because he had no active part in his own salvation? The redeemed one is re-created to glorify God, to tell of God's most glorious act, the redemption of the Devil's captives by Jesus Christ on the Cross (Isa. 43:21); the more the redeemed one communicates the Cross of Christ to a spiritually dead world, the freer he is.

True freedom is found only in Christ: *"For freedom Christ has set us free; stand firm therefore, and do not submit again to a yoke of slavery* [the Devil]*"* (Gal. 5:1). The natural man is a slave to sin, a Devil's hand puppet. But what could be more wonderful than to be held forever in the loving hand of the Almighty, to be His possession? No little child feels that he is a limited puppet because he belongs to his parents. He finds security in the arms of his parents. When his parents are out of his sight, he begins to cry. A small, helpless child does not want to be free from his parents, because he knows very well that without their care he would perish. Parents mean security to a little child, and similarly, God's little ones (Matt. 11:25) find life, security, and freedom only with their heavenly Father. If they "lose sight" of Him, they too begin to cry out in prayer. He not only delivered them from the bondage of Satan, but more than that, He has adopted them: *"Or do you not know that your body is a temple of the Holy Spirit within you, whom you have from God?* ***You are not your own****, for you were bought with a price. So glorify God in your body"* (1 Cor. 6:19-20). Such a statement has far-reaching implications. To become God's possession is to be His adopted son or daughter, to belong to the household of God.

Many Christians feel they do not want to be God's "robots," "puppets," or "slaves." This concern would be justifiable if God were not holy. In this context, let us not be concerned by the word slave—a slave is one who is the legal possession of another person. To be owned by the good and holy God Himself is the greatest privilege anyone can have! The born-again Christian should have no greater desire than to be a vessel for God's use, to be His devoted *doulos*, or slave. Most English and foreign language translations of the Bible translate the word *doulos* with the poor substitute "servant" out of historical, political correctness. The difference is profound—the slave is owned by the master, while the servant is the master's free employee.

I want to be owned by the Lord, to be bound to Him as His slave. I do not want to be a mere servant, to have "freedom" from the Lord and from His righteousness—which I previously had (Rom. 6:20). I want my freedom to be defined by the God who has no limits! I no longer want the natural "freedom" that kept me in bondage as Satan's puppet for almost 40 years. I am glad that God raised me from the dead and baptized me in Christ, giving me freedom in Christ and the desire for God's will in me. I want Him to transform me into His likeness, to make me His workmanship. I want to be the glove on Christ's hand, perfectly imitating the movement of His fingers. That is what I long for! Together we are one body, of which Christ is the head (Eph. 5:23b). Are the bodily organs puppets or robots of the head because the brain controls them? Do bodily organs long to be "free" of the body and no longer subject to the controlling impulses of the brain? Any amputated body part necessarily dies. I long exceedingly for the living nerve cords, those "threads and wires" that run from Christ's head down into His body to control me, so that if I were Christ's hand, I would respond as obediently as my fleshly hand obeys the commands of my brain!

WHAT TO REMEMBER WHEN EVANGELIZING

In chapter 3 we looked at requirements of Scripture that the natural man cannot meet[47]. Recall the opening verse: *"And they said, 'Believe in the Lord* ***Jesus, and you will be saved****, you and your household'"* (Acts 16:31). Here Paul and Silas were commanding the jailer: "Believe in the Lord Jesus, and you will be saved." We already know that the natural, spiritually dead man is unable to believe in Christ on his own unless and until God draws him to Himself (John 6:44) and imparts to him the whole of salvation[48], includ-

47 See chapter 3; section: The Inability of the Natural Man.

48 See chapter 3; section: "Salvation and Faith" According to the Reformation.

ing faith. Faith does not condition but confirms the rebirth and justification of the sanctified man of God, who through his active faith is moving toward the consummation, that is, the redemption and glorification of his body.

When Paul and Silas responded to the jailer: "Believe," they were basically saying: "You must be saved by God's grace to believe, and your faith will prove (not cause) that God has indeed drawn you to Himself." God's election, the cause of salvation, is invisible; only the fruit of salvation is visible (Matt. 7:16). In evangelism, it is therefore important to appeal to a visible result—believe, and bear fruit, as in the case of the jailer. We cannot appeal to God's hidden will to determine whether the person in question is written in His Book of Life from before the foundation of the world. In evangelism, we must invite everyone to the wedding feast of the Lamb, as if they were written in the Book of Life. We sow, and God gives or does not give the increase (1 Cor. 3:6-7). There are many verses in Scriptures that describe the activity of a person who has already been drawn by the Father; for example: *"Behold, I stand at the door and knock.* ***If anyone hears my voice and opens the door****, I will come in to him and eat with him, and he with me"* (Rev. 3:20).

When verses like Acts 16:31 and Rev. 3:20 are taken out of context in evangelism, they become half-truths. The natural man cannot hear the voice of God with his deaf ears (Rom. 11:8). These and similar verses are not isolated in the Bible; they must be consistent with other verses. Scripture is meant to be a harmonious chord. Only if these verses were isolated could Arminian conditional election hold true.

But the Reformed, Calvinistic interpretation teaches that man is irresistibly drawn to God only through the new birth, which is the sole, unilateral work of God (monergism). The above text, Rev. 3:20, is a prime example in Scripture, in this case in the voice of Christ, demanding a response from us that we cannot give without

His saving grace. So, who are the ones who hear His voice and open their hearts to Christ? Certainly not everyone. It is only His chosen people who can hear the voice of Christ: *"**My sheep hear my voice*** [and open to Me], *and I know them* [I have loved them from of old], *and they follow me. I give them eternal life, and they will never perish, and no one will snatch them out of my hand"* (John 10:27-28). Those who hear and open the door to the Lord Jesus are those and only those whom the Father has drawn by grace, those who belong to the flock of God (Luke 12:32). God's unconditional election stands. The spiritually dead, whom the Father has not drawn but has left to their own sin, do not open the door, they hear no voice because they are spiritually deaf. They do not know Christ because they have not been born-again through His Spirit: *"...but you do not believe because you are not among my sheep* [God gave them ears that would not hear; Rom. 11:8] *"* (John 10:26).

God does not choose anyone because of their interest in Him. The natural man is incapable of dealing with the question of who God really is, much less the question of efficacious salvation. There is no one who seeks God—there is truly no one (Rom. 3:11); therefore, God must draw to Himself those who have lacked interest in Him (there are no others): *"Then Isaiah is so bold as to say, 'I have been found by those who did not seek me; **I have shown myself to those who did not ask for me**'"* (Rom. 10:20). No natural man is capable of doing a "godly" deed to please God in order to be saved. Faith is not prompted by a natural human "spiritual" need to be saved, much less by a human need to know God: *"But God chose what is foolish in the world to shame the wise; God chose what is weak in the world to shame the strong; God chose what is low and despised in the world, even things that are not, to bring to nothing things that are, **so that no human being might boast in the presence of God**. And because of him* [not of your 'virtuous' will] *you are in Christ Jesus, who became to us wisdom from God, righteousness and* *sanctification and redemption, so that, as it is written, 'Let the one who boasts, boast in the Lord'"* (1 Cor. 1:27-31).

God has created all macro and micro events in the visible and invisible world, in heaven and on earth. Absolutely nothing except God Himself is self-sufficient; everything depends upon Him. All of history and the times in which we live are governed, controlled and sustained by God (Dan. 2:21). If there were anything in the visible or invisible world that was beyond His control, everything would collapse. Without God's sovereign choice, without His ultimate rule, even the smallest event would be utterly devastating.

11

DIVINE JUSTICE

IS GOD UNJUST?

ONE WILL BELIEVE AND THE OTHER WILL NOT

I have often thought: If I had been born in a different time and place, perhaps in the Amazon rainforest 700 years ago, I certainly would not have known Christ, I would never have heard the gospel. However, ifs will never happen. If I had been born an Amazon Indian, I would not be me. But by God's common grace, I was born a Czech, in the German Third Reich-dominated Protectorate of Bohemia and Moravia, in a different historical context. By God's common grace, I survived the war; Jewish children did not! By God's common grace, God has kept me alive to this day. By God's common grace, He brought me to the United States. It was by God's common grace that I heard—rather read—the gospel for the first time. The first chapter of Genesis was pure foolishness to me. I laughed at what I heard—a product of geological engineering and the evolutionary millions and billions of years of the world and the universe. Eight years passed, and unexpectedly God granted me "Salvation and Faith," no longer by God's common grace, but now through saving grace (1 Tim. 4:10). It was not a lottery win or random luck. All of this, common and saving grace from the cradle to the grave, is one continuous cord of God's election. It was divine providence so that God would be glorified in each of His elect, even in one who was formerly a wretched, wicked, and cunning man like me.

Also, by God's common grace, a classmate of mine from the same Prague grade school—we went to Catholic Sunday school together and were confirmed together—found himself in America, in Los Angeles where we met by "chance". We had lived in the same cities, and we shared the same geographical, historical and cultural background. He did not scoff at the gospel as much as I did, but he seemed indifferent to it and remains indifferent to this day.

Am I better than this friend? Absolutely not! What I am sharing through this personal experience is this: All whose names God has written in His Book of Life—from all eternity—God will then, according to His common grace, place into a historical and geographical context that enables them to hear the gospel and believe it, through the regeneration of the Spirit and through saving grace.

GOD HAS REVEALED THE GOSPEL TO MANY REPROBATES

Arminians, Semi-Pelagians, Pelagians, and atheists will object: "What about the 'poor people' who have heard the gospel but were not chosen by God, those whose names were not written in the Book of Life from the foundation of the world?" Coming from unbelievers who know neither God nor the Scriptures, this seems to be a logically coherent question, since their thinking proceeds from the humanistic belief that man is inherently good. All natural men, in addition to a large number of Pelagian "Christians", believe (in accordance with Islam) that men are born spiritually neutral; the lives that they live will reveal whether they are choosing good or evil. In this, they deny the biblical teaching of God's election and of man's spiritual inability and utter depravity[49]. The answer from Scriptures is clear: Man is not born clean, but filled with soot: *"Who can bring a clean thing out of an unclean? **There is not one**"* (Job 14:4). All men, without exception, even the elect, are active enemies of the true God from birth: *"And you* [the elect], *who once were alienated and hostile in mind, doing evil deeds, he* [Christ] *has now reconciled in his body of flesh by his death, in order to present you holy and blameless and above reproach before him* [justified]*"* (Col. 1:21-22).

So, if "erring wretches" who were not chosen come to a Godless end, is this not unfair? It would be unfair only if God turned His back on them while they were crying out to Him, longing for Him—if their hearts were seeking who God is instead of seeking what He can do for them and how He might alleviate their eternal suffering. In this case, they would indeed be unhappy, rejected wretches. But only those who are chosen by God want to know Him. For there is not one natural man who seeks God, not even one (Rom. 3:11-12). They all actively reject and stand against the true God (Col. 1:21-22). They are responsible for this[50].

I have classmates from high school, middle school, and college with whom I have shared the gospel, and thus far—how much longer(?)—God has kept their souls in their ignorance. We share a common geographical, historical, and cultural context; they, as I, have heard the gospel; we have received essentially the same common grace of God, which could not save them and did not save me. So many people hear the gospel by common grace, yet remain indifferent and do not believe (2 Cor. 2:15-16a). On the contrary, hearing and not believing will be to their loss and condemnation: ***"For it would have been better for them never to have known the way of righteousness** than after knowing it to turn back from the holy commandment* [all that Christ and His disciples taught]

49 See PART I.

50 See chapter 9; section: Man is Responsible—compatibilism.

delivered to them" (2 Pet. 2:21). If they had true concern about being saved from God's wrath, they would not argue that God is "unrighteous" in election, but would seek God and trust Him, thereby giving evidence that they are among the elect. It is not that God rejects people because they are not elect, but because they actively sin against God. Original sin, upon which all other sin is based, is natural man's refusal to believe in Christ out of pride, self-centeredness, self-love, self-will, and self-sufficiency (John 16:9). Original sin is in natural man's complete identification with Adam, who desired God-equality as we do today (Gen. 3:5), which led to a catastrophe of cosmic proportions.

GOD HAS NOT REVEALED THE GOSPEL TO MANY REPROBATES

Another objection to God's sovereign, unconditional election is "concern" for those who have never heard the gospel—what about those who have never had or will never have an opportunity to hear the gospel and to know Christ? *"For when Gentiles, who do not have the law* [today the law of Christ, Isa. 2:3; 1 Cor. 9:21], *by nature do what the law requires, they are a law to themselves, even though they do not have the law. They show that* ***the work of the law is written on their hearts****, while their conscience* [God's common grace] *also bears witness, and their conflicting thoughts accuse or even excuse them"* (Rom. 2:14-15). Two verses above we read: *"For all who have sinned without the law* [of Moses, and therefore of Christ] ***will also perish without the law****, and all who have sinned under the law will be judged by the law"* (Rom. 2:12). A chapter later, in the same letter to the Church in Rome, Paul makes it clear that there is no one who has not sinned: "*...**for all have sinned*** [even those who have not heard the gospel] *and fall short of the glory of God"* (Rom. 3:23). Anyone who has not heard the law of Moses or the law of Christ and has sinned, as he certainly has, will spend eternity far from the Glory of God. This is not because he did not hear, nor because he was not chosen, but because he deliberately sinned[51].

If we held to a conditional "election," i.e., that God knows in advance who will "freely" choose Him and therefore "elects" them, then we would be unable to answer the question: "What about those who have never heard?" For those who have never heard could not fulfill the "condition" of salvation, namely, belief in the gospel, which is necessary in Arminianism. However, some Pelagians, Semi-Pelagians, and even Arminians toy with the heretical idea that some Gentiles who, as sincere "believers" calling upon an unknown god, can be saved without having an intimate relationship with Christ. They believe this in spite of the text: *"This Jesus is the stone that was rejected by you, the builders, which has become the cornerstone.* ***And there is salvation in no one else****, for there is no other name under heaven given among men by which we must be saved"* (Acts 4:11-12).

The problem is that, as we have seen, there is no one who seeks God, not even one (Rom. 3:11). Natural men—pagans—seek and find only gods and idols of their own imaginations, golden calves and genies in bottles they hope might help them in their troubles. Those who have not heard the gospel have never been written in God's Book of Life, even though God's common grace has more or less included them. They will be judged justly according to their conscience (Rom. 2:12-16).

What is exceedingly disturbing, however, is the warning that these pagans—precisely because they have never heard the Law or the Gospel—are better off than those who have heard the Gospel but prefer destructive doctrines and despise the way of Truth (2 Peter 2:21). The destruction of Sodom and Gomorrah can be seen as a symbol of God's ultimate wrath against people hardened by sin, especially perverted sexuality, i.e., sodomy, zoophilia, homosexuality and lesbianism. The term "sodomy" is derived from city

51 See chapter 9; section: Man is Responsible—compatibilism.

of Sodom. And the inhabitants of Sodom and Gomorrah did not know the way of salvation. In contrast, Israel's Capernaum did know and rejected it—who was better off? *"And you, Capernaum* [who knew not only the Law of Moses], *will you be exalted to heaven? You will be brought down to Hades. For if the mighty works done in you* [through Jesus Christ] *had been done in Sodom, it would have remained until this day.* ***But I tell you that it will be more tolerable on the day of judgment for the land of Sodom*** [which did not know the law of Moses nor see the miracles of Jesus Christ] ***than for you*** [though you knew the law and saw the mighty works of God]"(Matt. 11:23-24). Yet today when we witness a vice, we do not identify it with Capernaum, but with Sodom and Gomorrah!

JUSTICE

In the biblical sense, we identify the concept of righteousness with sinlessness. Justification means that God has erased the record of His people's guilt—justification suggests a long list of sins that Jesus Christ paid for when they were nailed to His Cross (Col. 2:14). From that moment the sinner was justified, and now God sees him as clean, as white snow (Isa. 1:18). Here is the proof: "*...yet we know that a person is not justified by works of the law but through faith in Jesus Christ, so we also have believed in Christ Jesus,* ***in order to be justified by faith in Christ and not by works*** *of the law, because by works of the law no one will be justified*" (Gal. 2:16).

JUSTICE ACCORDING TO ARMINIANISM

Now we will deal with the Arminian question of whether it is just for God to save only His own—even though it should be clear to all of us that whatever God does is just because of His holy nature.

The Arminian looks at God's justice through a humanistic lens. He cannot understand how a Calvinist can believe in a God who has the power to save all men but does not save all men—for God is a God of boundless love! So, he accuses the Calvinist of believing in an unloving God. After all, only a cruel and heartless God would abandon someone whom He has the power to save. The Arminian rejects God's sovereign, monergistic election, and he places the responsibility for salvation on the "free" will of fallen man or on how man responds to God's prevenient grace.

JUSTICE ACCORDING TO CALVINISM

The Calvinist does not think this way because he does not see God's justice through a humanistic lens which sees man the centerpiece worthy of salvation. Rather, the Calvinist sees through the lens of an absolutely holy God who scrutinizes the wicked, the evil, the unworthy, and His holy soul hates them: *"The LORD tests the righteous, but his soul hates the wicked and the one who loves violence"* (Ps. 11:5). God does not punish sin; God punishes the sinner. The Calvinist believes in a God who not only has the power to save all men, but above all, has the moral right and absolute power to condemn all sinners. Sinners indiscriminately deserve condemnation, for rejecting evil is wholly good. The Calvinist remains in silent amazement at God's goodness (Ex. 33:19-23), for God has not condemned all, even though natural man is evil from his youth (Gen. 8:21). God's amazing Glory, goodness, and love—not His cruelty—is precisely revealed in the fact that God chose to save some, and that He chose a multitude so great that no one could number them, people from every race, tribe, nation, and language (Rev. 7:9).

WHY DOES NOT GOD SAVE OR CAST OUT ALL?

1. IF GOD WERE ONLY JUST

God would not have chosen anyone; we would all, without exception, be left in the condemnation we deserve. We would all be in the same position, groaning and far from God, for He would have shown love and mercy to no one. A decision not to save anyone would have been just, but it would not have glorified God at all.

2. IF GOD WERE ONLY GRACIOUS

As in the previous case, God would not have chosen anyone to save because He would have chosen to save all, which none of us deserve. We would all be equal, all enjoying God, and yet such choosing would have been incompatible with God's holy nature. If God's eternal purpose had been for all people, without exception, to spend eternity with Him in paradise, then He would not have needed to test Adam in the first place. Even more absurdly, had God prevented Adam from eating the fruit of the tree of the knowledge of good and evil in the test, there would have been no test.

3. GOD IS JUST AND MERCIFUL

God's justice and grace do not flow in the trough of human, humanistic egalitarianism. God is holy in all things, including in His justice and grace. He exercises both attributes for His supreme Glory, according to His holy, sovereign will, for which He is answerable to no one. He has bestowed upon His elect a grace that does not exceed His holy justice, for in justice He took upon Himself their sins. The Father poured out His wrath on the Son of Man, Jesus Christ, who took the place of His people, the Israel of God, in punishment. He left others in their sin. This decision glorifies God to the utmost, which is why He created such a history: "*'Now is my soul troubled. And what shall I say? 'Father, save me from this hour'? But for this purpose, I have come to this hour.* ***Father, glorify your name.' Then a voice came from heaven: 'I have glorified it, and I will glorify it again***" (John 12:27-28).

IS YOUR EYE ENVIOUS BECAUSE I AM GOOD?

Let us zoom in on the contrast between election and being left in sin with a clumsy simile. Suppose you, dear reader, are a creditor. Debtors come to hate you because you expect them to return your money. If you decide to forgive some of them their debts and bear the loss yourself, even though they hate you, your decision is based upon grace, not on law and justice. Then the remaining debtors will hate you even more: "How can you be so unjust and not even forgive us our debts?" *"Am I not allowed to do what I choose with what belongs to me?* ***Or do you begrudge my generosity*** [all my goodness shall pass before thee but I have mercy on whom I have mercy, and I have compassion on whom I have compassion; Ex. 33:19]*?' So, the last will be first, and the first last"* (Matt. 20:15-16).

We must constantly remind ourselves of God's amazing goodness in the fact that He saved anyone at all. But this is what disturbs the self-centered, anthropocentric, humanistic person. How dare God, before the foundation of the world, love someone like Jacob with a saving love and hate someone like Esau (Mal. 1:2-3), whom He—by the way—blessed with abundant common grace?

These two groups of people are seen throughout the pages of Scripture. Some remain the children of the Evil One, rejected by God; others are God's chosen, adopted children. There are the rejected children of Cain and the chosen children of Abel (Gen. 4:2-14). There is all the rejected antediluvian humanity and the chosen eight people of Noah's family (Gen. 6:5-10). There is all rejected humanity and the chosen Abram (Gen. 12:1-3). There are the reprobate Ishmaelites and the elect Isaacites (Gal. 4:22-31). There are the reprobate Esauites and the elect Jacobites (Mal. 1:2-3). On one side of the Cross of Christ there is a condemned criminal, sentenced to death, and on the other side there is a pardoned criminal, who though also sentenced to death on earth will be with his Savior in eternity (Luke 23:32-43). There are the reprobate people of the world and the elect Church (John 15:17-19). There are the reprobate goats, whom Christ places on His left on the day of judgment and the elect sheep, who are placed on His right on that day (Matt. 25:31-46).

PART III
CHRIST'S LIMITED, EFFICACIOUS, PURPOSEFUL REDEMPTION

12

CHRIST'S LIMITED, EFFICACIOUS, PURPOSEFUL REDEMPTION

DEFINITION OF THE TERM

The third point of Calvinism, and therefore of the Synod of Dort, responds to the second article of the Remonstrance. It concerns the sovereign, limited, efficacious, and purposeful salvation of God. It is inseparably and continuously connected with the previous two points:

1. ***The natural man, the offspring of Adam, is spiritually dead*** *as a result of original sin, separated from God, unable to understand the things of God. Everything man does in this state takes place on the stage of sin. He is a vassal of Satan, a slave to sin, and because of his corrupt nature is unable of his own accord to desire to follow God.*
2. *Therefore, out of inexpressible, amazing goodness, God had mercy on man.* ***God the Father has chosen*** *for Himself and for His own sake His promised people, His Church, whom He*

loved with an everlasting love from the whole fallen race of Adam before the foundation of the world and has set apart for salvation. His election is not based on merit or the "faith" of the natural man; it is based solely on God's sovereign grace.

3. *To fulfill the promises of God, God the Father sent His Son, Jesus Christ, into the world in the flesh. He gave His people to Him so that* ***God the Son could save them****. On the Cross, Jesus Christ took the place of God's chosen people in the judgment. He bore only their sins, not the sins of all mankind. In this way, He redeemed them from the bondage of sin and led the captives out of Satan's prison. God the Son did not make salvation possible for just anyone; He actually saved His entire people!*

Let us review some important elements from points 1 and 2 of Calvinism. The natural man is the property of the Devil; by nature, he rejects God, and he is incapable of seeking or choosing God. Therefore, God chose for Himself and for His own sake to save and redeem His elect people, His chosen, predestined, and called people. His people include not all without exception, but all without distinction—men, women, children, Jews, Greeks, poor, rich, healthy, sick, educated, uneducated, masters and slaves from all nations; simply put, He redeemed all kinds of people. Therefore, we should not be surprised that Christ's redemption on the Cross, like the Father's election, was limited in scope but unlimited in effect—it applied only to the Father's elect.

Arminians are most concerned about the concept of limited atonement, a term they do not like to hear. Most do not realize that both soteriological systems, Arminianism and Calvinism, understand God's atonement in a limited sense. Their view of salvation, their soteriology, tragically limits, without exaggeration, the efficacy of Christ's atonement, namely, His omnipotence. According to Arminians, Christ bore all the sins of all men on the

Cross so that everyone could be saved, though they admit that not everyone will be saved. They assert that human "free" will and the unbelief of many limit the efficacy of Christ's sacrifice for all. If this were true, it would mean that Christ died and suffered for many in vain. Although He paid and redeemed all, He could not receive all because many chose to remain in the bondage of Satan. It is as if you paid for goods you chose, but the merchant chose not to give them to you. As Arminians see God, He is not omnipotent because His power, including His prevenient grace, is limited by the power of man's "free" will. According to Arminianism, man can limit God from carrying out His purposes and plan to save all without exception. This deplorable view of our omnipotent God is an unfortunate consequence of Arminian salvation theology. In summary, Arminians limit Christ's redemption in efficacy, but not in scope; they limit the Cross in intensity, but not in extent.

Likewise, Calvinists understand salvation in a limited sense, since Christ died only for His chosen people. However, Calvinists believe the efficacy of His salvation on the Cross was 100%. Christ did not die and suffer in vain for anyone. Those for whom He paid, He redeemed for Himself, breaking them out of Satan's prison. Those for whom He has not paid will pay for all eternity in lake of fire. The limited atonement of Calvinism refers not to efficacy but to the scope of Christ's Cross. In summary, Calvinists limit the atonement of Christ in scope, not in efficacy; they limit the Cross in extent, not in intensity.

One of the most significant differences between Arminianism and Calvinism concerns the answer to this question: Who limits the entrance of God's Spirit into the sinner?

1. Is it man who, by his "free" will, **limits the efficacy** (intensity) of Christ's "universal" redemption, as man-centered Arminianism teaches?

2. Or is it God who, by His sovereign will, **limits the scope** (extensity) of Christ's redemption, that is Christ's fully efficacious redemption, as God-centered Calvinism teaches?

For clarity, let us recall both views in the table to discern the difference, which again is not in emphasis but in substance:

ARMINIANISM Remonstration	CALVINISM Synod of Dort
3. Universal Salvation through Christ God's salvation is unlimited in scope but limited by man in its efficacy. Salvation is only a possibility for all. Salvation only becomes efficacious when man believes. Those whom God foreknew would believe, He has also chosen. Man's faith precedes and conditions God's salvation.	**3. Efficacious Redemption through Christ** God's redemption is limited in scope but unlimited in efficacy. Salvation is perfect and complete because it has secured the "salvation and faith" of all whom God unconditionally chose and loved with an everlasting love before the foundation of the world. "salvation and faith" are God's simultaneous and inseparable gifts.

As the table shows, the argument is not about limited salvation—both groups believe that—but about who has the first and last word in salvation. Does the natural man decide by his act of faith, prompted or not by prevenient grace, or is it God who sovereignly decides according to his office over his creation? Is Christ's sacrifice for sin a mere potentiality, a possibility that may or may not be fulfilled in the lives of fallen, sinful men, or did Christ's sacrifice accomplish everything, i.e., "salvation and faith," regeneration, justification, sanctification, and the future redemption of the body? Let us answer this question again: What did Christ accomplish on the Cross? There are only two possibilities:

1. Christ did not save anyone, but He made salvation possible for all. He did not finish salvation; fallen, sinful man must finish it by faith; (Arminianism).
2. Christ accomplished the salvation of His people, including everything that is integral to salvation: *"When Jesus had received*

*the sour wine, he said, '**It is finished,**' and he bowed his head and gave up his spirit"* (John 19:30); (Calvinism).

Thus, the third point of Calvinism teaches that efficacious salvation applies only to the elect. Limited atonement means that the Lord Jesus Christ did not die for all men, but only for His own, those whose names were written in the Book of Life before the foundation of the world. It is this point that has the most opponents. If someone says that he rejects point 3, that he is a four-point "Calvinist," then he is not a Calvinist, but an Amyraldian, because Amyraldism rejects this very point 3.

ACQUAINTANCE WITH EFFICACIOUS REDEMPTION

DID CHRIST DIE FOR UNBELIEF?

Let us start with a famous reflection by John Owen (1616-1683). Think about which statement is closest to your heart:

1. Christ died for some of the sins of all men.
2. Christ died for all the sins of all men.
3. Christ died for all the sins of some.

The first statement—Christ died for some of the sins of all men—will be rejected by all, for all men would be utterly lost, each left with those sins which Christ did not atone for by His suffering on the Cross.

The second statement—Christ died for all the sins of all men—is gladly accepted by all Arminians, Semi-Pelagians, and Pelagians. But the Calvinist would object: "If Christ died for all the sins of all men, why are not all men saved?" The Arminian replies: "Because some have not believed." The Calvinist objects: "Unbelief is the cardinal sin." Christ defined it that way: *"...concerning* *sin, because they do not believe in me"* (John 16:9). If Christ died for all the sins of all men, then He must have died for the sin of sins, which is unbelief in Christ. If the Arminian agrees: "Yes, Christ died for all sins, including the sin of unbelief," the Calvinist will object: "Then why have not all believed? Why are not all saved?" The Arminian will be hard pressed to find a biblical answer to this. But if the Arminian answers: "No, Christ did not die for the sin of unbelief," then the Calvinist will object: "Then Christ did not die for all the sins of all men, but only for some of the sins of all men." See the first statement above, which any consistent Arminian will reject. Some may still object that unbelief is an unpardonable sin for which Christ did not have to die. Such an answer resolves nothing at all, for the first statement would again be true. There remains one more evasive maneuver that perhaps no sincere believer in Christ would dare to use. Namely, that unbelief is not sin, and therefore Christ did not have to die for it. To do so would be to deny John 16:9 and to make faith a blatantly self-serving human virtue, completely subject to fallen, "free" human will.

The third statement—Christ died for all the sins of some, He died for the unbelief of His elect. He thus sovereignly and unconditionally opened the way to "salvation and faith." Christ's sacrifice atoned for all sin exclusively for His elect Church, the ecclesia, whom He brought out of the darkness of Satan before His holy wrath against sinful, reprobate men (Rom. 9:22; 1 Thess. 5:9).

GOD DOES NOT NEED US TO PROTECT HIM

When I had been a Christian for about 16 years, it began to dawn on me from the Scriptures that Christ probably did not die for all men. I was very frightened at the thought. I asked God to forgive me for having such blasphemous thoughts in my mind. At that time, without realizing it, I was thinking in egalitarian, humanistic, and conditional categories—something for something, salvation for faith. I couldn't bear to think that God could be so merciless as to die only for His elect. Inwardly, I tried to protect God from this damning accusation that gnawed at me. I was soon relieved when I began to discover the Reformation doctrine of limited atonement in the books of R. C. Sproul. I gradually began to understand and believe without fear or protest in the almighty sovereignty of God and the utter spiritual impotence of man.

Without thinking much about it at the time, my previous sixteen-year view of God had been filtered through an Arminian protective lens:

- God the Father bears no guilt because He loves with the same redeeming love all who have ever been born; therefore, He gave them all to Christ to make salvation possible **on the condition of faith**.
- God the Son, Jesus Christ, bears no guilt, because by His death on the Cross, He made possible the salvation of all humanity given to Him by the Father, **on the condition of their faith,**
- God the Holy Spirit does not bear guilt because He convinces all—all humanity equally, silently, and convincingly by God's prevenient grace. By the Son's death on the Cross, prevenient grace makes possible the salvation of all, **on condition of their faith**.

Why then are not all saved? All have the same opportunity. The believer in the "free" will of man can answer only as follows: "God's universal, conditional plan of salvation is intended for all the souls of the world without exception, but it is continually thwarted by the 'free' will of man." Who, then, constrains the Cross of Christ? Is it not the Arminian?

CHARLES H. SPURGEON ON EFFICACIOUS REDEMPTION I

If Christ on His cross intended to save every man, then He intended to save those who were eternally lost before He died! If the doctrine of universal atonement is true, that He died for all men—then He died for some who were in Hell before He came into this world; for doubtless there were even then myriads there who had been cast away because of their sins.

Once again, if it was Christ's intention to save all men—then how deplorably has He been disappointed; for we have His own testimony that there is a lake which burns with fire and brimstone, and into that pit of woe have been cast some of the very persons who, according to the theory of universal redemption, were bought with His blood! That seems to me a conception a thousand times more repulsive than any of those consequences which are said to be associated with the Christian doctrine of special and particular redemption.

To think that my Savior died for men who were or are in Hell, seems a supposition too horrible for me to entertain. To imagine for a moment that He was the Substitute for all people, and that God, having first punished the Substitute, afterwards punished the sinners themselves—seems to conflict with all my ideas of divine justice. That Christ should offer an atonement and satisfaction for the sins of all men, and that afterwards some of those very men should be punished for the sins for which Christ had already atoned—appears to me to be the most monstrous iniquity that could ever have been imputed to Saturn, to Janus, to the goddess of the Thugs, or to the most diabolical heathen deities. God forbid that we should ever think thus of Jehovah, the just and wise and good!

We do not believe that Christ redeemed the damned. We do not believe that He poured out His life blood for souls already in Hell. We never can imagine that Christ suffered in the room

> *and stead of all men—and that then afterwards these same men have to suffer for themselves.*
>
> *We hold to this: that Christ laid down His life for His sheep, and secured the salvation of every one of them!*[52]

DOES GOD LOVE ALL PEOPLE WITHOUT EXCEPTION WITH A SAVING LOVE?

GOD'S SAVING LOVE EXTENDS ONLY TO HIS PEOPLE

We already know that God's love, i.e., His saving love, does not exist apart from Christ. God defines His saving love for His people as follows: *"In this is love, not that* ***we*** [who are in Christ] *have loved God* [while we were yet in perdition] *but that he loved* ***us*** *and sent his Son to be the propitiation for* ***our*** *sins* [for our sins, not for the sins of all]" (1 John 4:10). Try substituting the pronouns "we, us, our" for "all men without exception" in the previous verse, and you will not miss the absurdity. According to Scripture, as we have just read, saving love does not consist in the fact that the elect loved God, but in the fact that God loved them and sacrificed Himself for their sins and for the sins of no one else. God's saving love is defined by the very thing that humanistic believers are most opposed to. They object to the 100% efficacious, limited in scope, purposeful salvation of His people. They rail against the third point of Calvinism, not realizing that their soteriology "limits" the efficacy of the suffering of the Son of God on the Cross. This is anthropocentrism, man-centeredness in the deepest sense of the word.

God's redeeming love is identified with His Glory, which is identified with His goodness, and which is defined by His having mercy on whom He has mercy and compassion on whom He has compassion (Ex. 33:19). We are so often reminded of this: How is it even possible that God would have so much love that He would choose

52 https://www.gracegems.org/2015/09/thugs.html

to save anyone at all? We are just as bad, if not worse, than those who drowned in the worldwide flood (Gen. 8:21)? This is the proper perspective from which to view a holy God and an incorrigible self.

If God's saving love applied to all people without exception, how would we explain that God makes distinctions among people; some are children of light and others are children of darkness? Did He love Cain as much as Abel, pre-flood humanity as much as the eight members of Noah's family, Ishmael as much as Isaac, Esau as much as Jacob, Judas as much as Peter, goats as much as sheep? Scripture knows of no such universal, all-encompassing love of God, consummated in the "salvation and faith" of all. Jesus loves with a saving love only those of the world whom the Father has given to Him and who are His (John 17:9; 17:20). Other people God treats patiently (Acts 13:18) and leniently (Rom. 9:22), embracing them with common grace (Matt. 5:45). To repeat, outside of Christ there is no divine love, that is, saving love: *"As the Father has loved me* [the Son], ***so have I*** [the Son, Jesus Christ] ***loved you*** [whom the Father has given Me and who are in Me]. *Abide in my love"* (John 15:9). *"Now before the Feast of the Passover, when Jesus knew that his hour had come to depart out of this world to the Father,* ***having loved his own*** *who were in the world* [He did not love by saving love all of the world], *he loved them* [His own] *to the end* [by dying for them only and providing for them 'salvation and faith'] "(John 13:1).

God did not call His people to remain in bondage to Satan: ***"For God has not destined us*** [His people] *for wrath* [on the Day of Judgment], *but to obtain salvation through our Lord Jesus Christ"* (1 Thess. 5:9). God chose for His own sake, out of unconditional grace and love, to foreordain, predestine, call, justify, and bring His people out of the prison of sin into His Glory. It follows that a portion of humanity has not been loved, chosen, predestined, etc., from all eternity; they will remain in perdition until the Day of Judgment, when they fall under the righteous wrath of God

(Rom. 9:22), a permanent separation from God. There are about forty explicit references to the wrath of God in the New Testament, and more than three hundred in the Old Testament.

Even in the Old Testament, God's redeeming love was only for His people: *"God has not rejected* [not abandoned to reprobation] *his people* [the elect] *whom he foreknew* [unconditionally loved]. *Do you not know what the Scripture says of Elijah, how he appeals to God against Israel? 'Lord, they have killed your prophets, they have demolished your altars, and I alone am left* [Elijah did not see a single companion in the faith], *and they seek my life.' But what is God's reply to him? 'I have kept for myself seven thousand men who have not bowed the knee to Baal.'* ***So too at the present time*** [in this present Church Age] ***there is a remnant, chosen by grace.*** *But if it is by grace, it is no longer on the basis of works; otherwise grace would no longer be grace"* (Rom. 11:2-6).

On the Cross, the Lord Jesus Christ secured the gift of the Holy Spirit for all those for whom He died. By recreating the inner man, He secures for God's people "salvation and faith," that is, spiritual resurrection, justification, sanctification, and bodily resurrection into a glorified body. Created faith understands and sees the things of the Spirit of God (1 Cor. 2:14): *"Blessed be the God and Father of our Lord Jesus Christ,* ***who has blessed us*** [His people] *in Christ with every spiritual blessing in the heavenly places, even as he* ***chose us in him before the foundation of the world*** [loved us with an everlasting love], *that we should be holy and blameless before him. In love* [His saving love]*"* (Eph. 1:3-4). In fact, God's saving love extends only to God's chosen people. *The elect* and *God's saving love* are synonymous, expressing a consistent principle. To "elect" all the reprobate without exception would really be to elect no one; by analogy, to love with saving love all without exception would really be to love no one with saving love. To put it in popular terms, if we all loved each other equally without exception in this fallen world, we could never say that Johnny loves Molly, that she is his elect.

HOLY AND UNDEFILED IN LOVE

God gives every spiritual blessing in Christ to those whom He loves with redeeming love. These are encapsulated in Christ—baptized, immersed. And so positionally, not by their own strength, they follow Christ, doing what He does, and they are perfectly safe. No one can fly at 30,000 feet at 700 miles per hour. But if you jump into the airplane positionally, you will fly that high and that fast, though not by your own strength. Noah could not have stayed on the surface of the water flooding the entire earth for 375 days had God not put him in a safe place. He "dipped" him into the ark and saved him. If you were not in the ark, you were not floating; you would not be going anywhere. If you were not in the ark, you would drown. And those who are not in Christ will drown in the waters surrounding the multitude of nations (Rev. 17:15), forever separated from the meaning of existence, eternal knowledge of God (Rev. 20:14; 21:8).

God's redemptive love sent the Son of God into the world to redeem all of God's Israel from their sins—the promised Jews and Gentiles (Gal. 6:15-16; Eph. 2:12), those for whom He fought when on the Cross He delivered them from the Devil's grip: *"God exalted him* [Jesus Christ] *at his right hand as Leader and Savior, to give repentance* ***to Israel*** [the Israel of the God of Jews and Gentiles; not the whole world] *and forgiveness of sins"* (Acts 5:31). Christ was lifted up on the Cross to bring this commonwealth of the Israel of God, and only the Israel of God, out of the world to Himself (Gal. 6:15-16). The Israel of God consists of all who have been spiritually raised and baptized into Christ. It includes all new creatures in Christ, both Old Testament saints, mostly Jews, and New Testament saints, mostly Gentiles but Jews as well (Gal. 6:14-16).

God sent His Son into the world to save and cleanse only His special people through His death: *"...who gave himself* ***for us to redeem us*** [only for His people] *from all lawlessness and to purify for himself* ***a people for his own possession*** [the Cross purified only His own people] *who are zealous for good works"* (Titus 2:14). The commonwealth of Israel (Eph. 2:12), His Church, is set apart from the world, sanctified for Christ and because of Christ. It is His bride, being raised up before His face in love and knowledge of her Bridegroom (Eph. 1:3-4). If God loved all with His redeeming love, then He would have died for all, and all would be His possession, all would be zealous for good works, all would be cleansed by His blood, and all would be sanctified. But the blood of Jesus Christ sanctified only His people: *"So Jesus also suffered outside the gate in order to sanctify* ***the people*** [His particular nation] *through his own blood"* (Heb. 13:12). Full sanctification, alienation from the world, is not the result of human effort; it is the sovereign, purifying work of Jesus Christ on the Cross. All that Jesus Christ did in suffering for the people of God was established before the foundation of the world in the ministry of the triune God (Eph. 1:4): ***"For the love of Christ controls us*** [only us, His Church], *because* ***we have concluded this****: that one has died for* ***all****, therefore* ***all*** *have died; and he died for* ***all*** [Christ died for all who died in Him], *that those who live* [and live in Him] *might* ***no longer live for themselves but for him who for their sake died and was raised"*** (2 Cor. 5:14-15).

In the true, saving love of Christ, then, there are only those who no longer live for themselves, but live for Him who died and rose for them. Those who are in the power of Christ's saving love have been given to understand that Christ died for all who have died to sin in Christ. The love of Christ is not poured out on those who are perishing—hence the preceding terms, "all, all, all." The love of Christ is poured out only on the Body of Christ, His Church. Christ's redeeming love, therefore, cannot apply to absolutely all men, certainly not to those who have not been given to understand (Matt. 13:11) that they must die to sin in Christ and remain permanently in this spiritual death. God's eternal saving love extends only to those whom God loves with the same love that He loved Jeremiah: *"...the Lord appeared to him from far away.* ***I have loved you with an everlasting love****; therefore, I have continued my faithfulness to you"* (Jer. 31:3). Further, Paul's opening salutation in his letter to the Romans clearly communicates that he is addressing his letter to all those who are loved by God, not to those over whom God's wrath hovers: ***"To all those in Rome who are loved by God*** [other Romans were not loved by saving love] *and called to be saints* [only those who are loved by God are also called]*: Grace to you and peace from God our Father and the Lord Jesus Christ"* (Rom. 1:7).

GOD HATES THE SINNER

Sin is an integral part of the sinner's nature. A holy God cannot have loving fellowship with a spiritually dead, sinful man. Holiness and sinfulness cannot dwell together in the same household. God hates sinners because of their willfulness, self-centeredness, and unbelief. Every natural man is a wicked, self-willed wretch from birth: *"The Lord tests the righteous* [whom He hath justified, He imputes no sin], *but* ***his soul hates the wicked and the one who loves violence****"* (Ps. 11:5). There are only two categories of people in this Psalm—the righteous and the wicked. Although His soul hates wicked, violent people, He patiently embraces them with the abundant common grace that we so often confuse with saving love. Let us realize that the consequences of sin, iniquity, wickedness, and violence, that is, human nature, reach to the depths of hell (Heb. 10:31): ***"For the wrath of God*** *is revealed from heaven against all ungodliness and unrighteousness of men* [natural men are ungodly], ***who by their unrighteousness suppress the truth****"* (Rom. 1:18). God's wrath, not love, is revealed against every natural man, the promoter of ungodliness, who denies Christ—even if he is a Nobel Peace Prize winner for his kindness. There is a bottomless chasm between a holy God and sinful man that can only be bridged by God's unconditional grace, mercy, and saving love.

The natural man cannot dwell with God because he is evil from his birth, and as such God cannot endure him: *"For you are not a God who delights in wickedness;* ***evil may not dwell with you****"* (Ps. 5:4). "I hate the assembly of evildoers," is in fact a reflection of the mind of God. For whom God hates, He cannot love with a redeeming love: *"****I hate the assembly of evildoers****, and I will not sit with the wicked"* (Ps. 26:5). And in the following verse God explicitly reveals that whom He hates, whom He will not show love to: *"Every evil of theirs is in Gilgal; there* ***I began to hate them****. Because of the wickedness of their deeds, I will drive them out of my house.* ***I will love them no more****; all their princes are rebels"* (Hos. 9:15). Such verses are difficult to accept. They are unpleasant, and they should be unpleasant. God does not punish the effect—sin; He punishes the cause—the sinner whom He hates. On the day of judgment, the unforgiven sinner will be thrown into the lake of fire (Rev. 20:15) because his sin has rebelled against a holy God. A holy and righteous God must remove sinners because they offend Him through their sin. God's holy nature will not allow Him to simply turn a blind eye to the sinner and allow him to enter God's house.

The popular cliché, "God hates sin but loves sinners," contradicts Scripture. Those who are abhorrent to God cannot be loved with God's redeeming love: *"They were filled with all manner of unrighteousness, evil, covetousness, malice. They are full of envy, murder, strife, deceit, maliciousness. They are gossips, slanderers,* ***haters of God****, insolent, haughty, boastful, inventors of evil, disobedient to parents, foolish, faithless, heartless, ruthless"* (Rom. 1:29-31). The cliché, "God hates sin but loves sinners," should be reversed: "God hates sinners because they sin." Yet, in spite of their utter depravity and the heinousness of their deeds, He patiently endures and embraces all of them with common grace; and moreover, He has chosen a full number of His own, His remnant of "seven thousand" Jews and Gentiles, for His Glory, for His own sake, and for Himself, because He has loved them with an everlasting, redeeming love. This is God's amazing, wonderful, miraculous, unconditional grace. This displays all His Glory and goodness (Ex. 33:19).

Let us look at the following verses and examine our consciences. God's elect were once guilty of all seven things that the Lord hates. But it was God's amazing, special, unconditional, eternal, saving love that saved them from eternal destruction far from God, that saved them from God's righteous wrath (Isa. 43:21; Jer. 31:3): ***"There are six things that the Lord hates****, seven that are an abomination to him:* [1] *haughty eyes,* [2] *a lying tongue, and* [3] *hands that shed innocent blood,* [4] *a heart that devises wicked plans,* [5] *feet that make haste to run to evil,* [6] *a false witness who breathes out lies, and* [7] *one who sows discord among brothers"* (Prov. 6:16-19).

If we are not yet convinced that God does not love all sinners with a saving love, let us recall God's words about Esau: ***"...but Esau I have hated****. I have laid waste his hill country and left his heritage to jackals of the desert"* (Mal. 1:3). Yet He showed him an almost unbelievable common grace (Gen. 36).

SOME ARE LEFT TO THE WRATH OF GOD

Now let us see how it is with those to whom God's saving love and grace do not apply. If God's people have not been destined to fall into God's wrath (1 Thess. 5:9), then there must be others who have fallen into God's wrath: *"What if God, desiring to show his wrath and to make known his power, has endured with much patience* [through common grace] ***vessels of wrath prepared for destruction"*** (Rom. 9:22). The next two verses are even more relentless. The cause of the Fall is the rejection of the Lord Jesus Christ (John

16:9): *"So the honor is for you who believe, but for those who do not believe, 'The stone that the builders rejected* [Jesus Christ] *has become the cornerstone,' and 'A stone of stumbling, and a rock of offense.' They stumble because they disobey the word* [by nature], ***as they were destined to do*** [God withdrew from them; 1 Sam. 18:12]*"* (1 Pet. 2:7-8). Such truth is contrary to an innate, humanistic, Pelagian, Semi-Pelagian, and Arminian view of God. Let us be faithful to Scripture; let us all, without exception, suppress the natural image of the world that we create through human self-centeredness, the original sin of Adam's sins—pride, "knowledge" of what is good and what is evil, in short, the desire for God-equality (Gen. 3:5). Let us approach God with fear and trembling, knowing that God is sovereign in all things. He makes no mistakes, and that what He does is always right and absolutely holy: *"The Lord has made everything for its purpose* [to his Glory; Rom. 9:22-23], ***even the wicked*** [He withdrew from him] *for the day of trouble* [for the Day of Judgment, the Day of the Lord]*"* (Prov. 16:4).

God is patient, forgiving, and slow to anger. He shows common grace through the Cross of Christ even to those who are subject to His wrath and final condemnation, and often it surpasses the common grace with which He covers His elect. The historical experience of the rich man and Lazarus proves this to be true (Luke 16:25). We must take God's sovereignty as Scripture describes it, not as we would like to see it.

GOD'S SACRIFICE DID NOT MAKE SALVATION POSSIBLE, HIS SACRIFICE SAVED

WHAT DID JESUS CHRIST ACCOMPLISH ON THE CROSS?

The Arminian and Calvinist views of what Jesus Christ did on the Cross are diametrically opposed. The Arminian must believe that Christ's sacrifice did not save anyone, only making salvation possible for all on the condition of faith. In contrast, the Calvinist believes that Christ's sacrifice unconditionally saved the entire people of God, the entire Israel of God (Gal. 6:16; Eph. 2:12). Three things are very important in the study of Scripture—context, context, and more context. When interpreting Scripture, we must consider it as a whole; otherwise, the Bible "contradicts" itself. Dozens of verses clearly teach that Jesus' salvation was only efficacious for a certain category of people. Even Joseph, Mary's betrothed, was told that Jesus would only save His people and no one else. God told him clearly through the mouth of the angel: *"She* [Mary] *will bear a son, and you* [Joseph] *shall call his name Jesus, for he* [Jesus] ***will save his people*** [reprobates are not part of His people; He did not save them on the Cross] *from their sins"* (Matt. 1:21). If the Son of God had come into the world to pay the penalty for every person who ever lived, then God the Father would have been a most unjust judge, for on the last day of judgment He would have condemned myriads of people to the lake of fire to pay forever for their sins, for which Christ had already paid the penalty on the Cross. Only a usurer would collect again on a debt once paid. No honest restaurant asks you to pay a second time if a friend has paid your bill for you. Had Christ on the Cross redeemed all mankind from Satan's household, then no one would have to suffer for his sins in the lake of fire for all eternity.

CHARLES H. SPURGEON ON EFFICACIOUS REDEMPTION II

> *The greatness of Christ's redemption may be measured by the EXTENT OF THE DESIGN OF IT. He gave His life a "ransom for many." We are often told that we limit the atonement of Christ, because we say that Christ has not made a satisfaction for all men, or all men would be saved. Now, our reply to this is that, on the other hand, our opponents limit it: we do not. The Arminians say, Christ died for all men. Ask them*

> *what they mean by that. Did Christ die so to secure the salvation of all men? They say, "No, certainly not." We ask them the next question—Did Christ die so as to secure the salvation of any man in particular? They answer "No." They are obliged to admit this, if they are consistent. They say "No; Christ has died that any man may be saved if"—and then follow certain conditions of salvation. Now, who is it that limits the death of Christ? Why, you. You say that Christ did not die so as to infallibly secure the salvation of anybody. We beg your pardon, when you say we limit Christ's death; we say, "No my dear sir, it is you that do it." We say Christ so died that He infallibly secured the salvation of a multitude that no man can number, who through Christ's death not only may be saved, but are saved, must be saved, and cannot by any possibility run the hazard of being anything but saved. You are welcome to your atonement; you may keep it. We will never renounce ours for the sake of it*[53].

SALVATION IS NOT AN OPTION

There is no indication in Scripture that the sacrifice of Jesus is the means of salvation for all who willfully believe. The good news of the gospel reveals God's purpose, namely that Jesus' sacrifice secured for God's predestined people a perfect and complete, whole "salvation and faith," that is, regeneration, justification, sanctification, and future resurrection into a glorified body. God has not given anyone such a duty or privilege to complete the saving work done by Jesus Christ alone. No one, absolutely no male descendant of Adam, has the power to make God's sacrifice efficacious by his acceptance or useless by his rejection. Christ's Cross is 100% efficacious from all eternity! "Salvation and faith" is God's monergistic creation. If Jesus Christ had died for all merely to make salvation possible for all people, then the Cross of Christ

53 https://www.covenantbc.com/files/for_whom_did_christ_die.pdf

would have saved no one; it would still be a mere possibility, a potentiality, an eventuality dependent upon the utter spiritual corruption of mankind. Theoretically, the Cross of Christ could be accepted by all, by some, or by none. But Scripture teaches that Christ did not come to make salvation possible for all men, so that everyone could reach for it by his free choice, by his act of faith, but rather that He came to save His sheep, the children whom the Father gave Him (John 10:27-29).

SALVATION IS UNCONDITIONALLY EFFICACIOUS

The Son of God did not take on flesh like sinful man in order to make salvation possible for all. He was born to die in order that He might accomplish the salvation of the elect sinners, to save His people unconditionally. He came into this world to save what was already perishing. Christ was not born for the "free" will of man to do as he pleases with His sacrifice. He administered His sacrifice according to the will of His holy, sovereign office: *"For the Son of Man came to seek* [God seeks the lost, the lost do not seek God] ***and to save*** [He came not to make salvation possible, but to actually save] ***the lost****"* (Luke 19:10). Jesus' redemptive sacrifice on the Cross was and is perfectly finished. There is nothing that anyone can add to or subtract from it; it displays God's sovereign final decision, His final decree, His last words before He died: *"When Jesus had received the sour wine, he said, '****It is finished,****' and he bowed his head and gave up his spirit"* (John 19:30).

Jesus said: "It is finished." He did not say: "It shall be finished." He did not say: "Finish my offer of salvation with your 'free' decision." He did not say: "Make my sacrifice efficacious for all of you." He did not say: "I have done My part; now it is up to you what you do with My sacrifice." What did the Son of God actually accomplish on the Cross? Was the purpose of His death to save or to make salvation possible? Did He save His beloved people from all eternity, or did He save no one, but merely enable all men to dispose of His sacrifice according to their enslaved will? The Calvinist and the Arminian see the mission of the Cross and what Christ accomplished on the Cross through completely opposite lenses.

No one but God can decide what to do with the saving sacrifice of Christ. The Cross of Christ does not permit a spiritually dead person to either make God's saving sacrifice efficacious by accepting it or to render it powerless, ineffective, and useless by rejecting it. The efficacy of any divine purpose is not determined by natural, spiritually dead people enslaved to sin. The efficacy of Jesus' sacrifice cannot be conditioned on a natural, sin- and Satan-bound will (1 Cor. 2:14). The absolute efficacy of the Cross is determined by God's irrevocable decree.

13

FOR WHOM DID CHRIST DIE?

CHRIST'S REDEMPTION LIMITED IN EXTENT

CHRIST'S SACRIFICE DOES NOT SANCTIFY ALL WITHOUT EXCEPTION

"But when Christ had offered for all time a single sacrifice for sins, he sat down at the right hand of God, waiting from that time until his enemies should be made a footstool for his feet. For by a single offering, he ***has perfected for all time those*** [and only those] *who are being sanctified"* (Heb. 10:12-14). Christ's sacrifice brings to perfection only those whom He sanctifies. If His sacrifice applied to all in a general sense, then every person who ever lived would be sanctified, i.e., "saved and believing."

CHRIST SACRIFICED HIMSELF FOR HIS BRIDE ALONE

"Husbands, love your wives, as Christ loved the church and ***gave himself up for her*** [the Church alone, His bride alone]*"* (Eph. 5:25). Just as Christ has His one chosen people, His chosen and beloved bride from all eternity, for whom alone He gave Himself, so the believing man is to have only one chosen, beloved wife to marry and, if necessary, to lay down his life for her: "*"Therefore a*

man shall leave his father and mother and hold fast to his wife, and the two shall become one flesh [as the Head and members, Christ and the Church, are one flesh].*' This mystery is profound, and* ***I am saying that it refers to Christ and the church***" (Eph. 5:31-32). The marriage relationship between a man and a woman is an earthly type of the supreme marriage between Christ and His chosen bride, the ecclesia, the Church, all who are in Christ.

CHRIST REDEEMED FOR HIMSELF HIS SPECIAL PEOPLE

"*Grace to you and peace from God our Father and the Lord Jesus Christ, who gave himself* ***for our sins*** [our sins, not the sins of all] ***to deliver us*** [only us the elect] *from the present evil age* [Satan's age], ***according to the will of our God and Father*** [not according to the natural, "free" will of man]" (Gal. 1:3-4). The apostle Paul, himself a Christian, addresses his letter to his brothers and sisters in Christ, that is, to "us" Christians. Jesus gave Himself for "us," the people whom the Father gave to Him. Jesus redeemed "us," His Body, His Church, His elect, from the slavery of Satan, to dress "us" as His Bride, because we belong to His beloved people from all eternity, by the will of God the Father. The next text confirms this: "*...who gave himself* ***for us to redeem us*** [not make possible our redemption] *from all lawlessness and* ***to purify for himself*** [only the elect, beloved from of old] ***a people*** [not all mankind] ***for his own possession*** *who are zealous for good works*" (Titus 2:14).

God, for Himself and for His own sake, redeemed only His special people from the bondage of iniquity and cleansed them by the blood of His Son. The new Lord, Jesus Christ (the old lord was Satan) did not redeem His people with gold or silver, but with the ultimate price, His very life. He became a servant, and on the Cross He redeemed many, not all, from the bondage of sin by His blood: "*...even as the Son of Man came not to be served but to serve,* ***and to give his life as a ransom for many*** [not for all without exception]" (Matt. 20:28). Those who are not God's own, special, redeemed, and cleansed people have not been redeemed or cleansed by Jesus' sacrifice; they remain the property of the old lord, the Evil One. God's special people are the object of His eternal, sovereign, redeeming love and goodness (Ex. 33:19), without any human trappings, additions, or accessories. Everything He does, He does first and foremost for Himself and for His own sake. But whatever is good for Him is secondarily good for His children.

Do you "want" to be drawn to Christ by the Father? Do you "want" to belong to His special, redeemed and cleansed people? Do not be so self-absorbed (Rom. 8:7) that you doubt whether you belong to Him, whether you are chosen. Pray, study the Scriptures, then trust Him! If you believe and look to Christ, you are certainly God's elect in Him (Eph. 1:4), children of the promise. But if you think you belong to Christ by the "free" decision of your flesh and blood, then the time has come for your reformation—not necessarily for your salvation. All that you believe, all that you see with your spiritual eyes by faith, has been newly created in you and revealed to you by the Father in heaven, just as it was to the apostle Peter (Matt. 16:16-17).

When I told my aunt that God does everything for His own sake and Glory, she responded with irritation: "What a selfish person." She did not understand that it takes at least two people of the same category to be selfish. It cannot be that God is selfish; He is absolutely unique, in His own indefinable category. There is no one like God except Him: *"Who is like me? Let him proclaim it. Let him declare and set it before me, since I appointed an ancient people* [My chosen ones from all eternity, promised in Christ]. *Let them declare what is to come, and what will happen. Fear not, nor be afraid; have I not told you from of old and declared it? And you are my witnesses* [the royal priesthood; 1 Pet. 2:9]*!* ***Is there a God besides me? There is no Rock; I know not any"*** (Isa. 44:7-8). Since God is unique, everything He does is necessarily done for

Himself, for His own sake, for the glorification, joy and love of all three persons of God. He cannot share with anyone in His category because there is no one else in His category. To think that God is selfish is to drag Him down, out of His inaccessible Light, into space-time, into the dark murmur of human nature, into the sinful category where there are as many self-centered and selfish individuals as there are human beings born of human beings.

GOD SHOWS HIS REDEEMING LOVE ONLY TO HIS PEOPLE

"So, we have come to know and to believe ***the love that God has for us*** [for us, not for everyone without exception]. *God is love, and whoever abides in love abides in God, and God abides in him* [this love of God applies only to His people, the Church]" (1 John 4:16). Furthermore, when the apostle Paul who is in Christ is writing to a group of people who are also in Christ Jesus, he is writing to his spiritual family, his brothers and sisters. So, Paul addresses them in the first-person plural—*we* and *us*: *"...but* ***God shows his*** [redeeming] ***love for us*** [only for His elect] *in that while we* [His people] *were still sinners,* ***Christ died for us*** [His people only]. *Since, therefore,* ***we*** [His justified people] *have now been justified by his blood, much more shall* ***we*** [His people] *be saved by him from the wrath of God* [the others remain under God's wrath]" (Rom. 5:8-9). It is still the same principle. Christ loves with a saving love only His special, separate people for whom He gave His life.

The recipients of Paul's letters had received the whole "salvation and faith[54]", i.e., (1) regeneration, (2) justification, (3) sanctification, and (4) redemption of the body: *"And* ***because of him*** *you are in Christ Jesus* [(1) you are regenerated, raised up spiritually; John 5:24-25], *who became to us wisdom from God, righteousness* [(2) in Him we are justified, freed from sins] *and sanctification* [(3)

54 See chapter 3; section: "Salvation and Faith" According to the Reformation.

in Him we are sanctified, separated for Him, growing spiritually] *and redemption* [(4) in Him we will be raised up bodily]"(1 Cor. 1:30). Those who are not of His power in Christ Jesus are, by God's standards, (1) unregenerate, (2) unrighteous, (3) unsanctified, and (4) will not be redeemed into a glorified body (Rom. 8:23). If they never received full "salvation and faith," then the death of the Lord Jesus Christ cannot apply to them.

CHRIST WAS CURSED SOLELY FOR HIS PEOPLE

No man except the God-man, the sinless Son of Man, Jesus Christ, could or can keep God's law. To transgress the law is to die. The letter of the law kills (2 Cor. 3:6b). The law is a curse because it makes clear to every man that he cannot keep it. The law is a death sentence for all without exception: "***Christ redeemed us*** [his people, not all without exception] *from the curse of the law by becoming a curse for us* [his people and no one else]—*for it is written, 'Cursed is everyone who is hanged on a tree'*"(Gal. 3:13).

God's elect, though they perished in Adam and fell into Satan's bondage, were not left in the house of the Devil in perdition and were not destined for the final wrath of God (1 Thess. 5:9) at the judgment seat of God. Those for whom Christ was not cursed will remain cursed for all eternity (Rom. 9:22; 1 Pet. 2:7b-8). If Christ had taken the curse for all mankind in all ages, then He would be cursed for those who are already in hell today. In this incomprehensible case, all people without exception, even those who are already in hell, would yet enter the kingdom of God. This is universalism.

ON THE CROSS, GOD WAS RECONCILED ONLY TO HIS PEOPLE

Scripture declares that the result of Jesus' atoning work on the Cross is the reconciliation of God's enemies to God: "*For if while we* [His promised ones] *were enemies* [active voice] *we were reconciled* [passive voice] *to God by the death of his Son* [active work of God], *much more, now that we are reconciled* [passive voice], *shall we be saved* [passive voice] *by his life"* (Rom. 5:10). It is not we who are reconciled to God—He has not sinned against us; He has not offended us. On the contrary, we have offended a holy God by our sin. He who is offended has chosen to be reconciled to us, His people, through the sacrifice of the Lord Jesus Christ. The action is on His side. It is not in our power to be reconciled to God on our own.

Some of you will say—what about this verse? *"Therefore, we are ambassadors for Christ, God making his appeal through us* [to announce the good news to the world]. ***We implore you*** [active voice] *on behalf of Christ, **be reconciled to God"*** (2 Cor. 5:20). Only those who are saved can be reconciled to God; in fact, they are already reconciled. These two verses, Rom. 5:10 and 2 Cor. 5:20, do not contradict each other. We mentioned in chapter 3 that Scripture often requires us to do things that we cannot do in our sinful nature[55]. We can only act when Christ has taken us into Himself by the Spirit, and so the atonement is in God's hands. The death of the Son of God on the Cross does not apply to those who remain in sin to the end of their lives, unreconciled to God. If it did apply to them, God would be reconciled to them, and they would be reconciled to God: *"All this is from God, who through **Christ reconciled us*** [only us His people] *to himself **and gave us*** [active voice] *the ministry of reconciliation* [we act because we are already resting in Christ]*; that is, in Christ God was **reconciling the world to himself*** [without distinction not without exception], *not counting their trespasses against them, and entrusting to us the message of reconciliation"* (2 Cor. 5:18-19). This couplet is undoubtedly consistent with Rom. 5:10 and 2 Cor. 5:20 above. It is also deliberately included because of the word "world," which, taken out of context, seems to imply that the whole world may be involved, that

55 See chapter 3; section: The Inability of the Natural Man.

all men without exception have been reconciled to God in Christ. Bible verses are always complementary, never contradictory.

The "world" in this case cannot include every individual. If it did, then God would have made peace with everyone, and hell would be empty. No one would be thrown into the lake of fire on the last day of the Lord's judgment (Rev. 20:15). Furthermore, the preceding couplet (2 Cor. 5:18-19) makes it clear that only we who have been reconciled to God are entrusted with the Word of that reconciliation. If God had been reconciled in Christ to the whole perishing world, then the Word of His reconciliation would not have been entrusted to His people—to us—but to the whole world, which would take us back to universalism. Therefore, in chapter 14 we will explain the limited meaning of the words "world" and "all" in a biblical context.

CHRIST CAME INTO THE WORLD TO SAVE THOSE WHOM THE FATHER GAVE HIM

Those whom the Father has given to Jesus will surely come to Jesus. Not one of them will fall away from the faith; not one of them will be lost. Those whom the Father has not given to Him, those whom He has forsaken, will not come to Christ the Savior, because the Son of God did not die for them: *"Jesus said to them, 'I am the bread of life; whoever comes to me shall not hunger, and whoever believes in me shall never thirst. But I said to you that you have seen me and yet do not believe.* ***All that the Father gives me*** [all the Father's elect] ***will come to me****, and whoever comes to me I will never cast out. For I have come down from heaven, not to do my own will but the will of him who sent me. And this is the will of him* [Father] *who sent me,* ***that I should lose nothing of all that he has given me, but raise it up on the last day****. For this is the will of my Father, that everyone who looks on the Son and believes in him* [only those drawn by the Father are endowed with 'salvation and faith'] *should have eternal life, and I will raise him up on the last day'"* (John 6:35-40).

The Son has made the Father known to those whom the Father has given Him. The world may know about the Father, but it cannot truly know Him, and it cannot love Him. Christ died for those in whom He created a supernatural love, as the Father has for the Son: *"Father, I desire that they also,* ***whom you have given me****, may be with me where I am, to see my glory that you have given me because you loved me before the foundation of the world. O righteous Father, even though the world does not know you, I know you, and these know* [because you have given them to me] *that you have sent me.* ***I made known to them*** [those you have given me] ***your name, and I will continue to make it known, that the love with which you have loved me*** [God loves only his own] ***may be in them, and I in them"*** (John 17:24-26).

CHRIST LAYS DOWN HIS LIFE ONLY FOR HIS SHEEP

All who are His sheep are brought into the fold and drawn to Christ through the new birth, to hear His voice and follow Him: *"I* [Jesus Christ] *am the good shepherd.* ***The good shepherd lays down his life for the sheep"*** (John 10:11). *"I am the good shepherd.* ***I know*** [love] ***my own*** [those given to me by the Father] ***and my own*** [the promised Jews] ***know*** [love] ***me****, just as the Father knows* [loves] *me and I know* [love] *the Father; and* ***I lay down my life for the sheep****. And I have other sheep that are not of this fold* [the promised Gentiles]. *I must bring them also, and they will listen to my voice* [they will be given ears to hear—faith]. ***So there will be one flock*** [Jews and Gentiles], ***one shepherd*** [Christ]*"* (John 10:14-16). Jesus is concerned only with the lives of His sheep, both Jews and Gentiles. In Christ there is no distinction between them (Rom. 10:12); they are one flock. He does not lay down His life for those who are not His. Furthermore, the sheep do not come to Christ on their own; they are given to Him by the Father and are drawn by the Father (John 6:44). Who hears the voice of Christ? Only those who have the Holy Spirit, those who are His sheep: *"So the Jews gathered around him and said to him, 'How long will you keep us in suspense? If you are the Christ, tell us plainly.' Jesus answered them, 'I told you, and you do not believe. The works that I do in my Father's name bear witness about me,* ***but you do not believe because you are not among my sheep*** [I never knew you, never loved you; Matt. 7:23]. ***My sheep hear my voice, and I know them*** [love them], ***and they follow me. I give them eternal life*** [only to those for whom I die], *and they will never perish, and no one will snatch them out of my hand.* ***My Father, who has given them to me,*** *is greater than all, and no one is able to snatch them out of the Father's hand'"* (John 10:24-29).

Neither spiritual-intellectual pondering and searching of the Scriptures nor obvious miracles will convince the natural man. None of this leads to salvation for one simple reason—you are not My sheep, you will never hear My voice, you will never understand, even if you receive all the evidence in the world and witness supernatural miracles. The person who will never believe is not one of Christ's sheep. The person who is saved hears His voice and believes simply because he belongs to Christ's flock of sheep from all eternity. There is no fatalism here, as if everything were subject to a random, soulless, inexorable fate. Christ's death on the Cross has nothing to do with implacable, impersonal fate. Jesus died for specific individuals, those who were chosen by God's holy will! Can anyone resist His will, His decree (Rom. 9:18-21)?

Let us not gamble with eternal life by idly wondering whether we are the chosen sheep. Let us believe and thus demonstrate that we are His chosen sheep for whom He died. In this time of life's need, vain philosophy, idle speculation, and defiance cease, and holy fear with obedience comes in. Let us bow down to the Savior and, with trembling, work out our salvation (Phil. 2:12).

CHRIST PRAYS ONLY FOR HIS OWN, HE DOES NOT PRAY FOR THE WORLD

The Lord Jesus Christ, before His imminent death, prayed only for those whom the Father had given Him, those whom He loved with saving love, that is, His disciples and those who would believe through their word. Why did He not pray specifically for the whole world? Because His special saving grace, love, mercy, and compassion are for believers only (Ex. 33:19; Rom. 9:15). He did not pray for those who belong to the world, to the prince of the air (Eph. 2:2) until the end of their days. Jesus carried out the Father's plan of salvation; He did not make salvation available to all without exception, but He saved all who were His own. He fulfilled the mission given to Him by the Father: *"When Jesus had spoken these words, he lifted up his eyes to heaven, and said, 'Father, the hour has come; glorify your Son that the Son may glorify you, since you have given him authority over all flesh,* ***to give eternal life to all whom you have given him*** [not to all without exception]. *And this is eternal life, that they know you, the only true God, and Jesus Christ whom you have sent. I glorified you on earth, having accomplished the work that you gave me to do. And now, Father, glorify me in your own presence with the glory that I had with you before the world existed.* ***I have manifested your name to the people whom you gave me out of the world*** [the Father did not give Him the whole world]. *Yours they were, and you gave them to me, and they have kept your word. Now they know that everything that you have given me is from you. For I have given them the words that you gave me, and they have received them and have come to know in truth that I came from you; and they have believed that you sent me.* ***I am praying for them*** [the disciples and all those loved by You from all eternity]. ***I am not praying for the world*** [left in Satan's sonship] ***but for those whom you have given me, for they are yours.*** *All mine are yours, and yours are mine, and I am glorified in them. And I am* *no longer in the world, but they are in the world, and I am coming to you. Holy Father, keep them in your name, which you have given me, that they may be one, even as we are one'"* (John 17:1-11).

Jesus did not die for the whole world, for all sinners, but only for those sinners whom the Father had chosen to be saved. Jesus did not plead for the whole world; He pleaded exclusively for His disciples, for all generations of God's promised children, newly created for His Glory to tell of His mighty deeds: *"I do not ask for these only* [the disciples], *but also for those* ***who will believe in me through their word*** [the people of God, the Church, the ecclesia]*"* (John 17:20).

This certainly does not mean that we should not pray for the salvation of all. We witness to all with equal fervor and love because we do not know who are His. We treat all people as elect. But to some we will be a fragrance from death to death, and to the other a fragrance from life to life (2 Cor. 2:16). God's Word will never return empty (Isa. 55:11). Jesus' powerful prayer before His death continues: *"Father, I desire that they also,* ***whom you have given me****, may be with me where I am* [be in me], *to see my glory that you have given me because you loved me before the foundation of the world. O righteous Father, even though* ***the world does not know you*** [no one in Adam], *I know you,* ***and these know*** [all whom the Father has drawn to Christ and are in Christ] ***that you have sent me****. I made known to them your name* [to them only], *and I will continue to make it known, that the love with which you have loved me may be in them, and I in them* [God's love does not exist apart from Christ; 1 John 4:16]*"* (John 17:24-26).

GOD DECIDES WHO WILL BE ADOPTED AS A SON

Through the apostle Paul, Scripture declares that all the spiritual blessings the saints receive are due to their being kept in Christ, baptized, immersed in Christ, and thus sharing in His crucifixion.

God's will, not ours, determines who dies to sin in Christ to become His adopted son: *"Blessed be the God and Father of our Lord Jesus Christ,* ***who has blessed us*** [His people] *in Christ with every spiritual blessing in the heavenly places, even as* ***he chose us*** [His saving love extends only to His people] *in him before the foundation of the world, that we should be holy and blameless before him.* ***In love he predestined us*** [Ex. 33:19; Rom. 9:15] ***for adoption to himself*** *as sons through Jesus Christ,* ***according to the purpose of his will****, to the praise of his glorious grace, with which* ***he has blessed us*** *in the Beloved. In him we have redemption through his blood,* ***the forgiveness of our trespasses*** [we alone are justified], *according to the riches of his grace,* ***which he lavished upon us****, in all wisdom and insight* ***making known to us*** *the mystery of his will, according to his purpose* [to us alone and to no one else], *which he set forth in Christ as a plan for the fullness of time, to unite all things in him, things in heaven and things on earth. In him* ***we have obtained an inheritance****, having been predestined according to the purpose of him who works all things according to the counsel of his will,* ***so that we who were the first to hope in Christ might be to the praise of his glory****"* (Eph. 1:3-12).

There is nothing to do but to accept His absolute sovereignty with reverence. Whenever we read "in Christ" and "through Christ," let us always understand "in Christ's crucifixion" or "through Christ's crucifixion." Without the Cross, Christ's mission on earth is meaningless. Our focus must be Christ-centered, not primarily on the needs of man (Matt. 6:33). Believers become adopted children of God only through the Cross of Christ and the exclusive choice of His will. Natural man, by his own "free" will, can only choose a god or gods, never the true God, Jesus Christ (John 15:16). Therefore, all man-centered effort to please God, in hope of receiving salvation for good behavior, lead to destruction (Rom. 9:16). When the full number of His people come to God, earthly history will come to an end, including common grace which is the general blessing of the Gentiles. Then God's judgment will come.

THE BLOOD OF CHRIST WAS NOT SHED FOR ALL

Jesus Christ shed His blood only for His Church, for His Israel of God; He did not shed it for everyone: *"...for this is my blood of the covenant,* ***which is poured out for many*** [not for all the people of the world without exception] *for the forgiveness of sins"* (Matt. 26:28). If Jesus Christ had shed His blood for all people without exception, the following verse would be meaningless: *"Pay careful attention to yourselves and to all the flock* [the Church, His body], *in which the Holy Spirit has made you overseers, to care for the church of God,* ***which he obtained with his own blood*** [Christ's blood was shed for the Church alone]*"* (Acts 20:28).

If Jesus Christ shed His blood for all people without exception, why did His blood not redeem those who remain in the domain of the Evil One until death? In this case much of His blood would have been shed for nothing. But the Scriptures clearly teach that not one drop of His blood was shed in vain. It was shed efficaciously only for those who remember it throughout the generations: *"In the same way also he took the cup, after supper, saying, '****This cup is the new covenant*** [made only with His people; Heb. 9:15] ***in my blood*** [which was shed only for the Church of God; Acts 20:28]. *Do this* [only you who are my sheep], *as often as you drink it, in remembrance of me'"* (1 Cor. 11:25).

We could go on for a long time with similar proofs. Did the Lord Jesus enable all perishing men to complete the efficacy of His bloody sacrifice by accepting it? Or did He shed His blood with 100% efficacy only for those whom the Father gave Him, to give them "salvation and faith" with all that goes with it? How do we answer?

CONCLUDING REFLECTIONS

IS THE VALUE OF CHRIST'S DEATH UNLIMITED?

Arminians declare that since God is unlimited, the value of the death, obedience, and suffering of the Lord Jesus Christ must be (1) unlimited, and therefore (2) applicable in its extent to all men without exception.

On the first point, although Scripture is silent on the matter, many but not all Calvinists agree. Those who agree believe that if God had extended grace to absolutely everyone, Jesus Christ would not have had to undergo any greater degree of obedience or suffering, i.e., the sacrifice of the Lord Jesus would have been absolutely sufficient to save every sinner, every man, woman, and child who has ever lived on this planet. So, there is no fundamental disagreement between Calvinists and Arminians on this point.

The fundamental disagreement appears only in the second point. The infinite value of the death of the Lord Jesus Christ, which Scripture neither affirms nor denies by being silent about it, cannot, according to the Calvinist, be a reason for its being equally efficacious for all people without exception—for it is God who handles the redeeming death of the Son of God, according to his own office (not according to human office), and He limits it to the finite number of His elect.

WHO HOLDS THE KEY TO SALVATION?

We will not deal here with the keys of the kingdom of heaven, which, according to Catholic belief, are held by St. Peter (Matt. 16:19), the Pope, etc. That is another chapter.

Regarding the Arminian sequence of salvation, the following illustration comes to mind. Banks and hotels used to have safe deposit boxes in which customers could store valuables and documents. The box required two keys: A general key held by the teller or receptionist, and a personal key given to the customer or guest. First, general key could unlock any box, but it could not open any box. The safe-deposit box would only open if the customer chose to use his second, personal key. The two keys had to be used in sequence, first the General Key and then the Personal Key—both conditions were required for the box to open. This is like the Arminian, Semi-Pelagian, and Pelagian model of causal, conditional salvation. In this model, the sacrifice of Jesus on the Cross is the first condition, the first key by which Jesus Christ on the Cross made it possible for all people to open the gates of heaven. Subsequently, each person must either choose to open heaven with his or her second, personal key, or to keep it closed—he or she must choose to open it. This second key represents a human decision, an act of faith, an enlightenment, a desire, a need, a kind of necessary virtue—an affirmative response to a prevenient grace. The efficacy of God's sacrifice is thus activated and conditioned by this human action.

But the Scriptures teach that there is only one key to heaven and to the lake of fire, and the Sovereign God possesses that key: *"And to the angel of the church in Philadelphia write: 'The words of the holy one, the true one,* ***who has the key of David****, who opens* [the heavens] *and* ***no one will shut****, who shuts* [the lake of fire] ***and no one opens****'"* (Rev. 3:7). The Lord Jesus Christ died, gave His body and shed His blood only for His people; He unlocked the heavens with one key. He did not open the heavens for others. God will not share His absolute sovereignty with anyone; He alone decides who will enter heaven.

14

OBJECTIONS TO EFFICACIOUS REDEMPTION

DID JESUS CHRIST DIE FOR THE WHOLE WORLD?

The Holy Spirit often uses the words "world" and "all" in the New Testament. This seems to prove that Jesus Christ died for the whole world, that is, for all people without exception. So let us look at the first-century historical context that necessitated the use of these words, "world" and "all," in connection with the sacrifice of the Lord Jesus Christ.

WHY DOES SCRIPTURE OFTEN USE THE WORD "WORLD"?

Before the first coming of Jesus Christ, there was an insurmountable spiritual wall between Jews and Gentiles. Everything changed with His crucifixion. The wall between the God-near Jews and the God-far Gentiles was torn down at the Cross (Eph. 2:14-22). God thus established access to His kingdom for all righteous sinners without distinction, both Jews and Gentiles, the whole Israel of God (Gal. 6:15-16). However, the Israel of God, the Church, the ecclesia, has never included and embraced all ethnic Jews without exception, just as it has never included and embraced all Gentiles without exception: *"...through whom* [Jesus Christ] *we have received grace and apostleship to bring about the obedience of faith for the sake of his name among* ***all the nations*** [without distinction]*"* (Rom. 1:5) *"For he himself is our peace,* ***who has made us both*** [near Jews and far Gentiles] *one and has broken down in his flesh the dividing wall of hostility by abolishing the law of commandments expressed in ordinances* [fulfilled and nailed the Mosaic law to the Cross], *that he might create in himself* ***one new man*** [Jew and Gentile] *in place of the two, so making peace, and might* ***reconcile us both to God in one*** [Christ's] ***body through the cross****, thereby killing the hostility. And he came and preached peace to you who were far off* [Gentiles] *and peace to those who were near* [Jews]*"* (Eph. 2:14-17).

The Jews did not like this teaching at all. The Old Covenant Law guaranteed them a special, exclusive position before God that separated them from the world, from all the Gentile nations. They were convinced, as many still are, that they alone had the privilege of knowing the true God and being entitled to salvation. They did not want to share God with anyone in the world—especially not with the Gentiles: *"But when the Jews saw the crowds* [Gentiles], *they were filled with jealousy and* ***began to contradict what was spoken by Paul, reviling him****. And Paul and Barnabas spoke out boldly, saying, 'It was necessary that the word of God be spoken first to you. Since you thrust it aside and* ***judge yourselves unworthy of eternal life****, behold, we are turning to the Gentiles. For so the Lord has commanded us, saying, 'I have made you a light for the Gentiles, that you may bring salvation to the ends of the earth." And when the Gentiles heard this, they began rejoicing and glorifying the word of the Lord,* ***and as many as were appointed to eternal life believed****. And the word of the Lord was spreading throughout the whole region"* (Acts 13:45-49). The Jews were jealous of the

Gentiles, so they tried to prevent Paul from preaching the gospel to them. They were convinced that they and they alone possessed and knew the truth, and that they alone were the elect. Their minds could not accept that the Lord, whom they believed to be their Lord alone, could also be the God of the Gentiles. No wonder they were willing to use violence to maintain their privileged position: *"For you, brothers* [the Thessalonian Christians], *became imitators of the churches of God in Christ Jesus that are in Judea.* ***For you suffered the same things from your own countrymen as they did from the Jews,*** *who killed both the Lord Jesus and the prophets, and drove us out, and displease God* [most Jews] *and oppose all mankind* [without distinction, not without exception] *by hindering us from speaking to the Gentiles that they might be saved—so as always to fill up the measure of their sins. But wrath has come upon them* [the majority of the Jews, not all] *at last!"* (1 Thess. 2:14-16).

The Jews mistakenly believed that salvation was for them and no one else, that they were the only elect. It is as if they had never read in the Torah, the first five books of Moses, that God had appointed Abraham and made him the father of many nations (Gen. 17:5; Rom. 4:17-18), from whom elect would be endowed with the Abrahamic faith. These elect were God's promised children from all eternity (Rom. 9:6-8). The Jews, however, stubbornly insisted on keeping the Sinaitic, Mosaic Law, refusing to have anything to do with the Zionic Law of Christ, even though the Old Testament prophets had clearly foretold it to them: "*...and* ***many peoples shall come, and say****: 'Come, let us go up to the mountain of the Lord, to the house of the God of Jacob* [to the Church, the body of Christ], *that he may teach us his ways and that we may walk in his paths.'* ***For out of Zion shall go forth the law*** [the law of Jesus Christ; 1 Cor. 9:21], *and the word of the Lord from Jerusalem"* (Isa. 2:3).

It was inconceivable to Jews that the Gentile world could be saved outside of the sphere of the Sinaitic Mosaic Law of the Old

Testament. Therefore, the Holy Spirit put the words "world" and "all" into the pen of the New Testament writers' Zionic Christ Law, so that the Jews would realize that they were no longer an exclusive chosen people, that they could be united in Christ with elect from the Gentile world into one promised, spiritual people, the Israel of God (Gal. 6:16), regardless of ethnicity. That explains why the Holy Spirit emphatically demolished this self-centered Jewish prejudice with such phrases as "the whole world," "all nations," "the whole creation," etc.

These hyperbolic phrases were clearly intended to remind the Jews of the prophet Isaiah, who declared that Christ died for many nations, for all people without ethnic or social distinction; that is, He died for all the chosen Jews and for all the chosen Gentiles: *"Give attention to me,* ***my people*** [my chosen ones], *and give ear to me,* ***my nation*** [my chosen ones]; *for a law will go out from me, and* ***I will set my justice for a light to the peoples*** [I will give the right to dwell in my Son to my chosen ones from all the nations of the earth]"(Isa. 51:4).

The Jews did not want to comprehend such words because of their jealousy of the Gentiles (Rom. 10:19-20). They understood very well God's principle of unconditional election. After all, they thought they alone were the chosen people. All Jews had to "do" to be the chosen people was "merely" to be physically born into Jewish ethnicity, by God's will. Likewise, all that a Jew or Gentile must "do" on this side of the Cross to be spiritually chosen is "simply" to be born again of the Spirit—into God's "ethnicity"—and that, too, by God's will. I pray that this understanding of God's election will be embraced by Christians today. Most Jews did not, and still do not, recognize from Scripture that ethnically their people were God's carnal, unbelieving, "chosen" people, with only a small, figurative remnant of "seven thousand" (Rom. 11:4; 1 Kings 19:18) who are spiritually chosen, promised to Christ.

"THE WORLD" DOES NOT USUALLY MEAN "THE WHOLE WORLD"

The term "world" must always be understood in the context of Scripture as a whole. We have already seen several verses in which Christ's sacrifice is attributed only to a certain, limited group of sinners, those who believe, that is, those to whom God has given spiritual sight. The less clear passages of the text must always be interpreted by clear passages that simultaneously describe the same event, principle, or thing. The verses cannot be mutually exclusive. Let us first look at a few verses that Arminian brethren very often argue with. In none of the following verses can the word "world" include all the human souls that have ever walked, are walking, and will walk in this world:

EXAMPLE 1

"The true light [Jesus Christ], *which gives light to everyone,* ***was coming into the world*** [into all the Gentile nations without distinction, not only into ethnic Israel] *"* (John 1:9). The true light, Jesus Christ, does not enlighten all without exception, but all without distinction (Rom. 10:12; Gal. 3:27-29)—those whom He chooses to enlighten; those to whom He chooses to reveal Himself (Matt. 11:27). He enlightens all those whom the Father has given Him throughout the world (John 17:9), whether Jew or Gentile.

EXAMPLE 2

"The next day he saw Jesus coming toward him, and said, 'Behold, the Lamb of God, ***who takes away the sin of the world*** [all the Gentile nations without distinction, not only ethnic Israel]*!'"* (John 1:29). But Jesus Christ did not take away the sins of the whole world, of all the slaves of Satan. If He had literally taken away the sins of all the world, all would have believed in Him, and thus been delivered from the sin of sins, unbelief in Christ (John 16:9). On the Cross,

Jesus Christ justified only those of the world whom the Father gave Him (John 10:29).

EXAMPLE 3

"They said to the woman, 'It is no longer because of what you said that we believe, for we have heard for ourselves, and we know that ***this is indeed the Savior of the world****'"* [not of ethnic Israel only, but of all Gentile nations without distinction, as well]" (John 4:42). *"And we have seen and testify that the Father has sent his Son to be* ***the Savior of the world*** [not of ethnic Israel only, but of all Gentile nations without distinction, as well]" (1 John 4:14). Jesus Christ did not save the whole world; He did not save all the people of the world. There are many reprobates in the world who will die in that state. Had He saved the whole world without exception, in the Arminian sense, He could only have been a small "s" savior, because the efficacy of His "saving" work on the Cross would be continually thwarted by the "free" will of man.

EXAMPLE 4

"...that is, in Christ ***God was reconciling the world to himself*** [not of ethnic Israel only, but of all Gentile nations without distinction, as well], *not counting their trespasses against them* [against His people of the Jews and the Gentiles], *and entrusting to us the message of reconciliation*" (2 Cor. 5:19). Not all men without exception, but only those who have been reconciled through the death of His Son[56] are saved and have eternal life (Rom. 5:10). Again, we see that the defining noun "world" in the previous verse refers to Jewish and Gentile believers.

56 See chapter 13; section: Christ's Redemption Limited in Extent; heading: On the Cross, God was Reconciled only to His People.

EXAMPLE 5

*"He is the propitiation **for our sins*** [the sins of fellow saved Jews], *and not for ours only but also **for the sins of the whole world*** [the sins of those saved out of Gentile nations, without distinction]*"* (1 John 2:2). In this verse, we clearly see that the "sins of the whole world" does not include "our sins"; therefore, the "whole world" here cannot include everyone without exception. Jesus became the atoning sacrifice not only for the elect Jews, but also for the elect of whole world, i.e., all elect Gentiles for whom Abraham is the spiritual father (Gen. 17:5), from all the Gentile nations without distinction, in order to make one new man out of the two, Jew and Gentile, in Christ (Eph. 2:14-17).

"THE WORLD" DOES NOT USUALLY MEAN "ABSOLUTELY EVERYONE"

The term "world" in Scripture is not usually understood to be universal, because it does not include every individual. In fact, in many verses the word "world" refers to a specifically defined group of people:

EXAMPLE 1

*"**The world** cannot hate you* [my brothers], *but it hates me because I testify about it that its works are evil"* (John 7:7). Jesus is talking about two groups of people: First, His brethren, and second, the world. Therefore, "the world" in this verse cannot include everyone; it does not include Jesus' brothers, even though they did not yet believe in Him (John 7:5).

EXAMPLE 2

*"So the Pharisees said to one another, 'You see that you are gaining nothing. Look, **the world** has gone after him'"* (John 12:19). It is clear that most of the nations of the world could not follow Christ as He walked the earth. Most of Europe, Africa, Asia, America,

and Australia had never heard of Him. Therefore, "the world" here cannot mean all mankind, but only those who followed Him. We use similar exaggerations, especially when something revolutionary happens. Did not people say that the whole of Washington, D.C., was at the Lincoln Memorial when Dr. Martin Luther King, Jr. gave his historic "I Have a Dream" speech?

EXAMPLE 3

"First, I thank my God through Jesus Christ ***for all of you*** [all in Christ], *because your faith is proclaimed* ***in all the world*** [the then known world]*"*(Rom. 1:8). "All the world" meant the known world. Neither the Amazon rainforest nor the Bohemian Basin was being preached to in Paul's day, although these areas are certainly part of the world. "For all of you" certainly does not mean for all the people of the world, but only for all of you who belong to Jesus Christ.

EXAMPLE 4

"For I think that God has exhibited us apostles as last of all, like men sentenced to death, because we have become a spectacle ***to the world,*** *to angels, and to men"*(1 Cor. 4:9). In the apostolic times and today, there have been and are myriads of people in the world who have never heard of the apostles. Optimistically speaking, there are at least three to four billion people in the world today who have never heard of the apostles; how could the apostles have been a spectacle to them? But even those ignorant people were part of the world. Again, the world certainly does not include everyone without exception.

EXAMPLE 5

"And I will ask the Father, and he will give you another Helper, to be with you forever, even the Spirit of truth, ***whom the world cannot***

***receive**, because it neither sees him* [does not believe in Him] *nor knows him* [does not love Him]. *You* [who are in Christ] *know him, for he* [the Holy Spirit] *dwells with you and will be in you"* (John 14:16-17). Again and again, "the world" here cannot include absolutely everyone. If it did, then no one could receive the Holy Spirit, no one could be saved, because it clearly says, "The Spirit of truth, whom the world cannot receive, because it neither sees nor knows Him."

EXAMPLE 6

Here are two seemingly "contradictory" verses: (1) *"Behold, the Lamb of God, who **takes away the sin of the world!**"* (John 1:29b); and (2) *"even the Spirit of truth, **whom the world cannot receive**, because it neither sees him nor knows him"* (John 14:17a). How do we reconcile these two verses? Does the word "world" have the same meaning in these two verses? Of course it does not. If we understand "world" here in the universal, Arminian sense of including all men without exception, then in the first verse (John 1:29b) Christ died for all men, and in the second verse (John 14:17a) all men cannot receive the Spirit of truth. If we always understood the word "world" in an all-inclusive sense, we would inevitably come to absurd conclusions. If all mankind (the world) cannot receive the Spirit of truth (John 14:17a), it is because Christ took away the sin of all mankind (the world) (John 1:29b)! When the word "world" is not specific, it must almost always be understood in a limited, particularistic sense. We too say, "The whole world has gone mad," but we exclude ourselves from the world's madness.

When the Bible speaks of Christ's crucifixion for the world, it does not mean that He died for everyone without exception, but that He died for the elect in the many possible pagan nations of the world. Thus, it is clear from Scripture that the term "world" usually, but not always, includes sinful, natural people who are not spiritually baptized into Christ. If Christ came to save the world, it means that He came to save from the whole world the remnant of His Jews and Gentiles, in short, His people from all different nations, from all walks of life, those whom He has loved from all eternity.

EXAMPLE 7

"I am the living bread that came down from heaven. If anyone eats of this bread, he will live forever. And the bread that I will give ***for the life of the world is my flesh*** [here the 'world' is even referred to as those who have life in Christ]*"* (John 6:51). In the context of this verse, the term "world" does not refer to those who are natural and dying in Adam, but just the opposite; it refers to those who have spiritual life in Christ. As we see, depending on the context, the word "world" can also have a completely opposite meaning.

WORLD–TEN MEANINGS

According to John Samson[57], the noun "world," Greek "kosmos," occurs 185 times in the New Testament: 78 times in John, 8 times in Matthew, 3 times in Mark, and 3 times in Luke. Thus, most occurrences are in the Gospel of John. In addition, it occurs 24 times in John's epistles, but only 3 times in Peter's epistles. John's use of the word "world" has ten different meanings in his Gospel:

1. THE ENTIRE UNIVERSE

"He was ***in the world****, and* ***the world*** *was made through him, yet the world did not know him* (John 1:10). *"And now, Father, glorify me in your own presence with the glory that I had with you* ***before the world existed****"* (John 17:5).

57 https://effectualgrace.com/2011/01/21/world-johns-ten-uses-of-the-word/

2. THE PHYSICAL EARTH

"Now before the Feast of the Passover, when Jesus knew that his hour had come ***to depart out of this world*** *to the Father, having loved his own who were in the world, he loved them to the end"* (John 13:1). *"Now there are also many other things that Jesus did. Were every one of them to be written, I suppose that* ***the world itself*** *could not contain the books that would be written"* (John 21:25).

3. THE WORLD SYSTEM

"Now is the ***judgment of this world****; now will* ***the ruler of this world*** *be cast out"* (John 12:31). *"I will no longer talk much with you, for* ***the ruler of this world*** *is coming. He has no claim on me"* (John 14:30). *"...concerning judgment, because* ***the ruler of this world is judged****"* (John 16:11).

4. ALL HUMANITY MINUS BELIEVERS

*"****The world cannot hate you, but it hates me*** *because I testify about it that its works are evil"* (John 7:7). *"****If the world hates you****, know that it has hated me before it hated you"* (John 15:18).

5. A BIG GROUP BUT LESS THAN ALL PEOPLE EVERYWHERE

"So the Pharisees said to one another, 'You see that you are gaining nothing. Look, ***the world has gone after him****'"* (John 12:19).

6. THE ELECT ONLY

"For God did not send his Son into the world to condemn the world, but ***in order that the world might be saved*** *through him"* (John 3:17).

7. THE NON-ELECT ONLY

"I am praying for them. ***I am not praying for the world*** *but for those whom you have given me, for they are yours"* (John 17:9).

8. THE REALM OF MANKIND

*"He was **in the world**, and the world was made through him, **yet the world did not know him**"* (John 1:10).

9. JEWS AND GENTILES (NOT JUST ISRAEL BUT MANY GENTILES TOO)

*"They said to the woman, 'It is no longer because of what you said that we believe, for we have heard for ourselves, and we know that **this is indeed the Savior of the world**'"* (John 4:42).

10. THE GENERAL PUBLIC (AS DISTINGUISHED FROM A PRIVATE GROUP)—NOT THOSE IN SMALL PRIVATE GROUPS

*"So his brothers said to him, 'Leave here and go to Judea, that your disciples also may see the works you are doing. For no one works in secret if he seeks to be known openly. If you do these things, **show yourself to the world**'"* (John 7:3-4).

This selection of verses can be very helpful, especially where tradition and misinterpretation prevail in people's minds that the term "world" includes all people without exception. This is true in some cases, but in most occurrences it is not. Although this tradition is strongly rooted, it cannot stand up to a careful study of Scripture.

FOR GOD SO LOVED THE WORLD

Let us take the most frequently quoted verse in all of Scripture to show the limits of the meaning of the word "world": *"For God so loved the world, that he gave his only Son, that whoever believes in him should not perish but have eternal life"* (John 3:16). A table can help clarify both the Arminian and Calvinistic interpretations of this verse. The two interpretations differ not in emphasis, but in substance. The first, the Arminian interpretation, is man-centered, focusing on man, his benefit, and his salvation. The second is God-centered, focusing on the glory of a holy, sovereign God and His unchanging, decretive will. Read slowly from top to bottom, one column at a time:

	ARMINIAN VIEW	CALVINISTIC VIEW
	Salvation Made Possible	Finished Salvation
For God so loved	God had such unlimited, infinite love and desire for the joy and happiness	In His most sovereign, unconditional love, God chose some out of His supremely holy will and for His own sake,
the world,	of the whole fallen, sin-laden world, of absolutely all human beings without exception, that for their good, out of His mercy and compassion for them	out of the whole perishing, sin-drenched world, out of all nations, not just the Jews, to save for Himself and His glory His chosen, beloved people from all eternity,
that he gave his only Son,	He had His Son crucified to bear the sins of all men without exception, thus enabling every man who has ever lived	by having His Son crucified to bear their sins exclusively, to become their efficacious Savior, thus perfecting their 'salvation and faith;'
that whoever believes in him	to choose by his natural free will, assisted by prevenient grace, the gentle call of the Holy Spirit to believe in Christ crucified, thus enabling God to grant him redemption from the Devil's grasp and to regenerate him by the Holy Spirit,	by His sacrifice on the Cross, He delivered His people from the Devil's prison, raised them from death to life, unconditionally created a new heart in them, so that each one of His redeemed, freed from the Devil's bondage, born of the Holy Spirit, believes in Christ crucified,
should not perish but have eternal life.	that he should not perish but have eternal life.	and thus, he should not perish but have eternal life.

DID JESUS CHRIST DIE FOR ALL?

"ALL" OR "EVERYONE" USUALLY DOES NOT MEAN "ALL" OR "EVERYONE" WITHOUT EXCEPTION

The term "all" or "everyone" must always be understood in its full context, as must the term "world." The verses below in the first six examples seem to teach that Jesus Christ died for absolutely everyone. The seventh example, on the other hand, shows isolated instances where the term "all" includes absolutely every soul. Let us look at them:

EXAMPLE 1

"But we see him who for a little while was made lower than the angels, namely Jesus, crowned with glory and honor because of the suffering of death, so that by the grace of God he might taste death for ***everyone****"* (Heb. 2:9). From the immediately adjacent context, we see again that the term "everyone" does not include every created human soul, for the very next verse defines the term "everyone" as follows: *"For it was fitting that he, for whom and by whom all things exist, in bringing* ***many sons*** [not all without exception] *to glory, should make the founder of their salvation* [the salvation of many sons only] *perfect through suffering"* (Heb. 2:10).

EXAMPLE 2

"The Lord is not slow to fulfill his promise as some count slowness, but is patient toward you, not wishing that any should perish, but that ***all*** [of us] *should reach repentance"* (2 Pet. 3:9). This text, which is most often used by Arminian brethren to argue that it is God's will that all be saved without exception, has already been thoroughly analyzed in chapter 10.[58]

EXAMPLE 3

"...one God and Father ***of all****, who is* ***over all*** *and* ***through all*** *and* ***in all****"* (Eph. 4:6). The context of the Bible clearly teaches that God is the Creator of all, but the Father of only His children (1 John 3:10). The Devil is the father of the world, the father of natural man (John 8:44; 1 John 3:10). The Spirit of God does not

58 See chapter 10; section: God's Will.

dwell in all men, but only in those who are born-again. Here, then, the designation "Father of all" refers only to the category of His children, the citizens of the kingdom of God.

EXAMPLE 4

"And in this way ***all Israel*** [all the elect] *will be saved, as it is written, 'The Deliverer* [the Redeemer of both Jews and Gentiles] *will come from Zion, he will banish ungodliness from Jacob'"* (Rom. 11:26). No Christians, no matter what theology they hold, believe that every ethnic Jew and every Gentile will be saved (universalism). Only one category of people will be saved, that is, only those of God's newly created Israel of Jews and Gentiles will be saved (Gal. 6:15-16). Again, we see that the term "all" is not absolute; it includes all, but only from a certain category, the category of God's people.

EXAMPLE 5

"And they shall not teach, each one his neighbor and each one his brother, saying, 'Know the Lord,' for they shall ***all*** [whom the Father has given Me] *know me, from the least of them to the greatest"* (Heb. 8:11). We cannot conclude from the preceding text that all people who have ever lived, from the least to the greatest, will know the Lord Jesus Christ. Only some people from every nation, family, language, and tribe on earth will know the Savior. All these together make up the special people of God, the special group of people promised by the Father to the Son. This passage shows that the term "all" very often expresses the full number of all those who belong to a particular group, category, set, or class of people.

EXAMPLE 6

"And I, when I am lifted up from the earth, will draw ***all*** [whom the Father has given me] *people to myself"* (John 12:32). Here the interpretation is the same as in the previous example. Jesus was

lifted up from the earth to the Cross. Did He draw all to Himself? Of course not. He drew only His bride, the Church, the ecclesia, those whom He plucked out of the fire like a brand (Zech. 3:2).

EXAMPLE 7

*"**All*** [without exception] *have turned aside; together they have become worthless; no one does good, not even one"* (Rom. 3:12). This verse uses the term "all" in an inclusive, all-encompassing, absolute sense. The exceptions prove the rule. Again, context, context, and more context. We do not have to look far—the last three words of the verse are the key to proper interpretation. If there is no one who does good, then the term "all" must include every person without exception.

"ALL" IN ROMANS 5:18

THE FIRST INTERPRETATION INVOLVES TWO SETS OF MEN:

The term "for all men" occurs 2 times in Rom. 5:18. In the first occurrence it includes a definite group, all who are born of Adam. In the second occurrence it includes another definite group, all who are born of the Holy Spirit: *"Therefore, as one trespass led to condemnation* ***for all men*** [without exception], *so one act of righteousness leads to justification and life* ***for all men*** [without distinction, those for whom Christ died]*"* (Rom. 5:18). In this interpretation, "all" includes everyone in each of the two distinct groups. Adam's one transgression brought condemnation to all men without exception; but Christ's act on the Cross brought justification to all men without distinction. Paul had to tell the Jews, and therefore the Jewish Christians, that God applies the Cross of Christ to all men without distinction; that is, He applies it not only to them, the chosen Jews, but also to all nations, to all social classes, to children, women, men, rich, poor, masters, slaves, etc. If a single act of righteousness brought justification and life to all men without exception, then every man must be saved. This verse does not teach that eternal life and justification are prepared for all in a universal sense. Note that in a verse with multiple occurrences of "for all men," the meanings may or may not be identical.

We see the exact same principle in the following verse, where the term "all" again includes all in each of the two distinct sets: *"For as* ***in Adam all*** [without exception] *die* [the carnal category], *so also* ***in Christ shall all*** [without distinction] *be made alive* [the spiritual category, those born of the Spirit]*"* (1 Cor. 15:22).

THE SECOND INTERPRETATION INVOLVES ONE SET OF MEN:

Since the apostle Paul, himself a Christian, is writing to his brethren in Christ in Rome and Corinth, this is not only possible, but a more acceptable interpretation of Rom 5:18 and similar verses: *"Therefore, as one trespass led to condemnation* ***for all men*** [us, God's people], *so one act of righteousness leads to justification and life* ***for all men*** [us, God's people]*"* (Rom. 5:18). Likewise: *"For as* ***in Adam all*** [even the elect] *die, so also* ***in Christ shall all*** [all the elect] *be made alive"* (1 Cor. 15:22).

In the spirit of this interpretation, then, both occurrences of "all" include the same group of people—Christians, the Church, the Israel of God—but they certainly do not include absolutely everyone without exception.

SUMMARY

For the word "all" we must apply the same principle of interpretation as for the word "world." The words "world," "all," and "everyone," as we have already seen, were intended by the writers of Scripture primarily to help the Jews understand that the Messiah was not theirs alone, but that He belonged to the whole "world," to "all." A new era was dawning for the Israel of God, the Church, the Body of Christ, in which there was no longer a distinction between peoples, between Jews and Greeks; the priesthood had changed, and with it, necessarily, the Law (Heb. 7:12)—the Sinaitic, Mosaic law, which no man could fulfill except the Son of God, Jesus Christ, who was nailed to the Cross (Col. 2:14). The new, Zionic law is Christ Himself (1 Cor. 9:21; Mic. 4:2).

PART IV

IRRESISTIBLE GRACE, EFFICACIOUS CALLING OF THE SPIRIT

15

IRRESISTIBLE GRACE, EFFICACIOUS CALLING OF THE SPIRIT

DEFINITION OF THE TERM

The fourth point of Calvinism, that is, of the Synod of Dort, responds to the fourth article of the Remonstrance. It concerns God's irresistible grace, the efficacious calling of the Holy Spirit. It is inseparably and continuously connected with the previous three points:

1. ***The natural man, the offspring of Adam, is spiritually dead*** *as a result of original sin, separated from God, unable to understand the things of God. Everything man does in this state takes place on the stage of sin. He is a vassal of Satan, a slave to sin, and because of his corrupt nature is unable of his own accord to desire to follow God.*
2. *Therefore, out of inexpressible, amazing goodness, God had mercy on man.* ***God the Father has chosen*** *for Himself and for His own sake His promised people, His Church, whom He loved with an everlasting love from the whole fallen race of*

Adam before the foundation of the world and has set apart for salvation. His election is not based on merit or the "faith" of the natural man; it is based solely on God's sovereign grace.

3. *To fulfill the promises of God, God the Father sent His Son, Jesus Christ, into the world in the flesh. He gave His people to Him so that* ***God the Son could save them****. On the Cross, Jesus Christ took the place of God's chosen people in the judgment. He bore only their sins, not the sins of all mankind. In this way, He redeemed them from the bondage of sin and led the captives out of Satan's prison. God the Son did not make salvation possible for just anyone; He actually saved His entire people!*
4. *In order that God's people might be in obedient union with God, believing that God the Father had chosen them, and God the Son had saved them, God the Son sent a Helper to earth, God the Holy Spirit, who, like God the Son, proceeds from God the Father.* ***God the Holy Spirit has rebirthed, recreated, raised to new life with Christ the full number of God's promised people****. Thus, the Spirit of God has accomplished an unconditional, that is, irresistible grace in which all three persons of the triune God participate. The creative power of the Holy Spirit, the efficacious calling of the Spirit, the rebirth of the new man in Christ, cannot be resisted any more than physical birth can be resisted.*

Let us let the Scriptures speak again so that we may learn what God's triune, perfect cooperation, what irresistible grace, what the efficacious calling of the Spirit means:

1. The Father in Eternity, according to His purpose, has chosen to save those whom He unconditionally loves: *"Blessed be the* ***God and Father*** *of our Lord Jesus Christ, who has blessed us in Christ with every spiritual blessing in the heavenly places, even*

*as he **chose us in him before the foundation of the world,** that we should be holy and blameless before him*" (Eph. 1:3-4).

2. The Son of God on the Cross redeemed all whom the Father had given to Him from the bondage of sin and Satan: "*I* [Christ] *have manifested your name* [Father] *to the people whom you gave me out of the world.* ***Yours they were, and you gave them to me****, and they have kept your word*" (John 17:6).
3. The election of the Father and the redemption by the Son are completed by God's third act of cooperation. This is the rebirth of the Holy Spirit, which makes the Father's election and the Son's redemption efficacious in the history of time and thus necessarily irresistible to every elect and redeemed person: "*That which is born of the flesh is flesh, and* ***that which is born of the Spirit is spirit***" (John 3:6).

For clarity, let us recall both views in the table to see the difference, which again is not in emphasis but in substance:

ARMINIANISM Remonstration	CALVINISM Synod of Dort
4. Resistible Grace God's grace is offered without merit. However, people have the God-given freedom through prevenient grace to resist and reject His offer.	**4. Irresistible Grace** The grace that God unconditionally gives to His people cannot be refused, cannot be resisted, because it is not a matter of accepting an ordinary offer but of the Holy Spirit creating a new inner man who lives his new life in Christ irresistibly.

The resistible prevenient grace of Arminianism is abysmal when contrasted with the irresistible grace of Calvinism. Arminianism has a disjointed chaos in its understanding of God's triune cooperation, or, more precisely without exaggeration, an incoherence.

According to Arminianism, the Father only chooses those whom He knew (in advance) would believe, even though His desire was then, and remains, that everyone should believe. The Son paid the ransom for all men without exception, including those whom the Father knew would not believe! Thus, the efficacy of the Spirit's prevenient grace is nebulous. It is not clear whether He persuades all equally convincingly or persuades only those whom He knows will believe. Arminian soteriology is unclear about whether He persuades those who have never heard and never will hear the gospel. It is unclear whether, by His prevenient grace, the Holy Spirit convinces those who were already in hell when Jesus Christ died for them! In any case, the Spirit cannot regenerate without exception all those for whom Christ paid the ransom. It is as if the right hand of God does not know what the left hand is doing. Arminian salvation, then, depends solely on the "free" will (arbitrary willfulness) of fallen man.

THE NEW CREATION CANNOT RESIST GOD

THE HOLY SPIRIT COMPLETES THE COOPERATION OF THE TRIUNE GOD

Let us examine more closely the efficacious calling of the Spirit. Each person of the Triune God—Father, Son, and Holy Spirit—has a specific role in each area of God's work. Scripture shows that every purpose of the Father is perfectly carried out by the Son, and that the Son's work is mediated by the Holy Spirit: *"...according to* ***the foreknowledge of God the Father*** [The Father loved them and chose them], *in* ***the sanctification of the Spirit*** [they are born irresistibly of the Spirit and are 'saved and believe,' i.e., the first resurrection], ***for obedience to Jesus Christ and for sprinkling with his blood*** [Christ shed his blood for them alone, baptizing them, immersing them in Himself by the Holy Spirit; Matt. 3:11b]*: May grace and peace be multiplied to you"* (1 Pet. 1:2). Notice the timeless logic of the preceding verse. The Father has sought out and chosen His Church, the Holy Spirit has sanctified it, that is regenerated it, so that it might see Christ, believe in the finished sacrifice of His blood that has justified and redeemed it from Satan's bondage to sin, and then obediently surrenders to Him. In Calvinistic soteriology, "salvation and faith" are an indivisible, timeless gift, a timeless integrity of being—born-again, justified, sanctified and bodily resurrected[59]. Salvation does not precede faith, and faith does not precede salvation. We believe because we are saved, and we are saved because we believe.

That, in a nutshell, is irresistible grace, the efficacious calling of the Spirit. This is God's unilateral, monergistic creation of the Church, His people (Isa. 66:8). When God works, He always works in interoperation according to the office of His Trinity. None of the three Persons can stand outside the accomplishment of any of God's purposes. Each Person of Triune God always accomplishes His mission perfectly. What pleases God, He will perform with absolute consistency (Isa. 46:10). So it must be, and so it is, when it comes to the salvation of His elect.

In Arminian soteriology, on the other hand, God's prevenient grace is resistible because the death of Jesus Christ did not save anyone but made salvation possible for all. In this system, salvation is preceded by temporal causality: When a person believes (through prevenient grace, which can be resisted as a result of "free" will), only then can the Spirit of God save that person, i.e., regenerate him or her. This explains why some Arminians do not believe faith is a gift, since through faith believers receive the gift of salvation.

IRRESISTIBLE GRACE IS GOD'S CREATIVE ACT

The good news, the gospel, cannot and does not invite God and salvation to those who have not heard it (Rom. 2:12; 10:13-14), but it does invite all who hear it, making no distinction between those who are elect and those who are not. It promises salvation

59 See chapter 3; section: "Salvation and Faith" According to the Reformation.

to all who repent and believe. This universal, external invitation of the gospel is rejected by every natural man[60] without exception, because he cannot and will not submit to the law of God (Rom. 8:7). In contrast, God's saving grace, the inward calling—circumcision of the heart—of the promised, is produced by the Holy Spirit only in those who have been chosen by the Father and redeemed by the Son (Rom. 9:23-24).

The special inward calling, rebirth of the Holy Spirit, is a divine decree which, by its very definition of creation, is always 100% efficacious; it cannot be resisted. That someone might refuse the new birth is as absurd as it would be for someone to refuse his own physical birth. A person who has not yet been created, either physically or spiritually, cannot exercise any will.

Only God, by His creative sovereign power and absolute will, creates both physical life—uniting the body with the inner man—and spiritual life—uniting the inner man with the Spirit of God. The non-existent or the dead cannot wish to be or not to be. The clay cannot negotiate with the potter as to what kind of vessel he should make of it (Rom. 9:20-21). The Creator alone is active in the creation of anyone or anything new. True salvation is not some kind of repair of the old inner man.

The old inner man is spiritually dead, so he must be recreated "out of the broken skeleton" as Ezekiel described in chapter 37: *"Then he said to me, 'Prophesy over these bones, and say to them, O dry bones, hear the word of the Lord. Thus says the Lord God to these bones: Behold,* ***I will cause breath to enter you, and you shall live****. And I will lay sinews upon you, and will cause flesh to come upon you, and cover you with skin, and put breath in you, and you shall live, and you shall know that I am the Lord'"* (Ezek. 37:4-6). At this point, as has happened to me many times, some will argue that Ezekiel is speaking here of the general salvation of the Jews during

60 See chapter 8; section: Chosen Wedding Guests.

the Great Tribulation, not of the Church. We cannot agree with this. Let us always remember that the Old Testament represents the physical foreshadowing of Christ; the New Testament represents the spiritual reality, that is, Christ Himself. Therefore, Ezek. 37:4-14 refers to the Church, a new man made up of Jews and Gentiles, the body of Jesus Christ. Let Moses be our argument. The Lord offered salvation through Moses' mouth to ethnic Israel only, on the condition of obedience and perfect keeping of His covenant: *"'Now therefore,* ***if you will indeed obey my voice and keep my covenant*** [the Old, Sinaitic Covenant], *you shall be my treasured possession among all peoples, for all the earth is mine; and* ***you shall be to me a kingdom of priests and a holy nation****.' These are the words that you shall speak* [Moses] *to the people of Israel"* (Ex. 19:5-6). The Lord here conditions Israel's salvation on obedience, which no natural man can keep[61]. None of the Jews or Gentiles could or can obey God 100%; none of them except the true God and true man, the Lord Jesus Christ, has been able to keep the covenant. He did not come to abolish the Old Covenant or the Law or the Prophets, but to fulfill them (Matt. 5:17). He alone obeyed the Father in everything and kept the Law in everything. And so, every born-again person whom Christ has baptized (immersed) into Himself by the Holy Spirit, sealed by the Holy Spirit in Christ, is positionally now doing all that Christ does—by dwelling in Christ: ***"For if we have been united with him in a death like his, we shall certainly be united with him in a resurrection like his.*** *We know that our old self was crucified with him in order that the body of sin might be brought to nothing, so that we would no longer be enslaved to sin"* (Rom. 6:5-6). All that Christ fulfilled is positionally fulfilled for anyone who spiritually dwells in Him, even though he is totally unable to keep the whole law in the flesh. Let us again recall our familiar illustration: When a car is going 100

61 See chapter 3; section: The Inability of the Natural Man.

miles an hour, if we are in it, we are also going 100 miles an hour, even though we are totally incapable of running that fast in the flesh. The condition that the Lord imposed on the Jews, the Israel of God (Gal. 6:15-16)—on the whole commonwealth of Israel, both Jew and Gentile (Eph. 2:12)—Christ fulfilled for His chosen people, Jew and Gentile alike. Therefore, it is because of His work, not our works, that God can declare today: "Not that you *should be* to Me a kingdom of priests and a holy nation, but you *are* a chosen race, a royal priesthood, a holy nation." Thus, Ezek. 37:4-14 refers to the whole Church, the whole Israel of God: ***"But you are a chosen race, a royal priesthood, a holy nation, a people for his own possession*** [you are His slaves, owned by Him], *that you may proclaim the excellencies of him who called you out of* [Satan's] *darkness into his* [Christ's] *marvelous light"* (1 Pet. 2:9).

Without the new birth, without the new creation, no one can see the kingdom of God (John 3:3). Paul was essentially telling the Corinthian believers the same thing: *"Therefore, if anyone is in Christ, he is a new creation* [God has created a new spirit in His promised ones, a new heart that already communicates with the Spirit of God]. ***The old has passed away; behold, the new has come. All this is from God,*** *who through Christ reconciled us to himself and gave us the ministry of reconciliation"* (2 Cor. 5:17:18). God declares His absolutely sovereign will, His unconditional decree, that He Himself will give a new heart to His people, whom He has loved with redemptive love from eternity, taking out their heart of stone and putting in a new heart of flesh (Ezek. 36:26). His people are made new by God's irresistible grace, by His efficacious calling. God has created for Himself and for His Glory a noble, royal, priestly, holy nation; a nation that belongs to God, adopted by Him, redeemed by the blood of Christ and brought out of the darkness of Satan into the marvelous light of Christ to proclaim the mighty works of God in salvation (1 Peter 2:9). After all, the Old

Testament prophet Isaiah prophesied of God's irresistible grace, His creative work: "*...**the people whom I formed*** [in Christ] *for myself that they might declare my praise* [the Church; the Jews did not and do not evangelize the Gentiles]"(Isa. 43:21).

PAUL'S IRRESISTIBLE PARDON AND EFFICACIOUS CALLING

The way in which God spiritually recreated the sinful Saul of Tarsus, Satan's slave, to dwell in Christ can be applied to every promised soul. Saul did not seek Christ, he did not long for Him; on the contrary, he pursued Him. He was on his way to Damascus to destroy those who had believed and were following Christ. Without warning, a light and a voice from heaven intervened in Saul's life (Acts 9:1-22). Saul was paralyzed, blinded, overwhelmed, and terrified. None of his companions was able to speak. It was God's eternal ordinance, God's decree, God's irresistible grace that called Paul with 100% efficacy to preach the Cross of Christ to the Gentiles: *"But when he who had set me apart* [chose me] *before I was born, and who called me by his grace* [by sovereign and unconditional saving love], ***was pleased to reveal his Son to me****, in order that I might preach him among the Gentiles, I did not immediately consult with anyone* [whether I would 'freely' consider His calling and then accept or reject it]"(Gal. 1:15-16).

God chose Paul for a predetermined purpose before he was born. In the same way, He sets apart each of His promised ones in the womb, according to His sovereign, holy purpose: *"Before I formed you in the womb I knew you* [loved you with saving love], *and before you were born I consecrated you;* ***I appointed you a prophet to the nations****"*(Jer. 1:5). Every elect, promised soul has been endowed by God with irresistible grace, "salvation and faith," an efficacious calling by the Holy Spirit, from the ages, before the foundation of the universe; it happens not by the determination of his own sinful will, but by the predetermination of the holy, sovereign will of God: "*...who saved us and called us to a holy calling,* ***not because of our works but because of his own purpose and grace****, which he gave us in Christ Jesus before the ages began* [before the creation of the world]" (2 Tim. 1:9).

Again and again, we see that the sovereign God alone, from eternity, decides upon whom He has mercy (Ex. 33:19), whom He loves with an eternal redeeming love, and whom He passes over. That Saul became the apostle Paul was not Paul's choice, but God's choice, i.e., God's irresistible grace, the efficacious calling of the Spirit. Spiritual rebirth does not come from the enslaved will of man—see the archetype of Ishmael—but from the sovereign, free will of God—see the archetype of Isaac. If it had been up to man—if he had consulted his own flesh and blood regarding what to do with the Cross of Christ—no one in the world would have walked in God's way; all would have gone astray (Ps. 58:4).

NOT ONLY SPIRITUAL BUT ALSO PHYSICAL RESURRECTION IS IRRESISTIBLE

A most apt foreshadowing of irresistible grace, of the Spirit's efficacious calling, is the physical revival of Lazarus' dead body. Lazarus could neither resist nor choose his physical resurrection, because he was dead: "*Then Jesus, deeply moved again, came to the tomb. It was a cave, and a stone lay against it. Jesus said, 'Take away the stone.' Martha, the sister of the dead man, said to—him, 'Lord, by this time there will be an odor, for he has been dead four days.' Jesus said to her, 'Did I not tell you that if you believed you would see the glory of God?' So they took away the stone. And Jesus lifted up his eyes and said, 'Father, I thank you that you have heard me. I knew that you always hear me, but I said this on account of the people standing around, that they may believe that you sent me.' When he had said these things, he cried out with a loud voice, '***Lazarus, come out***.' The man who had* *died came out, his hands and feet bound with linen strips, and his face wrapped with a cloth. Jesus said to them, 'Unbind him, and let him go.' Many of the Jews therefore, who had come with Mary and had seen what he did, believed in him, but some of them went to the Pharisees and told them what Jesus had done* [the self-righteous will not believe even if they witness the resurrection; Luke 16:27-31]" (John 11:38-46). The body of Lazarus lay in the tomb, and the only thing that hung over it was the stench, just as spiritual decay is the stench of every natural man[62]. Only God's supernatural intervention could change this hopeless situation. Only when Lazarus was revived did he begin to show signs of life. He began to hear, see, and walk. Was Lazarus brought back to life against his will? Could the dead Lazarus have resisted God's creative, life-giving action if he had no active will? Does the newborn baby protest that he was born against his will—that no one asked him? Of course not! He is viable; he has an innate, God-created will to live.

It is similar with those newborn of the Spirit. Just as no one can resist his conception and physical birth, so no one can resist his spiritual birth. The spiritual newborn is endowed with a God-created, true free will that already longs for Christ (John 8:36): *"But what does the Scripture say? 'Cast out the slave woman and her son* [Ishmael], *for the son of the slave woman* [Hagar] *shall not inherit with the son* [Isaac] *of the free woman* [Sarah]. *'So, brothers, we are not children of the slave* [of Satan] *but of the free woman* [of God]. ***For freedom Christ has set us free;"*** (Gal. 4:30-5:1a). The spiritually resurrected man manifests spiritual activity through faith, through spiritual sight and hearing, following his Shepherd, obeying Him and doing His will. Both physical birth and spiritual rebirth are God's creation of the new man, a unique, monergistic, creative expression of God's sovereign, decretive will in sanctification.

62 See chapter 4; THE TOTAL SPIRITUAL INABILITY, THE CORRUPTION OF MAN

CHRIST IS THE IRRESISTIBLE BRIDEGROOM

Christ is the perfect Bridegroom of His bride, His chosen people, His Church, His ecclesia. His perfection lies in His total irresistibility—such a Bridegroom cannot be rejected. If His bride did not love Him, His people would not be faithful; He would become a reprobate suitor and cease to be God.

Where did the pagans of the world get their fairy tales, legends, and fables? The allegorical, even apocalyptic language of pagan tales and fables often originates in distorted truth. As a child, I listened with bated breath to variations of the same story—how a prince rescued his beloved princess from the prison of the seven-headed dragon, where she was imprisoned, deprived of her freedom. The prince won her and set her free so that he could enjoy her as a bridegroom enjoys his beloved bride, so that she too would love him faithfully and stand by him. And they lived happily ever after. The resemblance of pagan stories to divine revelation is certainly not accidental.

The Lord Jesus Christ is the Prince, King, Wonderful Counselor, Mighty God, Everlasting Father, Prince of Peace, the Bridegroom who fought for His bride, the Church, and overcame the seven-headed dragon (Rev. 12:3), the Evil One, Satan. He chained him up and plundered his dragon's lair (Matt. 12:29; Mark 3:27; Isa. 49:24-25), snatched and freed His Bride, His Church. He redeemed His people for Himself by a fierce battle on the Cross, plucking them like a brand from the fire (Zech. 3:2). All of heaven was involved in this spiritual battle on the Cross, including God's first servant, the archangel Michael: *"Now war arose in heaven, Michael and his angels fighting against the dragon.* ***And the dragon and his angels fought back, but he was defeated, and there was no longer any place for them in heaven.*** *And the great dragon was thrown down, that ancient serpent, who is called the devil and Satan, the deceiver of the whole world—he was thrown down to* *the earth, and his angels were thrown down with him* [bound for a figurative 1000 years so that he could not deceive God's people; Rev. 20:1-3]. *And I heard a loud voice in heaven, saying, '**Now the salvation and the power and the kingdom of our God and the authority of his Christ have come*** [Christ reigns with his redeemed people for a figurative 1000 years, today, between His two advents; Eph. 2:6], *for the accuser of our brothers* [Christ's bride, God's people] *has been thrown down, who accuses them day and night before our God. And they have conquered him **by the blood of the Lamb and by the word of their testimony*** [Matt. 28:19], *for they loved not their lives even unto death'"* (Rev. 12:7-11).

RESURRECTION IS IRRESISTIBLE

JESUS TEACHES TWO KINDS OF RESURRECTION

The Lord Jesus Christ explained two kinds of resurrection in the 5th chapter of the Gospel of John. When the Scriptures mention the resurrection, we must always keep His interpretation in our hearts and minds. Any resurrection concerning a person necessarily belongs to either the spiritual or the physical category. The Lord Jesus clearly speaks of a twofold resurrection in John 5:24-29:

THE FIRST IS THE SPIRITUAL RESURRECTION

According to Jesus it concerns only God's people: *"Truly, truly, I say to you, whoever hears my word and believes him who sent me has eternal life. He does not come into judgment, but has passed from death to life. 'Truly, truly, I say to you, an hour is coming, **and is now here**, when the dead* [spiritually dead] *will hear the voice* [only His sheep hear His voice and follow Him; John 10:27] *of the Son of God, and those who hear will live* [the first resurrection, the new birth, is spiritual and is already taking place between the two advents of Christ]. *For as the Father has life in himself, so he has granted the Son also to have life in himself'"* (John 5:24-26).

THE SECOND IS THE BODILY RESURRECTION

According to Jesus it applies to all without exception: *"And he has given him* [Jesus Christ] *authority to execute judgment, because he is the Son of Man. Do not marvel at this,* ***for an hour is coming*** [when He returns to earth as Judge] *when all who are in the tombs will hear his voice and come out, those who have done good to the resurrection of life, and those who have done evil to the resurrection of judgment* [the general bodily resurrection of both the saved and the reprobate will take place at the second Advent of Christ; Dan. 12:2-3]" (John 5:27-29).

DEDUCTION

1. Those who have been spiritually raised, that is, **those who have been born twice**, the first time bodily of Adam and the second time of the Spirit (John 3:6-7), will be bodily raised on the last day in a glorified body to eternal life with Christ; **they will die only once, bodily**.
2. Those who have not been raised spiritually, **those who have been born only once**, bodily of Adam, will also be raised bodily on the last day; but **they will die twice, the first time bodily and the second time spiritually** to eternal damnation and condemnation in the lake of fire, far from Christ (2 Thess. 1:8-9).

Both the first, spiritual, and the second, bodily, resurrection are the monergistic, one-sided work of the Creator. No one can resurrect himself! The first, the spiritual resurrection, the bestowal of "salvation and faith," is through irresistible grace; it is the efficacious calling of the Holy Spirit, and it is the heart of Calvinism's 4th point.

THE FIRST MAN–ADAM; THE LAST ADAM–JESUS CHRIST

"Thus it is written, 'The first man Adam became a living being [natural man]*'; the last Adam* [Jesus Christ] *became a life-giving* [irresistibly baptizing from spiritual death to spiritual life] *spirit* [the Son and the Spirit with the Father is the triune God]. *But it is not the spiritual that is first but the natural, and then the spiritual* [efficacious calling, i.e., birth of the Spirit]. *The first man was from the earth, a man of dust; the second man is from heaven" (1 Cor.15:45-47).* In these verses, the last Adam, the Son of Man, the Son of God, Jesus Christ, is identified with the quickening Spirit, one of many obvious proofs that the Father, Son, and Holy Spirit are one triune God. Adam was the first man, the representative of all fleshly, natural humanity. Christ is the last Adam, the representative by whose Spirit all whom the Father gave Him are spiritually born-again (John 3:6-7). These are those who are spiritually resurrected, "saved and believing" in history between the two advents of Christ, and are ushered into the heavenly throne to reign with Christ[63] during the figurative 1,000 years; i.e., the first resurrection (Eph. 2:6; 1 Cor. 15:47b).

The sinless Christ was identified with sin (2 Cor. 5:21), in a body like that of a sinful man, that He might take the place of His people in judgment (Rom. 8:3), so that by His death He might save all who are of His flock: ***"For if, because of one man's*** [Adam's] *trespass, death reigned through that one man* [through Adam], *much more will those who receive the abundance of grace and the free gift of righteousness reign in life* ***through the one man Jesus Christ"*** (Rom. 5:17). In Adam, all died physically and spiritually. Just as through one man sin entered the world—the wages were the physical and spiritual death of all (Rom. 6:23)—so through Jesus Christ,

63 See SUPPLEMENTS; I. EVANGELIZATION IN THE REFORMED CONCEPT; section: Generally About Evangelization; heading: God's People Evangelize—Reign with Christ.

the Son of God (Heb. 10:29; 1 John 5:12), the Son of Man (Gen. 3:15; Rom. 8:3; John 12:23), the gift of resurrection has come to all who are His: *"For as by a man came death, by a man has come also the resurrection of the dead.* ***For as in Adam all die*** [physically and spiritually], ***so also in Christ shall all*** [all for whom Christ died] ***be made alive*** [spiritually in the first resurrection; physically on the last day in the second resurrection]*"* (1 Cor. 15:21-22).

If death had not entered the world through one man, Adam, salvation could not have been accomplished through one man, the second Adam, the sinless Son of Man, the Lord Jesus. With this causal dependence falls any notion that God creates through evolution. Adam was unique, the first man created, and he certainly had no common ancestry with the apes (Luke 3:38). Theistic evolution, in whatever form it is accepted, seeks to please the world by burying the saving gospel of Jesus Christ and relegating the biblical doctrine of salvation (and the authority of Scripture) to the realm of human speculation and fable. Humanistic Christians who buy into theistic evolution are believing in another gospel that lacks power to save anyone (Gal. 1:9-12). If we accept the assumption of theistic evolution that death was before Adam, then we must negate the preceding couplet (1 Cor. 15:21-22). The result is sheer absurdity and the consequences are damnation, not salvation: "For as by a man came 'NO' death [if any evolution holds], by 'NO' man has come also the resurrection of the dead. For as in Adam 'NOBODY' dies [because 'Adam' dies in a primordial protein], so also in Christ shall 'NOBODY' be made alive [because nobody dies in 'Adam,' but in a primordial protein]" (This would negate 1 Cor. 15:21-22).

Both the spiritual and physical death of all in Adam and irresistible grace, the efficacious calling by the Spirit, for all who are in Christ seem unjust from a humanistic point of view—why are all men sinful and subject to death because of the one sin of their ancestor Adam? Similarly, why would God consider many sinners sinless simply because He chose them, adopted them, through the atoning death of His Son? And yet in their natural state, His promised children were unworthy (Rom. 10:20).

God created all-natural mankind from Adam. Therefore, all humanity is in Adam, his representative, and thus is an indivisible whole, a group, in which all are born naturally fallen and sinful. Likewise, all the promised, spiritual people in Christ, in His Representative, are likewise one indivisible whole, one group, in which all who are born-again of the Spirit of God are efficaciously, unconditionally, monergistically, without merit, irresistibly "saved and believing."

THE FIRST, SPIRITUAL RESURRECTION OF THE PEOPLE OF GOD

In John 5:24-26, the Lord Jesus speaks of salvation, that is, the first, spiritual resurrection, which God is doing in these days between the two appearances of Christ. Whoever believes in the word he has heard has eternal life at this very moment. Although he was dead, he has already passed from death to life. To make this clear, Jesus emphasizes in verse 25: *"Truly, truly, I say to you, an hour is coming,* ***and is now here, when the dead*** *will hear the voice of the Son of God, and those who hear will live"* (John 5:25). That is, they will pass from death to life, they will be raised. These are His sheep, the people who already hear (John 10:27); their state of death and their resurrection, therefore, must have to do with the spiritual and not the physical side of their being. The first resurrection concerns only those spiritually dead and physically alive sinners whom the Father has chosen and the Son has redeemed. This miracle happens around us every day. Spiritual resurrection forms a new human spirit united with the Spirit of God, and it is an integral part of the "salvation and faith" that culminates in the glorification, that is, the bodily resurrection of all who are in Christ. Jesus Christ secured the resurrection of His own by His sacrifice on the Cross; to Martha He said: *"I am the resurrection and the life. Whoever believes in me, though he die* [bodily], *yet shall he live* [eternally spiritually and bodily after the resurrection of the body]*"* (John 11:25).

God's people died with Christ on the Cross. When His chosen people, the Church, shared in His death, they also shared in His resurrection. The old man died with Christ; a new man was born of the Spirit, a new man who was created in Christ. This is the first resurrection, the spiritual resurrection: *"And you were dead* [spiritually] *in the trespasses and sins"* (Eph. 2:1). *"even when we were dead* [spiritually] *in our trespasses,* ***made us alive*** [spiritually raised, made alive, i.e., the first resurrection] ***together with Christ****—by grace you have been saved—****and raised us up with him*** [translated us from spiritual death to spiritual life] ***and seated us with him in the heavenly places*** *in Christ Jesus"* [God's people are now reigning with Christ, they are His ambassadors on earth]*"* (Eph. 2:5-6).

Jesus is the resurrection and the life. In Him His elect, His ecclesia, share in the first resurrection and eternal life. They are united with God, no longer living for themselves, no longer living for sin, but living for God, ripening for eternity: *"We know that Christ, being raised from the dead, will never die again; death no longer has dominion over him. For the death he died he died to sin, once for all* [His one sacrifice removed the sin He bore for His people], *but the life he lives he lives to God* [I and the Father are one]. ***So you also must consider yourselves dead to sin*** [separated from sin] *and alive to God in Christ Jesus* [sealed by the Spirit]*"* (Rom. 6:9-11). Therefore, the second, spiritual death, the lake of fire, no longer has a claim on God's people who have been spiritually raised: *"This is the first resurrection* [salvation and faith]. ***Blessed and holy is the one who shares in the first resurrection*** [who is born of the Spirit]*!* ***Over such the second death*** [the lake of fire] ***has no***

***power**, but they will be priests of God and of Christ* [1 Pet. 2:9], *and they will reign with him for a thousand years"*[64] (Rev.20:5b-6).

SPIRITUAL RESURRECTION, BAPTISM IN CHRIST IS IRRESISTIBLE

The first, spiritual resurrection, the baptism into Christ, this irresistible, creative act of God, is called in Scripture the new birth (John 3:3), and the new birth is not conditioned by the will of the natural man. This is precisely what the Lord Jesus Christ explains to Nicodemus, the teacher of Israel; he will not enter the kingdom of God, eternal life, unless he is born-again, unless the old man is first raised from natural, corrupt, and unable[65] condition of utter spiritual death into a new man: *"Truly, truly, I say to you,* ***unless one is born again*** [spiritually raised, immersed in Christ] *he cannot see the kingdom of God"* (John 3:3b). To this Nicodemus replied: *"How can a man be born when he is old? Can he enter a second time into his mother's womb and be born?"* (John 3:4b). Nicodemus understood that a man who does not exist cannot actively initiate his own physical birth: *"For you* [God] *formed my inward parts; you knitted me together in my mother's womb"* (Ps. 139:13). Jesus reiterated and specified his demand, which Nicodemus could never meet:[66] *"Truly, truly, I say to you,* ***unless one is born of water and the Spirit****, he cannot enter the kingdom of God"* (John 3:5b).

If the knitting of the carnal man in the mother's womb (Ps. 139:13) is the exclusive, monergistic work of God, how much more must this be true when the Spirit of God circumcises the heart of natural man to bring forth the new, spiritual man! The text "unless one is born of water" is not clear; it can have at least three interpretations. In none of them does being born of water

64 See SUPPLEMENT; I. section: Generally, About Evangelism; heading: God's People—Reigning with Christ.

65 See chapter 4

66 See chapter 3; section: The Inability of the Natural Man; heading: Scripture Demands what the Natural Man Cannot Do.

mean that we must be baptized in water to be saved. Water baptism is but a physical illustration of the spiritual baptism that truly saves (1 Pet. 3:21), that is, being baptized into Christ, to be in Christ, to be drenched by Him, to be inundated by Him, to be marinated in Him, to taste as He does, to die with Him and be raised with Him. It is simply to be sealed in Christ by the Holy Spirit (Eph. 1:13) and thus to do without ceasing what He does in us.

When eight of Noah's family found refuge in the ark, they were saved from certain destruction. The ark was a physical representation of Christ. Those who were inside were saved; those who remained outside were destroyed in the waters of the flood. Those whom God places in Christ through the Holy Spirit are safe from the coming judgment on the Day of the Lord. At the second coming of the Lord Jesus Christ, the age of grace will end. Then no one can be saved, for "the door of the ark will be slammed"; the day of judgment will come. To be kept in Christ, to be hidden in Him, is the true baptism that saves us: ***"Baptism*** [being immersed in Christ], *which corresponds to this* [the eight saved in the ark], *now saves you* [we are saved by being baptized into Christ, not into water], *not as a removal of dirt from the body* [as in being bodily immersed in water] ***but as an appeal to God for a good conscience****, through the resurrection of Jesus Christ"* (1 Pet. 3:21). Without an outward confession and commitment based on the resurrection of Jesus Christ, the baptismal font would be a mere tub of water that would only wash away our physical filth, not our inner filth. This is not to diminish the importance of water baptism and the table of bread and the fruit of the vine as a memorial of His crucified body and shed blood; after all, baptism and communion are His commands! Anyone who confesses Jesus Christ, who is truly in Him, should obey the command of the Lord and not delay water baptism! But saving spiritual baptism, immersion in Christ, is an inescapable and irresistible necessity that precedes water baptism—

a sign of confession as to whom we belong. The baptism that saves us, which is certainly not removing the filth of the flesh with water, is like a holy "sandwich"—God the Holy Spirit in us and us in God the Son. In this sonship we are so secure and blissful: *"You shall suck the milk of nations; you shall nurse at the breast of kings* [His children feed on God]*; and you shall know that I, the Lord, am your Savior and your Redeemer, the Mighty One of Jacob"* (Isa. 60:16).

God created His children for His holy arms, not only to show His love and mercy, but to glorify Himself, so that the whole being of God's people, every thought, every action, would glorify His holiness. Christians are born-again, immersed in Christ, not because of their own choice, but by God's choosing: *"**Of his own will*** [not of our will] *he brought us forth by the word of truth, that we should be a kind of firstfruits of his creatures* [God's creative activity cannot be resisted]*"* (James 1:18). If the Holy Spirit gave birth to someone only after receiving their permission, then His grace would be resistible. God does not wait for our consent—He would not get it; He is the Lord of life and death.

GOD IRRESISTIBLY SPIRITUALLY RESURRECTS HIS PROMISED ONES

The following text does not refer only to Old Testament Jerusalem or Israel. It describes in general the spiritual condition and incapacity of every natural man who has been born only once, that is, in the flesh. It is one of the most impressive pictures of God's irresistible saving grace, His decreed will, His efficacious call to eternal life, which natural, spiritually dead children of the Evil One cannot resist: *"And as for your birth* [daughter of Jerusalem], *on the day you were born* [of Adam] ***your cord was not cut*** [by which you feed on the Evil One], *nor were you washed with water to cleanse you, nor rubbed with salt, nor wrapped in swaddling cloths* [a picture of utter spiritual corruption and uncleanness]. *No eye pitied you, to do any of these things to you out of compassion for you, but you* *were cast out on the open field, for you were abhorred* [the natural man has not a single quality by which he pleases God], *on the day that you were born. "'**And when I passed by you and saw you wallowing in your blood*** [you were bleeding to death], ***I said to you in your blood, 'Live!' I said to you in your blood, 'Live!'"*** (Ezek. 16:4-6). Twice the Lord repeats: "I said to you in your blood, 'Live!'" Can anyone describe the condition of the natural man and his deliverance from the deadly grip of Satan better than God Himself? This is irresistible grace, the efficacious calling of the elect by the Spirit par excellence. The one who understands this and experiences the Spirit in his heart has an irresistible, God-implanted "salvation and faith." He has been chosen! He has also settled once and for all the questions of Calvinism vs. Arminianism, Monergism vs. Synergism, and Reformation vs. Catholicism.

The natural man is lost, self-centered, and therefore unwilling and unable to submit to the law of God (Rom. 8:7). No one will ever repent of his own will, no one will turn to the true God of his own accord unless it is given to him from above: *"And when he* [Apollos] *wished to cross to Achaia, the brothers encouraged him and wrote to the disciples to welcome him. When he arrived, he greatly helped **those who through*** [God's] ***grace had believed*** [saw Christ irresistibly]" (Acts 18:27). Notice the text above. Apollos benefited all to whom he witnessed. His hearers did not philosophize. They did not consult flesh and blood as to whether it was right to believe in Christ, but they believed by God's irresistible grace and power. The following text goes on to show in an amazing way that the first, spiritual resurrection of God's people, the efficacious calling of the Spirit, "salvation and faith," are irresistible; no one can resist God's decreed will: *"For as the Father raises the dead and gives them life, **so also the Son gives life to whom he will*** [to whom the Father has given Him]" (John 5:21). Again and again we are assured that the

Creator of the first, spiritual resurrection, the new birth, "salvation and faith," is the Triune God alone: *"But to all* [the promised and elect] *who did receive him* [Christ], *who believed in his name, he gave the right to become children of God,* ***who were born, not of blood nor of the will of the flesh nor of the will of man, but of God*** [God's irresistible will]*"* (John 1:12-13).

Let us recall again the not accidental but deliberate similarity between the archetypes of Ishmael, born of the will of man, and Isaac, born of the will of God (Gal. 4:23-26). Only those who are spiritually born of the will of God become children of God, solely because they are children of the promise (Rom. 9:8). Only the born-again man, empowered by the Spirit to know this, can receive God by faith, by spiritual sight: *"...**he saved us, not because of works done by us in righteousness,** but according to his own mercy* [Ex. 33:19], *by the washing* [not by physical water, but of the Spirit] *of regeneration and renewal **of the Holy Spirit, whom he poured out on us richly through Jesus Christ our Savior, so that being justified by his grace** we might become heirs according to the hope of eternal life"* (Titus 3:5-7). Jesus Christ, in one creative moment, washes and seals His people with the Holy Spirit, that is, He incorporates them into Himself and baptizes them to dwell in Him forever. From that moment on, everyone who belongs to His elect is saved, sees Christ, believes, is justified, and begins his process of sanctification, obedience, and growth in the knowledge of God, culminating in his resurrection to a glorified body (Rom. 8:23). Through His wounds, Christ awakens His spiritually resurrected people, the Church, to discipline (1 Cor. 9:27), that with fear and trembling they will work out their irresistible and irrevocable salvation (Phil. 2:12): *"For everyone who has been born of God* [God is the irresistible cause] *overcomes the world* [the house of Satan]. ***And this is the victory that has overcome the world—our faith*** [spiritual sight, the first, spiritual resurrection, the result of God's irresistible creative grace]*"* (1 John 5:4).

The faith of the born-again, a faith given by God (Phil. 1:29), overcomes the world. But he who is not born of God and does not believe cannot understand the things of God (1 Cor. 2:14) but is overcome by the world. The nature of the irresistible, first, spiritual resurrection can be beautifully illustrated by God's surgical intervention. No patient operates on himself, and under anesthesia he cannot resist the incisions of the surgeon's scalpel: *"**And the Lord your God will circumcise your heart and the heart of your offspring*** [in the seed of Abraham, Isaac, and Jacob shall all the nations of the earth be blessed; Rom. 9:6-8], *so that you will love the Lord your God with all your heart and with all your soul, that you may live* [you will know me]*"* (Deut.30:6). Only after this spiritual, divine, monergistic surgery do the chosen people love the Lord their God irresistibly with all their heart and with all their soul and with all their strength and with all their mind. Ezekiel described this sovereign operation, this creation of a new inner man, as follows: *"And **I will** give you a new heart, and a new spirit* [God's Spirit] ***I will*** *put within you. And **I will** remove the heart of stone* [the spirit of the Devil] *from your flesh and give you a heart of flesh. And **I will put my Spirit within you*** [you will be born-again inwardly of Him] *and cause you to walk in my statutes and be careful to obey my rules"* (Ezek. 36:26-27). God will "plant" a new heart in all of God's Israel (Rom. 9:6-8; Gal. 6:16; Eph. 2:12), Jew and Gentile alike. The Holy Spirit works on the new, God-created will so that the born-again person does not follow his own will or the letter of the law, which only pointed to Christ but condemned him to death (Col. 2:14), but now he follows the law of Christ (1 Cor. 9:21). This is the goal and ultimate fulfillment of God's redemptive purpose, which no promised child of God can resist.

THE SECOND, BODILY RESURRECTION OF THE SAVED AND THE REPROBATE

The bodily resurrection of all, of the saved and unsaved, will take place on the last day of judgment, the second advent of Christ. Like the first, spiritual resurrection, the second, bodily resurrection, is irresistible. Since the Son of Man is the Judge of all, at the hour of His second coming, all the departed, whether in Christ or out of Christ, will hear His voice and be bodily resurrected. This second, future, bodily resurrection awaits everyone who has ever been born, without exception. This is how Jesus' words will be fulfilled (John 5:27-29).

1. The Old Testament prophet Daniel prophesied this truth: *"But at that time* ***your people shall be delivered, everyone whose name shall be found written in the book*** [elected before the foundation of the world]. *And many of those who sleep in the dust of the earth shall awake, some to everlasting life, and some to shame and everlasting contempt"* (Dan.12:1b-2). Daniel's prophecy is completely consistent with Jesus' statements in John 5:28-29. Even Martha testified that her brother Lazarus would rise bodily on the last day: *"Jesus said to her, 'Your brother will rise again.' Martha said to him, 'I know that* ***he will rise again in the resurrection on the last day****.' Jesus said to her, 'I am the resurrection and the life'"* (John 11:23-25a). Thus, Jesus affirmed that the bodily resurrection would indeed take place on the last day of judgment, the day when the Church would be caught up in the clouds in glorified bodies to meet the Lord (1 Thess. 4:17).

2. Furthermore, in his defense in Acts, Paul affirmed that there were even Jewish religious leaders who believed in a certain bodily resurrection of the righteous and the unrighteous: "... *having a hope in God, which these men themselves accept,* ***that***

***there will be a resurrection of both the just and the unjust*"** (Acts 24:15).

3. Another verse that proves a bodily resurrection of the righteous and the unrighteous on the last day, i.e., at the second advent of the Lord Jesus Christ, is the following: ***"Let both grow together until the harvest****, and at harvest time I will tell the reapers, 'Gather the weeds first* [the reprobate] *and bind them in bundles to be burned* [in the lake of fire, the second death; Rev. 21:8], *but gather the wheat into my barn* [John 14:2]'" (Matt. 13:30). This verse implies that the wicked will be separated first, and only then will the righteous be gathered around the Lord Jesus Christ. The order is not important. What is important is that there will be a bodily resurrection of all, a harvest on the last day.
4. Likewise: *"So it will be at the end of the age.* ***The angels will come out and separate the evil from the righteous*** [on the last day] *and throw them into the fiery furnace. In that place there will be weeping and gnashing of teeth* [Rev. 21:8]" (Matt. 13:49-50).
5. John the Baptist saw the Day of Judgment, saw clearly the Second Advent of the Lord Jesus Christ, saw the resurrection of all people, both the righteous and those who remain in sin, and saw the Last Judgment: *"John answered them all, saying, 'I baptize you with water, but he who is mightier than I is coming, the strap of whose sandals I am not worthy to untie.* ***He will baptize you*** [his people] ***with the Holy Spirit*** [between his two comings, in inter-advent] *and fire* [the reprobate when He comes the second time; Rev. 20:15]. *His winnowing fork is in his hand, to clear his threshing floor and* ***to gather the wheat into his barn, but the chaff he will burn with***

unquenchable fire'" (Luke 3:16-17). From the foregoing, it follows that when Jesus baptizes with the Holy Spirit, He places the righteous into Himself, and when He baptizes with fire, and He throws the unrighteous into the burning lake. Wheat and chaff, salvation and damnation, these are both of the same harvest, the same bodily resurrection.

6. We see the same principle of one harvest, one bodily resurrection in these verses: *"When the Son of Man comes in his glory, and all the angels with him* [the second advent], *then he will sit on his glorious throne. Before him will be gathered all the nations* [on the last day of judgment], *and he will separate people one from another as a shepherd separates the sheep from the goats. And* ***he will place the sheep on his right, but the goats on the left****. Then the King will say to those* ***on his right****, 'Come, you who are blessed by my Father,* ***inherit the kingdom prepared for you from the foundation of the world*** [I have loved you with an everlasting love]'" (Matt. 25:31-34). *"Then* ***he will say to those on his left, 'Depart from me, you cursed, into the eternal fire*** *prepared* [from all eternity] *for the devil and his angels'"* [Rev. 19:20b] (Matt. 25:41).

Just as none of the elect have resisted the first, spiritual resurrection, so none will resist the general bodily resurrection at the sound of the last trumpet (1 Cor. 15:51-54). God will clothe the saved with glorified bodies and bring them into eternal life (Dan. 12:2a); He will clothe the unsaved with bodies of shame and send them into everlasting terror (Dan. 12:2b). All Glory and goodness belong to Him alone! Humanity is passive in its creation and resurrection. The monergistic activity in all things is His alone. Let us bow down before our Creator, for we are merely clay in His holy hands (2 Cor. 4:7)!

THE UNIQUENESS OF REVELATION AND UNDERSTANDING OF THE GOSPEL

GOD REVEALS HIS KINGDOM ONLY TO HIS PROMISED CHILDREN

Those who are never born-again of the Spirit will never understand the mysteries of the kingdom of God because God has hidden them from them: *"At that time Jesus declared, 'I thank you, Father, Lord of heaven and earth,* ***that you have hidden these things*** [the things of the Spirit of God, the irresistible understanding and acceptance of the gospel] *from the wise and understanding* [according to this world] ***and revealed them to little children*** [the children of God born of the Spirit]*; yes, Father, for such was your gracious will. All things have been handed over to he by my Father, and* ***no one knows the Son except the Father, and no one knows the Father except the Son and anyone to whom the Son chooses to reveal him*** [for no one desires the true God by nature]'" (Matt. 11:25-27). God hid the mysteries of the kingdom of God because it pleased Him to do so. The things of the kingdom are understood only by those to whom the Son was willing to reveal them, those whom He called (Matt. 13:10-11; 13:16). It is not God's "arbitrariness," as the natural man sees it, but the most holy decretive will of God, to which no one can resist. *"And he* [Jesus] *said to them, '****To you has been given*** *the secret of the kingdom of God,* ***but for those outside everything is in parables****'"* (Mark 4:11). *"...he* [Jesus] *said, '****To you it has been given*** *to know the secrets of the kingdom of God, but for others they are in parables,* ***so that 'seeing they may not see, and hearing they may not understand****'"* (Luke 8:10).

The preceding verses are in perfect harmony with the context of all of Scripture. The sovereign God gives irresistible grace and efficaciously calls His promised people: *"What then? Israel failed to obtain what it was seeking. The elect obtained it, but the rest were hardened, as it is written,* ***'God gave them a spirit of stupor, eyes that would not see and ears that would not hear, down to this very day*** [God has withdrawn from them and left them in their natural, unbelieving state]'" (Rom. 11:7-8).

At this point, many Arminians argue that there is no point in evangelizing if everything is already given by God. In fact, the opposite is true. None of us is omniscient like the Lord Jesus; we do not know who is included in His saving, irresistible grace and who is left out. It is not our responsibility to test who will believe and who will not. Therefore, we sow the Word of God and share it with everyone without prejudice, believing that it will not return empty (Isa. 55:11). We know that our power to persuade or save is nil, but our efforts are not in vain, for it is God who attracts the sinner. If we were able to persuade someone with our eloquence, they would surely end up in hell: *"So* ***neither*** *he who plants* [who witnesses for Christ] ***nor*** *he who waters* [who teaches and preaches the gospel] *is anything,* ***but only God who gives the growth*** [the One who creates the new man of the Spirit]" (1 Cor. 3:7). He is the beginning and the end. The seeds of faith that I sow are only given to me, they are not of me; whether they sprout and grow is not by my merit, but by the will of the Sovereign God. As for me, I am supremely reassured and happy that I have neither the power nor the skill to convince anyone that I am anything other than a laborer in God's vineyard. The Lord God knows why He made me this way. He knows I would not have been able to bear success—I would have succumbed to the impression that I was somehow a good "savior." I am nothing, even though I preach the good news that Jesus Christ came to save what was lost. We who have been translated from the darkness of Satan into the light of Christ—we who are His royal priesthood—invite everyone without exception from outside (common grace). This explains why the Gospel, the Good News, is more often resisted than accepted. But when His promised ones are invited from inside by God the Holy Spirit (saving grace) on the basis of seed that was sown by us, they cannot resist God's saving grace, His new birth of the Spirit.

THE SON OF GOD IS IRRESISTIBLY REVEALED BY THE FATHER TO THE ELECT

True spiritual knowledge can only be given by the Triune God (Heb. 1:2). Every chosen royal priest (1 Pet. 2:9) has been spiritually resurrected and is a new creation; he now recognizes and sees his Messiah in Jesus Christ: *"He* [Christ] *said to them, 'But who do you say that I am?' Simon Peter replied,* ***'You are the Christ, the Son of the living God.'*** *And Jesus answered him, 'Blessed are you, Simon Bar-Jonah!* ***For flesh and blood has not revealed this*** [that I am the Messiah] *to you* [your fallen, 'free' will and mind], ***but my Father who is in heaven'"*** (Matt. 16:15-17). "Salvation and faith" consist of God's efficacious calling by the Spirit, His irresistible grace that delivers the elect from the Devil's prison. Peter was not saved by rational reasoning, but by God's revelation to him, and he believed, seeing Jesus as the Christ, the Son of the living God, the Savior, the Messiah. If this is how Peter was saved, how much more do we need God's revelation? From birth we are all enemies of God, antichrists. In his heart the natural man denies that Jesus is the Christ, the anointed Messiah: *"Who is the liar* ***but he who denies that Jesus is the Christ*** [Messiah]*?* ***This is the antichrist,*** *he who denies the Father and the Son"* (1 John 2:22). He who does not believe that Jesus is the Christ, the anointed Messiah, the Son of the living God, the Savior, has not had it revealed to him by the Father in heaven, and therefore he remains God's enemy, the antichrist (1 John 2:22). In believing this lie, natural man is held by his father, the Devil (1 John 3:8; 3:10). Just as the newborn child of the Spirit obeys his heavenly Father by God's irresistible grace (1 John 3:9), so the natural man cannot help but obey his father, the Devil (Eph. 2:2). Knowing the Son of God, the Messiah, comes not from the will of man, but from God (John 6:65-69). Irresistible grace, the efficacious calling of the Spirit, is our sovereign God's most wonderful creative work, His gift flowing from His holiness, Glory, goodness, and love: *"And we know that the Son of* ***God has come and has given us understanding*** [which we could not resist], *so that we may know* [see, believe] *him who is true; and we are in him who is true, in his Son Jesus Christ.* ***He is the true God and eternal life****"* (1 John 5:20). The natural heart is useless to God because it is irredeemably monstrous, most wicked and evil, who knows it (Jer. 17:9)? Therefore, God creates in us a new heart, from the ground up: *"Of his own will* [not that we made our rebirth possible to Him by our will] ***he brought us forth*** *by the word of truth, that we should be a kind* ***of first fruits of his creatures****"* (James 1:18).

THE GOSPEL CANNOT MISS THE MARK

The good news, the gospel we proclaim, always accomplishes what God intends, always accomplishes God's purpose (Isa. 55:11). Everyone who is efficaciously called and drawn by the Father, who comes to Christ (John 6:37), is a new creation. Knowledge of the mysteries of the kingdom is not for every sinner, but only for those who are drawn and taught in perfect cooperation with the Triune God. Sometimes the called are taught by the Father (John 6:45), sometimes Christ is their teacher (Matt. 23:10), and sometimes the Holy Spirit teaches them (John 14:26). Indeed, the Father, Son, and Holy Spirit are one triune God. Let us bow before His sovereign majesty. The proclamation of the gospel of God will never be in vain. It is a life-giving fragrance to some and a deadly odor to others (2 Cor. 2:16). God can never be harmed; He always glorifies

Himself. His people never talk to the wind: *"...so shall my word be that goes out from my mouth* [God's Word is being spread today by His royal priesthood; 1 Pet. 2:9]*; it shall not return to me empty, but* ***it*** [His word] ***shall accomplish that which I purpose, and shall succeed in the thing for which I sent it"*** (Isa. 55:11). Man's ability to receive the gospel is irresistibly granted from heaven. Therefore, the one newborn of the Spirit has been equipped to receive the Lord Jesus Christ as his Lord and Savior.

GOD'S GRACE IS IRRESISTIBLE, LEST ANYONE SHOULD BOAST

God's people have eternal life because the Father has appropriated them and adopted them for His own sake (Isa. 43:25), out of His sovereign love which no one can comprehend or understand. It all comes from above: *"A person cannot receive even one thing* [not even faith] ***unless it is given him from heaven"*** (John 3:27b). For many years I lived under the illusion that though enslaved by sin, I had believed with my "free" will and thus received God's grace. Like every Pelagian, Semi-Pelagian, and Arminian, I considered my faith to be my natural virtue: When I believed, I did not resist the call of God's prevenient grace. I bragged, because others did resist. Let us read Paul's uncompromising hyperbole with a shudder: *"For who sees anything different in you* [the efficacious, unconditional calling of the Spirit is God's most special and different gift]*? What do you have that you did not receive* [for everything is from the Creator]*? If then you received it,* ***why do you boast as if you did not receive it****? Already you have all you want!* ***Already you have become rich! Without us you have become kings! And would that you did reign****, so that we might share the rule with you!"* (1 Cor. 4:7-8).

As far as true spiritual knowledge is concerned, the natural man has nothing of himself. The whole "spiritual" life of the natural man is distorted, false and idolatrous; man creates gods in his own image. It does not matter whether his idol is set up on mountains, fields, crossroads, stadiums, events, etc., or in temples where the Most High does not dwell (Acts 7:48), or in the hearts of natural men where covetousness dwells (Col. 3:5).

PART V
THE PERSEVERANCE OF THE SAINTS, THE PRESERVATION OF THE SAINTS BY GOD

16

THE PERSEVERANCE AND PRESERVATION OF THE SAINTS BY GOD

DEFINITION OF THE TERM

The fifth point of Calvinism, and therefore of the Synod of Dort, corresponds to the fifth article of the Remonstrance. It concerns the perseverance and preservation of the saints by God. It is inseparably and continuously connected with the previous four points:

1. ***The natural man, the offspring of Adam, is spiritually dead*** *as a result of original sin, separated from God, unable to understand the things of God. Everything man does in this state takes place on the stage of sin. He is a vassal of Satan, a slave to sin, and because of his corrupt nature is unable of his own accord to desire to follow God.*

2. *Therefore, out of inexpressible, amazing goodness, God had mercy on man.* ***God the Father has chosen*** *for Himself and for His own sake His promised people, His Church, whom He loved with an everlasting love from the whole fallen race of Adam before the foundation of the world and has set apart for*

salvation. His election is not based on merit or the "faith" of the natural man; it is based solely on God's sovereign grace.

3. *To fulfill the promises of God, God the Father sent His Son, Jesus Christ, into the world in the flesh. He gave His people to Him so that* ***God the Son could save them****. On the Cross, Jesus Christ took the place of God's chosen people in the judgment. He bore only their sins, not the sins of all mankind. In this way, He redeemed them from the bondage of sin and led the captives out of Satan's prison. God the Son did not make salvation possible for just anyone; He actually saved His entire people!*

4. *In order that God's people might be in obedient union with God, believing that God the Father had chosen them and God the Son had saved them, God the Son sent a Helper to earth, God the Holy Spirit, who, like God the Son, proceeds from God the Father.* ***God the Holy Spirit has rebirthed, recreated, raised to new life with Christ the full number of God's promised people****. Thus, the Spirit of God has accomplished an unconditional, that is, irresistible grace in which all three persons of the triune God participate. The creative power of the Holy Spirit, the efficacious calling of the Spirit, the rebirth of the new man in Christ, cannot be resisted any more than physical birth can be resisted.*

5. *God's people have been chosen by God the Father, redeemed by God the Son, and regenerated by God the Holy Spirit; they have been rescued from the abyss of spiritual death by the Triune God for God's sake and for God's Glory. Therefore, the Church,* ***the whole people of God, is permanently sealed, kept by the Holy Spirit in Christ*** *according to the Father's purpose, to endure to the end of her earthly days in the faith and works that God has prepared for her. Those who fall away from "the faith"*

have never received faith from God. God never knew them; therefore, He did not choose them, redeem them, or regenerate them.

The perseverance of the saints, as the name implies, emphasizes the supernatural, God-maintained perseverance of the faith and good works of His children, which confirms the irresistible call of the Spirit, the "salvation and faith" of God's people. God accomplishes the whole of salvation and never forsakes His children for a moment. Thus, the main theme of Calvinism's fifth point is not the goal, i.e., the certainty of salvation (modern Arminianism), but God's continuing power to cause His peculiar and separate people to persevere in holiness to the end.

For clarity, let us recall both views in the table to see the difference, which again is not in emphasis but in substance:

ARMINIANISM Remonstration	CALVINISM Synod of Dort
5. Conditional Guarantee and Assurance In God's grace, there is the assurance that all who choose to accept Jesus Christ are guaranteed salvation. However, this assurance is conditional upon faith to the end. One is free both to accept Jesus Christ and later to reject Him by falling away. (There is no agreement among Arminians on this point.)	**5. The Perseverance of the Saints** The elect cannot lose their salvation or their faith, because "salvation and faith" are the work of the Triune God. The Father chose His elect, the Son redeemed the elect, and the Holy Spirit regenerated the redeemed. God's work cannot be thwarted because it is God who perseveres in faithfulness and causes His elect, redeemed, and regenerated saints to persevere to the end.

APOSTASY AND ASSURANCE VS. GOD'S PRESERVATION OF THE SAINTS

Surely you have heard stories of believers, especially those who are young, who used to be passionate for Christ and very active in the Church, but then they disappeared, went back to the world, and never came back. Was such a person saved or not? Let us study the following three positions taught in Protestant churches today:

1. FALL FROM GRACE (TRADITIONAL ARMINIANS)

DEFINITION

The believer who has freely chosen to believe in Christ and to do good works also has the free will to deny Christ again, to abandon his original decision, and thus to lose his salvation (Heb. 6:4-6). Prevenient grace can be resisted both before and after salvation.

APPLICATION

Traditional Arminians, in keeping with the Arminian concept of salvation, have always believed that a person who has fallen away, fallen from grace, has lost the salvation once gained. If a person is "free" to vote yes, he is also "free" to vote no. He can fall away from the faith and live in a worldly way, even though it was the Holy Spirit who helped him to his initial faith by the working of prevenient grace.

OBJECTION

No one can snatch God's elect out of Christ's hand, for the Father, who is greater than all, has given them to Him (John 10:28-29). How often can a person change his mind about what to do with Christ's sacrifice? Will the Holy Spirit condescend to be repeatedly invited into the heart and cast out according to the willfulness of the natural man? Is it not rather the man of the Adamic nature who obeys the rulers of this world? Is it not rather that the "salvation" once obtained was not true salvation?

2. ASSURANCE OF SALVATION (MODERN ARMINIANS)

DEFINITION

A true believer can never lose his salvation. Once he has accepted Jesus Christ as his Savior, the saying is true: "Once saved, always saved." Modern Arminianism recognizes two types of Christians. First, those to whom Jesus Christ is Lord are spiritual Christians doing the works God has prepared for them, building on Christ with gold, silver, and precious stones (1 Cor. 3:12a). Second, those to whom Jesus Christ is not Lord are carnal, fleshly Christians who live in the world, even in gross sin, building on Christ with wood, grass, and straw (1 Cor. 3:12b). Though their works will burn, they will not lose eternal life (1 Cor. 3:15).

APPLICATION

Modern Arminians inconsistently believe that even an apostate is eternally saved because he previously accepted Christ. But this belief is inconsistent with their Arminian view of salvation—the apostate was "free" to vote yes, but he is no longer "free" to vote no. He is seen as a carnal, fleshly Christian who does not necessarily bear fruit because although he knows Christ as his Savior, he does not know Him as his Lord.

OBJECTION

Those who oppose such "assurance" of salvation are, first and foremost, unbelievers who rely on their natural "decency"; then the religiously inclined, who trust in their good works—without Christ, or with Him; and born-again believers who rely solely on Christ, who works good deeds in them. All rightly object: "You say that if you accept Christ, your troubles are over; now you can do whatever you want. Even if you murder, you believe you are still forgiven, still above reproach?" Surely you have heard similar objections, especially from unbelievers. Modern Arminianism's assurance of salvation—the concept of the carnal, fleshly Christian—should be rejected on biblical grounds by both traditional Arminians and Calvinists.

3. PERSEVERANCE OF THE SAINTS (CALVINISTS)

DEFINITION

The man of God, whom God has created with a new heart, will continue in faith and good works in Christ, which God has prepared for him (Eph. 2:10). He will be preserved by the power of God, by the new creation, so that his "salvation and faith" will endure to the end of his earthly days (1 Cor. 1:8).

APPLICATION

Calvinists believe in the perseverance of the saints, that is, the saints' preservation by God. Their understanding of God's sovereignty in election by the Father, redemption by the Son, and regeneration of the Spirit is in complete disharmony with both the traditional Arminian idea of apostasy from grace and the modern Arminian assurance of salvation for all who once confessed faith in Christ with the mouth alone. The promise of perseverance of the saints is not given to those who have received Christ informally—intellectually only, or emotionally only—but only to those who have received Christ transformationally, having been transformed by the Spirit of God into a new creation. Perseverance to the end, in faith, growth, and works, is accompanying inward and outward evidence of salvation (Matt. 7:16). The perseverance of the saints is ongoing sanctification, an inseparable part of "salvation and faith." It is impossible for a born-again person to receive Jesus Christ as his Lord and Savior by the power of God and to remain unchanged, to not persevere in faith and works.

SUMMARY

A person who "forsakes" Christ has only known about Him and has never belonged to Him, never having known Him in the true sense of the word. This is the person of whom Christ will speak on the Day of Judgment: *"I never knew you; depart from me, you workers of lawlessness"* (Matt. 7:23b). Such an apostate never accepted Christ as his Lord and Savior because he was never touched by the regenerating power of the Holy Spirit. He could not lose God's salvation because he never had it. He made his decision for Christ only by the power of his own natural mind, consulting only his own flesh and blood (Matt. 16:17). He may have confessed faith with his mouth, he may have been baptized, become a member of a church, and even be an elder or a preacher, but the circumcision of his heart by the Holy Spirit never took place. In such a case, the seed of the gospel fell along the path where it was picked up by birds, or on rocky soil where it withered without moisture, or among thorns where it was choked out (Luke 8:5-14).

THE PERSEVERANCE OF THE SAINTS IS EVIDENT IN THE SANCTIFIED LIFE

Those who are truly in Christ and therefore persevere in the good works prepared by God, are sanctified to the end—not to be saved at the end, but because they are already "saved and believing." Persevering to the end in Christ and His good works does not cause salvation but is an integral part of salvation. The only cause and guarantee of "salvation and faith" is the Triune God—the Father, Son, and Holy Spirit. Those who by the power of God keep the faith to the end and bear fruit (Matt. 7:20) are true partakers of Christ: *"For we have come to share in Christ,* ***if indeed we hold our original confidence firm to the end****"* (Heb. 3:14). Or: *"****But the one who endures to the end*** *will be saved"* (Matt. 24:13). The perseverance of God's people in faith comes not from their natural strength, even though it dwells in natural, sin-infested bodies. Perseverance of the saints is the act of God's unconditional creative grace: "*...**who*** [God] ***will sustain you to the end****, guiltless in the day of our Lord Jesus Christ* [at His second coming]*"* (1 Cor. 1:8).

Again, we do not believe man's good works lead to salvation, even good works that endure to the end, but we do believe that good works in Christ accompany every truly saved person as proof that the Spirit of God is at work in him. Only those who are sealed in Christ by the Holy Spirit (Eph. 1:13) will endure to the end. The seal of the Holy Spirit is the only guarantee and assurance of the endurance of the child of God: ***"For we are his workmanship*** [new creation], *created in Christ Jesus* [for this purpose] *for good works, which God prepared beforehand, that we should walk in them"* (Eph. 2:10).

In a parallel way, every worldly belief is accompanied by corresponding actions, deeds that confirm what we believe. If a stockholder believes that the value of his stocks is going to fall, he sells them as soon as possible. If he were to say, "Yes, I believe they will fall," yet he did not sell them, what he actually believed in his heart was that they would not fall. Conversely, if he said: "No, I do not believe they will fall," and yet he sold them, he actually believed in his heart that they would fall. What we say is not as important as how we act: "*'What do you think? A man had two sons. And he went to the first and said, 'son, go and work in the vineyard today.' And he answered, 'I will not,' but afterward he changed his mind and went. And he went to the other son and said the same. And he answered, 'I go, sir,' but did not go. Which of the two did the will of his father?' They said, 'The first.' Jesus said to them, 'Truly, I say to you, the tax collectors and the prostitutes go into the kingdom of God before you'"* (Matt. 21:28-31). And so, every kind of faith, spoken or unspoken, secular, religious, and even the God-created faith of the born-again, is accompanied by corresponding works that confirm and are in harmony with such faith.

CAN A SAVED PERSON COMMIT A SIN?

Those redeemed by Christ are created to do good works prepared by God. Nevertheless, they are still capable of committing a sin. All have sinned—disciples, apostles, those dear to God, and even saints in Christ today may occasionally sin. But those in Christ are no longer enslaved by sin (i.e., the Devil), as they once were; Christ has freed them from the Devil's economy, so unlike natural men, they can now rebel against the Devil (James 4:7). They are redeemed and have a new Lord. Sin is no longer their lifestyle for them, but an individual, personal failure that leads to a spiritual, painful disaster. By faith, they see Christ and they turn to Him with a broken heart and repent. In Christ they have the power not to sin. They are not motivated by their carnality, but by God the Holy Spirit. Therefore, they love God with all their heart, with all their soul, with all their strength, and with all their mind (Luke 10:27).They do not want to grieve Christ; they do not want to lay more and more of their sins on Him: *"And do not grieve the Holy Spirit of God, **by whom you were sealed for the day of redemption*** [our whole salvation will be consummated in the redemption, the resurrection of the glorified body] "[67] (Eph. 4:30).

God's people who are sealed by the Spirit in Christ do not take personal failure lightly. Yes, Christians can commit sin because of the weaknesses of the flesh, but they cannot continue in sin permanently. When God's people commit a sin, they have a way out and an Advocate in God: *"My little children, I am writing these things to you so that you may not sin. But if anyone does sin, **we have an advocate with the Father, Jesus Christ** the righteous"* (1 John 2:1).

Peter also persevered to the end in the good work to which he was predestined and called. Yet his sin of denying the Lord Jesus

67 See chapter 3; section "Salvation and Faith" According to the Reformation.

Christ might seem not that much different from Judas' betrayal of Christ. Peter was cowardly, where Judas was greedy. It might look like, in the flesh, both repented of their sin, but God's awesome power sustained Peter's relationship with Christ. Peter's regret or remorse did not sustain his faith, and for Judas, remorse did not help (Matt. 27:3-5). Peter's faith did not fail, only because of Jesus' powerful intercession: *"Simon, Simon, behold, Satan demanded to have you, that he might sift you like wheat,* ***but I have prayed for you*** *that your faith may not fail"* (Luke 22:31-32a).

The man of God, whether he is Peter, Job, or the Christian of today, who undergoes testing in the furnace of affliction will persevere, even though for a time he may fail. The cause of his perseverance—of his continued sanctification—is God: *"For God, who said, 'Let light shine out of darkness* [the Light, Christ, has delivered His people from Satan's darkness], *' has shone in our hearts* [by the Holy Spirit] *to give the light of the knowledge of the glory of God in the face of Jesus Christ* [God is revealed to us in Christ]. ***But we have this treasure*** [Christ] ***in jars of clay*** [our bodies not yet glorified], *to show* ***that the surpassing power belongs to God and not to us****"* (2 Cor. 4:6-7).

The saved, newly created inner man will occasionally sin, in violation of his liberated will, because the inner man is still trapped in a fallen body. Therefore, he awaits the second resurrection—the redemption of his body—with joy and groaning in his heart; he longs to put on the new, glorified body (Rom. 8:23; Phil. 1:23). He looks forward to the consummation of his "salvation and faith," when God will clothe him with a body similar to that of the risen Christ here on earth: *"Beloved, we are God's children now* [we have already been raised for the first time—spiritually], *and what we will be has not yet appeared; but we know that when he* [Christ in His second advent in the flesh] *appears* ***we shall be like him*** [we shall be raised a second time—to a glorified body], *because we shall see* *him as he is"* (1 John 3:2). In the glorified heavenly body, man will be completely free from sin because he will no longer be trapped in this corruptible body. God's people will thus be made fit to behold the face of God, Jesus Christ.

GOD IS THE CAUSE OF THE PERSEVERANCE OF HIS PEOPLE

THE PERSEVERANCE OF THE SAINTS ACCORDING TO THE OLD TESTAMENT

The Old Testament testifies in many places that the endurance of God's chosen people is eternal because they are created by the Lord: *"But now thus says the Lord, **he who created you*** [who created your new spirit and will create your new glorified body], ***O Jacob**, he who formed you, O Israel: '**Fear not, for I have redeemed you*** [delivered you on the Cross from the Devil]*; I have called you by name, you are mine. When you pass through the waters, I will be with you; and through the rivers, they shall not overwhelm you; when you walk through fire you shall not be burned, and the flame shall not consume you. For I am the Lord your God, the Holy One of Israel* [of all children of promise; Rom. 9:6-8], *your Savior'"* (Isa. 43:1-3a). The Holy Spirit did not say through Isaiah that these promises apply only to the person of Jacob; nor did He say that they apply only to the "seven thousand" redeemed remnant of ethnic Israel. Isaiah was seeing all who are in Christ, regardless of their ethnicity, regardless of the historical context in which they lived. He had in mind the entire promised, spiritual seed of Abraham, Isaac (Gen. 17:19; Rom. 9:6-8) and Jacob (Isa. 65:9), both Jew and Gentile (Gen. 17:5)—all of God's people, the Israel of God (Gal. 6:16; Eph. 2:12).

The Old Testament foreshadows in physical images Christ and His Body, that is, all who are in Christ, of whom carnal, ethnic

Israel was merely a shadow: ***"I will bring forth offspring from Jacob*** [the promised seed of Abraham, Isaac, and Jacob, God's people, God's Israel, the Church], *and from Judah possessors of my mountains* [the lion of Judah, Christ, is heir of the kingdom of God; Heb. 1:2]*; my chosen* [joint heirs with Christ; Gal. 4:7] *shall possess it, and my servants* [slaves] *shall dwell there"* (Isa. 65:9). It is not Jacob's physical seed that belongs to God, but his spiritual, promised, chosen seed, from the Jews and Gentiles (Rom. 9:8). No matter what trials come upon this chosen seed, their faith will be preserved; they will persevere because they are called by God, and their Creator and Redeemer is with them. God protects them and stands by them in all circumstances. All those in "Jacob, Isaac, and Abraham" are in Christ, created to do His will, His purpose, to the end: *"'For the mountains may depart and the hills be removed, but **my steadfast love shall not depart from you**, and my covenant of peace* [1 Cor. 11:25] *shall not be removed,' says the Lord, who has compassion on you"* (Isa. 54:10). From him who is the Lord's, God's mercy will not depart, though the mountains fall.

God's covenant with His elect is permanent and unchangeable: *"I will make with them an everlasting covenant* [This cup is the new covenant sealed with my blood, which is shed for you; Luke 22:20b], *that I will not turn away from doing good to them. **And I will put the fear of me*** [Myself, the Holy Spirit] *in their hearts, **that they may not turn from me*** [that they may persevere]*"* (Jer. 32:40). The preceding verse is incompatible with both the carnal, fleshly Christian of modern Arminianism and the free-will Christian of traditional Arminianism. The unshakeable position of the regenerate is guaranteed by God's eternal covenant. God essentially makes this covenant with Himself; He will not cease to do good to His people, that they may not depart from Him, but persevere. This covenant is asymmetrical because God is the first mover—He will do eternal good to His people, and His people will be the sovereign recipients of that good. His true people cannot denounce or question this covenant. Because it is eternal and immutable, the perseverance of the saints is sustained by God who puts "fear"—that is, His Spirit—into the hearts of His specially created people: *"Serve the Lord with fear, and rejoice with trembling"* (Ps. 2:11).

THE PERSEVERANCE OF THE SAINTS ACCORDING TO THE NEW TESTAMENT I

Christ is the Good Shepherd; He has in His fold a complete number, a roll call, of His special people, figuratively one hundred sheep (Matt. 18:12), whom He called out of Satan's darkness into His marvelous light before the foundation of the world (1 Pet. 2:9). If even one of the sheep strays, the Good Shepherd will seek it out and bring it back to the fold, rejoicing over it more than over the ninety and nine that did not stray (Matt. 18:13). God will preserve even the "last" of His elect saints, for it is His irresistible, decreed will that none of His sheep should stray and perish: *"My* [chosen] *sheep hear my voice, and* ***I know them*** [unconditionally loved them with an everlasting love], *and they follow me. I give them eternal life, and they will never perish, and* ***no one will snatch them out of my hand*** [not even the Devil]. *My Father, who has given them to me, is greater than all, and* ***no one is able to snatch them out of the Father's hand"*** (John 10:27-29). Only the sheep of Jesus hear His voice and follow Him faithfully. The Spirit of God has regenerated them, creating them for "salvation and faith," that is, giving them ears to hear His voice. How could they go back to the Evil One who rules this world? God would have to cast them out, or they would have to slip from God's grasp. What a contradiction! As if the Almighty were so "weak" that He could not keep those whom He has chosen, created and redeemed by His blood.

Let us look at another argument from Scripture that testifies to the preservation of the saints in Christ: *"Jesus said to them, 'I am the bread of life;* ***whoever comes to me shall not hunger****, and whoever believes in me* ***shall never thirst****. But I said to you that you have seen me and yet do not believe* [the Father has not given you to Me]. *All that the Father gives me will come to me, and* ***whoever comes to me I will never cast out****. For I have come down from heaven, not to do my own will but the will of him who sent me* [the Father]. ***And this is the will of him*** *who sent me,* ***that I should lose nothing*** *of all that he has given me* [His elect], *but raise it up on the last day* [into a glorified body]. *For this is the will of my Father, that everyone who looks on the Son and believes in him should have eternal life, and* ***I will raise him up on the last day*** [because by the power of God he will endure to the end] '" (John 6:35-40).

Anyone who is chosen by the Father will surely be irresistibly and permanently drawn to Jesus, because he is redeemed by Him to be born-again of the Spirit of God and raised to spiritual life in the Kingdom of God. Anyone who is drawn to Christ is assured that, by God's power, he will endure to the end, for Jesus will efficaciously do the will of His Father, i.e., He will not lose any of His sheep: *"And I am no longer in the world, but they* [the apostles] *are in the world, and I am coming to you.* ***Holy Father, keep them in your name*** [that they may persevere by Your power], *which you have given me, that they may be one, even as we are one. While I was with them* [the apostles], *I kept them in your name, which you have given me.* ***I have guarded them, and not one of them has been lost*** *except the son of destruction* [Judas], *that the Scripture might be fulfilled"* (John 17:11-12). *"I do not ask that you take them out of the world, but that you keep them from the evil one* [Satan]*"* (John 17:15). ***"I do not ask for these only, but also for those who will believe in me through their word*** [all the elect]*"* (John 17:20). The preservation of the saints by God applied to the apostles as it also applies to all of God's elect. The history of salvation, the perseverance of the saints, God's preservation of the saints in Christ until the end, is ordained by God's will—not by human need, though worldly eyes often see it that way.

Furthermore, Paul assures the Roman Christians that eternal condemnation can no longer befall them because they are permanently sustained by the power of the Spirit in the Lord Jesus Christ: *"There is therefore now no condemnation* [on the last day at the judgment seat] *for those who are in Christ Jesus* [being in Christ guarantees the perseverance of the saints]*"* (Rom. 8:1). The Israel of God, the Church, all who are in Christ, must persevere; they must be preserved, for they are beloved members of the body of Christ, which no one can amputate: *"What then shall we say to these things? If God is for us, who can be against us? He who did not spare his own Son but* ***gave him up for us all*** [all the elect], *how will he not also with him graciously give us all things?* ***Who shall bring any charge against God's elect****? It is God who justifies. Who is to condemn? Christ Jesus is the one who died—more than that, who was raised—who is at the right hand of God,* ***who indeed is interceding for us*** [that we may persevere]. *Who shall separate* ***us*** [who are in Christ] ***from the love of Christ****? Shall tribulation, or distress, or persecution, or famine, or nakedness, or danger, or sword? As it is written, 'For your sake* ***we are being killed*** *all the day long;* ***we are regarded as sheep to be slaughtered.****' No, in all these things we are more than conquerors* ***through him who loved us*** [who wrote us indelibly in the Book of Life]. *For I am sure that neither death nor life, nor angels nor rulers, nor things present nor things to come, nor powers, nor height nor depth,* ***nor anything else in all creation, will be able to separate us from the love of God in Christ Jesus our Lord****"* (Rom. 8:31-39). Here it is in black and white! God's eternal love is only, solely, entirely, and merely in Christ Jesus. God's love does not exist outside of Christ. Outside of Christ there is only God's common grace, which is more than generous to natural men (Luke 16:25; 1 Tim. 4:10), but also wrath and judgment at the last day: *"...whoever does not obey the Son shall not see life,* ***but the wrath of God*** [not love] ***remains on him"*** (John 3:36b).

Sometimes I think about this verse: *"No temptation has overtaken you that is not common to man. God is faithful, and he will not let you be tempted beyond your ability,* ***but with the temptation he will also provide the way of escape****, that you may be able to endure it"* (1 Cor. 10:13). This verse was misused during the Inquisition. In its torture practices, it was assumed that if the "heretic's" doctrine was from God, he could withstand any torture; if he could not withstand the torture, then his doctrine was not from God and he deserved death. Many endured, but others did not. Others recanted, believing in their hearts that God had not forsaken them. How do you think we would have responded? So, we pray: "And lead us not into temptation, but deliver us from evil." God's chosen one relies on the One who is source of his strength to sustain him.

THE PERSEVERANCE OF THE SAINTS ACCORDING TO THE NEW TESTAMENT II

We continue with other verses that confirm the perseverance of the saints to the end, and again, we see that God is victorious on all fronts: *"...so that you are not lacking in any gift, as you wait for the revealing of our Lord Jesus Christ, who will sustain you to the end, guiltless in the day of our Lord Jesus Christ* [because you will endure to the end]. *God is faithful,* ***by whom you were called into the fellowship of his Son****, Jesus Christ our Lord"* (1 Cor.1:7-9). God is the guarantee that His people will overcome the world and their flesh, that they will cross the finish line and not be condemned on the last day of judgment, because they were not destined for God's wrath but for "salvation and faith" (1 Thess. 5:9). It is the Father who calls His own into fellowship with the Lord Jesus Christ. Therefore, His Church is permanently bound by the presence of the Holy Spirit.

Only those who are called are God's children, and He works in them the desire to love Him: *"...by the blood of the eternal covenant,* [Jesus] ***equip you with everything good that you may do his will****, working in us that which is pleasing in his sight* [love the Lord with all your heart, soul, and mind, and love your neighbor as yourself], *through Jesus Christ, to whom be glory forever and ever. Amen"* (Heb. 13:20b-21). Everything His people do comes from Him. He brings it to perfection, culminating in the second resurrection, the redemption of the body: *"Since we have the same spirit of faith* [we have already been raised spiritually] *according to what has been written, 'I believed, and so I spoke,' we also believe, and so we also speak, knowing that* ***he who raised the Lord Jesus will raise us also with Jesus*** [bodily; we are already spiritually raised] *and bring us with you into his presence* [Rev. 22:4]*"* (2 Cor. 4:13-14). The Scriptures give us assurance—He who raised the Lord Jesus will also raise those who are in Him. The man of God cannot fall away because the certainty of the second resurrection into a new, glorified body has been guaranteed by the resurrection of the Lord Jesus.

The hope of God's people is not in vain: *"If in Christ we have hope in this life only, we are of all people most to be pitied. But in fact, Christ has been raised from the dead, the first fruits of those who have fallen asleep. For as by a man came death, by a man has come also the resurrection of the dead.* ***For as in Adam all die, so also in Christ shall all be made alive****"* (1 Cor. 15:19-22). What greater guarantee and assurance can God's people have? Anyone who doubts that God cannot by His power preserve His people to the end, so that His will may be done, may also doubt that He raised His Son at all.

"In him you also, when you heard the word of truth, the gospel of your salvation, and believed in him, were sealed with the promised Holy Spirit [therefore you shall endure], *who is the guarantee of our inheritance* ***until we acquire possession of it, to the praise of his glory"*** (Eph. 1:13-14). God's people are sealed in Christ. The Holy Spirit sealed those whom God the Son rescued from Satan's grip on the Cross for the praise of His Glory. How could they not persevere; how could they permanently fall away when they bear His seal? Who can break the seal of the Spirit of God? Can God's people erase themselves from the Book of Life? *"Now may the God of peace himself sanctify you completely, and* ***may your whole spirit and soul and body be kept blameless*** *at the coming of our Lord Jesus Christ* [He will cause you to endure]. *He who calls you is faithful;* ***he will surely do it"*** (1 Thess. 5:23-24).

What is there to add? The Scriptures are full of verses that speak of the perseverance of the saints. He causes a people chosen by the Father, redeemed by the Son, and called by the Spirit to persevere to the end. God's power will preserve them for eternal life: *"Blessed be the God and Father of our Lord Jesus Christ! According to his great mercy, he has caused us to be born again to a living hope through the resurrection of Jesus Christ from the dead, to an inheritance that is imperishable, undefiled, and unfading, kept in heaven for you,* ***who by God's power are being guarded through faith for a salvation*** *ready to be revealed in the last time."* (1 Pet. 1:3-5).

17

OBJECTIONS TO THE PERSEVERANCE OF THE SAINTS

IS IT POSSIBLE FOR A SAVED PERSON TO LOSE SALVATION?

ELECTION AND FALLING AWAY ARE MUTUALLY EXCLUSIVE

Let us first look at a number of verses that speak of individuals and groups of people who walked with the Lord but later turned away from Him, as if they were saved and later lost their salvation. However, these verses do not speak of losing salvation, but rather serve as a warning to all within the visible church to examine themselves—to see whether they are truly baptized into Christ and genuinely part of the true Church, His body. There are more than a few deceived people in churches who think that all is well with their spirituality, and therefore everyone should examine the depths of his soul: *"Examine yourselves, to see whether you are in the faith. Test yourselves. Or do you not realize this about yourselves, that Jesus Christ is in you?—unless indeed you fail to meet the test!"* (2 Cor. 13:5).

In the next three headings we will look at verses dealing with these "apostates," verses that traditional Arminian brethren believe are about the loss of salvation. Some have compared those saved and later lost to a person who conceives and then aborts a child. But we must always interpret verses in the context of Scripture as a whole. The following three points of Reformed soteriology, mentioned throughout this book, are crucial:

1. God the Father has chosen.
2. God the Son redeems all whom the Father has chosen.
3. God the Holy Spirit regenerates all those redeemed by the Son who were chosen by the Father.

If people were only conditionally saved and could later lose their salvation if they failed to keep the condition of salvation, i.e., they fell away from the faith, then this all-perfect cooperation of all three persons of the triune God in salvation, as understood by the Reformation, would be absurd. Consider the following three points as exaggerations, but again, not far from the implications of traditional Arminian soteriology:

1. God the Father elected only on trial—let's see whether the faith of the saved will endure.
2. God the Son redeemed all those tentatively elected by the Father, knowing that His suffering on the Cross would be in vain for many.
3. God the Holy Spirit regenerated all those uncertainly elected by the Father and questionably redeemed by the Son.

The question that remains both unanswered and unthinkable is how God could make His "born-again" children "dead again" if they were to change their minds and decide not to remain "born-again."

ENLIGHTENED "APOSTATES"

Traditional Arminians who believe that truly saved people can fall away and lose their salvation most often cite the following verse:

> *"For it is impossible, in the case of those* [1] ***who have once been enlightened,*** [2] ***who have tasted the heavenly gift,*** *and* [3] ***have shared in the Holy Spirit,*** *and have tasted the goodness of the word of God and the powers of the age to come, and* [4] ***then have fallen away,*** [5] ***to restore them again to repentance,*** *since they are crucifying once again the Son of God to their own harm and holding him up to contempt"* (Heb. 6:4-6).

This text seems to contradict countless verses that clearly teach the perseverance of the saints. At first glance, it appears that those referenced in these verses were truly saved. A closer look, however, reveals that these seemingly "saved" ones were never really saved. Scripture cannot contradict itself:

1. ***who have once been enlightened***—they had been taught and they understood the gospel intellectually, but they had not been born-again of the Holy Spirit.
2. ***who have tasted the heavenly gift***—to have tasted is a verb in perfective aspect, meaning to do or experience something only briefly, only once. To taste the gift of salvation is not the same as to perpetually eat the body and drink the blood of the Lord Jesus Christ (John 6:54-56), being nourished by God forever (Isa. 60:16). I remember an absurd slogan on bumper stickers in the U.S. that said: "Try Christ"—"try Him, taste Him and see." Such a bumper sticker is basically saying: "If you do not like Him, you can spit Him out." The absolute God never allows sinful man to profane Him in this way!

3. [who] ***have shared in the Holy Spirit***—they have sampled without actually experiencing the truth of God's Word and the power of the age to come. They have shared but disliked the truth of God's Word, seeing only briefly the power of the gospel around them and the transformation of saved sinners; in the end, they did not like either.
4. ***then have fallen away***—this Greek word is found only here in the New Testament. In the Septuagint it was used to translate terms expressing serious unfaithfulness and apostasy. These, then, are people who, with full knowledge and conscious experience, have rejected Christ. Their hearts became a stumbling block, a rock, and a thorn because the Word of God had not taken root in them (Luke 8:11-14; Matt. 13:21).
5. [It is impossible] **to restore them again to repentance**—in the beginning these people received the gospel and had even been led to repentance, but the gospel was a deadly smell to them (2 Cor. 2:16a). Christians had sown the Word of God in their hearts and watered it with prayers, but God had not given this ministry an increase.

Neither of the two verses quoted (Heb. 6:4-6) confirms that they refer to truly born-again believers who later apostatized. In the visible church, as in ethnic Israel, there have always been many on whom the gospel shines, people who take note of it, understanding the response it requires of them, but they do not take it seriously; gospel realities have not become their guide. Had they been chosen, redeemed and born-again, they would believe and bear the fruit of the Spirit. Not everyone who hears the gospel and enters the fellowship of Christians will have eternal life and know God forever.

In other words, these people had the Word of God preached to them, heard it with their ears and considered it, but were never transformed by it. There is no "salvation and faith" apart from

God's monergistic intervention, supernatural circumcision of the heart. By their very nature, these people despised the glorious salvation and thus will not escape the righteous wrath of God. Such contempt for Christ remains and continues in the stony hearts of those who have been present among God's people, "belonging" to Him for a time for various humanistic reasons, but never belonging to Him in their heart (1 John 2:19). It is like a fickle "love", here today and gone tomorrow, when their heart will belong to someone else. They tried Christ out, they tasted Him to see if they liked Him, but they no longer feed on Him because they do not like Him. The text (Heb. 6:4-6) is in perfect harmony with Heb. 2:1-4, which interprets it at its core: *"Therefore we must pay* ***much closer attention to what we have heard, lest we drift away from it*** [examine ourselves; 2 Cor. 13:5]. *For since the message declared by angels proved to be reliable, and every transgression or disobedience received a just retribution, how shall we escape if we neglect such a great salvation? It was declared at first by the Lord, and it was attested to us by those who heard* [the apostles], *while God also bore witness by signs and wonders and various miracles and by* ***gifts of the Holy Spirit distributed according to his will****"* (Heb. 2:1-4).

KNOWING THE GOSPEL BY REASON ALONE

A good friend and classmate of mine does not accept the biblical belief in Christ's substitutionary death, and he has his reasons. He says with a kind of Czech playful cunning: "I could never do such a thing to Him; I could not bear that an innocent man should be punished for me, the guilty one. It would not be fair; I have to serve my sentence alone." In his eyes, Christians do not have the courage to take responsibility and punishment for their sins. You see, he understands the gospel message better than many Christians. Nevertheless, the Spirit of God has not transformed him, has not yet made him a new man. My friend still despises God's glorious salvation. Well-informed and untransformed people like him would be better off not knowing the truth at all (2 Pet. 2:21).

Another frightening example of a very knowledgeable but untransformed man is Billy Graham's former associate, Charles Templeton. He died in 2001, six years after writing the disturbing book "Farewell to God—My Reasons for Rejecting the Christian Faith," from a biblical perspective. This great evangelist became an atheist, a critic, and an opponent of the God of the Bible. In so doing, he confirmed the judgment he would face.

THEY WENT OUT FROM US, BUT THEY WERE NOT OF US

OLD TESTAMENT ISRAEL

"But it is not as though the word of God has failed. For not all who are descended from Israel [the natural, physical descendants of Abraham, Isaac, and Jacob] *belong to Israel* [to the Israel of God belong only the born-again, spiritual descendants of Abraham, Isaac, and Jacob]*"* (Rom. 9:6). Only the Israel of God (Gal. 6:16), i.e., the commonwealth of Israel, knows Christ; those who do not know Christ are separated from the real, true, divine commonwealth of Israel: *"...remember that* ***you were at that time separated from Christ, alienated from the commonwealth of Israel*** *and strangers to the covenants of promise, having no hope and without God in the world"* (Eph. 2:12). Only the Israel of God, that is, all the promised of Jew and Gentile—the entire spiritual seed of Abraham, Isaac, and Jacob, regardless of ethnicity or nationality—will receive the content of God's Word, Jesus Christ, as God (Rom. 9:7-8). Thus, it is clear that not all ethnic Jews were part of the Israel of God.

CHURCHMEN

The same is true of the Church in New Testament times. Not all who have been part of the visible church belong to Christ. There have always been people in the Church who intellectually identify with the visible church; acting like Christians, they may have been members, pastors, or even elders, but they received the Scriptures with "moderation and reason." They are convinced that neither the Church nor anyone else has a say in their lives. They have never been and will never be spiritually identified with the Body of the Lord Jesus Christ. This is how John describes these "members" of the Church: *"They went out from us, but they were not of us; for if they had been of us, they would have continued with us. But they went out, that* ***it might become plain that they all are not of us.*** *"*(1 John 2:19).

Those who have "fallen away" from Christ have not lost their salvation, because they never had it. Though they were with Christ for a time, they were never in Christ. Those who do not persevere to the end were not children of God; they never truly believed because they were never saved. The Scriptures give us many examples of "believers" who were not true believers.

SIMON

When the popular Simon the magician saw the many miracles performed by Philip, he "believed" on the basis of reason: *"Even Simon himself believed* [really?], *and after being baptized he continued with Philip. And seeing signs and great miracles performed, he was amazed"* (Acts 8:13). Simon believed only intellectually, for personal gain. His body was baptized, immersed in water, but he was not spiritually baptized, immersed in Christ by the Holy Spirit. The Spirit did not transform him, did not regenerate him. There are many Simons in the world who "believe," come into the fellowship of the Church, are baptized, do "good works" in their flesh, live a superficial Christian life—not an inner Christian life, because their heart is not circumcised.

Let us look at the motivation for Simon's action: *"Now when Simon saw that the Spirit was given through the laying on of the apostles' hands, he offered them money, saying, 'Give me this power also, so that anyone on whom I lay my hands may receive the Holy Spirit.' But Peter said to him, '**May your silver perish with you*** [Simon did not really believe], *because you thought you could obtain the gift of God with money! You have neither part nor lot in this matter, for your heart is not right before God. Repent, therefore, of this wickedness of yours, and pray to the Lord that, if possible, the intent of your heart may be forgiven you'"* (Acts 8:18-22). Simon wanted to buy the gift of the Holy Spirit. He thought that God the Holy Spirit would obey him and serve his own popularity. How do we know that he acted carnally? The words "pray to the Lord that, if possible, the intent of your heart may be forgiven you" prove that although Simon "believed," he was not a child of God at that time. Only God knows if he was truly one of God's elect, whom He loves with an everlasting love. If Simon was one of the elect, then surely he was drawn to God in a saving way after this unfortunate experience.

JUDAS

Judas also falls into the category of those who were in the presence of Christ, but not in Christ. Judas was enlightened by the gospel at first hand. Although he received knowledge directly from the mouth of God, he did not belong to God from the beginning: *"'But there are some of you who do not believe.' (**For Jesus knew from the beginning who those were who did not believe**, and who it was who would betray him)"* (John 6:64). Judas never believed with saving faith, even though he walked and ate with Christ, and for a time he seemed credible as His disciple. Judas is a type of all man-centered church members who "went out from us, but they were not of us." Yet such "believers" may not ever fall away from the visible church. For their own personal reasons, they can appear to remain in Christ until they die, even though they have never truly been in Christ, for God's sake.

SPIRITUAL NARCISSISTS

In churches today, a significant number of people believe God has given them more than they deserve, responding as if they have a direct phone line to heaven. They feel that God speaks to them personally: "God has told me"; He "sends" them extra-biblical prophecies, allowing them to add to the Scriptures; they stir up "spiritual gifts" within themselves and impart them to each other through courses designed to make them more spiritual (and more admirable). In this, they completely ignore the truth that the gifts are given by the Spirit of God alone, as He wills (1 Cor. 12:11). They live as Christians on thin ice (Rev. 22:18-19). So, this may be said of some of them: Could they lose their "salvation" if they were never saved? *"On that day many will say to me, 'Lord, Lord, did we not prophesy in your name, and cast out demons in your name, and do many mighty works in your name?' And then will I declare to them, '**I never*** [since the foundation of the world] ***knew you*** [I never loved you with an everlasting, saving love]*; depart from me, you workers of lawlessness'"* (Matt. 7:22-23).

Christ addressed "believers" who were never part of His flock. Christ never shepherded them because He never knew them, even though people viewed them as distinguished for their zeal in the visible church, doing many mighty works and miracles and overflowing with "gifts" exercised in Jesus' name. People who use religion to build their own glory and realize their own ambitions, like Simon (Acts 8:18-22), completely miss the fact that it is God who calls, not man. They have not yet grasped God's monergistic, one-sided grace. They have not grasped the essence of the Christian faith, nor recognized their own sinfulness and utter lostness and their need for forgiveness and rebirth. Gaining understanding of God's holiness, sovereignty, and goodness and God's sacrificial love, saving grace, and sealing of the elect through the Holy Spirit in Christ leads them to spiritual transformation, immense gratitude, true humility, and faithful perseverance in sanctification to the end.

DOES GOD ERASE SINNERS FROM THE BOOK OF LIFE?

We know that traditional Arminians believe that a saved person can lose his salvation. Therefore, they must also believe that God can and does erase "saved" apostates from the Book of Life. When we speak of the Book of Life, we are not referring to a bound or paperback book, a physical scroll, or a book printed on paper. Nor is it a card catalog that contains all members of the visible church, many of whom were never written in the Book of Life. The Book of Life is God's list of the elect, His redeemed, those He has regenerated. The timeless, all-knowing God does not need to write their names in books. He does not need ledgers to weigh good and bad deeds, to tally them up and close them out. He needs no reminders, makes no revisions, and has no forgetfulness (as we fallen humans do). The biblical image God's book conveys to us is of God's absolute, unchanging mind, something humans can scarcely comprehend and grasp. Let us remember again, for the umpteenth time, that the God we know from Scriptures is independently sovereign, unchanging, and timeless: *"Your eyes saw my* [David's] *unformed substance; in your book were written, every one of them, the days that were formed for me, when as yet there was none of them* [God has woven the thread of history]*"* (Ps. 139:16).

No one imagines that God sits at a desk with a pen and inkwell, or a pencil, or a computer, and writes out his plans, so that he will not forget how every human life (not just David's) will unfold second by second (Ps. 139:16). He certainly does not print His "books" on a printing press or on laser printer. God exists in the third heaven (2 Cor. 12:2), outside of space, time, and matter, i.e., He is not bound by the coexisting elements of this three-dimensional universe. It is inconceivable that God would make His history on the fly, in the time and space He created. It would be absurd to think that God had to discover in time that this "William Rebelton" had rejected Him, when previously in eternity past, He had written his name in the Book of Life. It would be even more absurd to think that if, after "discovering" that he had forsaken the faith, God were to reach for an eraser, turn to the appropriate page, and erase the ungrateful Billy from the Book of Life.

God's will is as unchangeable as solid rock—singular, unique, exclusive in all things, and yet optimally dynamic. The will of God has been given once and for all. The Triune God will surely fulfill His eternal purpose in earthly, temporal history. In order that we, fallen creatures limited by time, space, and flesh—and forgetful—may understand that the unchanging will of God is stored in His eternal, holy mind, the Holy Spirit communicates it to us in an intelligible manner in Scripture, in a such way that God's will can be discerned in "books" or on "scrolls." But on the day of judgment, His eternal books will be opened (Dan. 7:10; Rev. 20:12) and the absolutely sovereign, eternal, timeless will of God will be revealed: *"The beast that you saw was, and is not* [Rev. 20:3], *and is about to rise from the bottomless pit* [Rev. 20:7] *and go to destruction. And the dwellers on earth* ***whose names have not been written in the book of life from the foundation of the world*** [God has not had mercy or compassion on them since the beginning of time; Ex. 33:19] *will marvel to see the beast, because it was and is not and is to come* [to fight the Lamb; Rev. 17:13-14]"(Rev. 17:8).

Those who have not been enrolled in His holy mind from all eternity, according to His sovereign will—those whom He never knew, those whom He did not love with redeeming love—will be condemned. This negative statement also makes it clear that God has in His "book" of life (in His mind), a specific, named "list" of all who were chosen for eternal life through the new birth of the Holy Spirit. These are those whom God has loved with an eternal redeeming love, whom He has stored up in His loving heart, by His sovereign will. They were written in His Book of Life from all eternity (Eph. 1:4; Ps. 139:16): *"Yes, I ask you also, true companion, help these women* [Euodia and Syntyche], *who have labored side by side with me in the gospel together with Clement and the rest of my fellow workers,* ***whose names are in the book of life"*** (Phil. 4:3). Or: *"...and to the assembly of the firstborn* ***who are enrolled in heaven*** [in the mind of God, in His book], *and to God, the judge of all, and to the spirits of the righteous made perfect"* (Heb. 12:23). Traditional Arminians will point to the book of Revelation, where God says He will not blot out the names of those who overcome, to assert that God can blot someone out of the Book of Life: *"The one who conquers will be clothed thus in white garments, and* ***I will never blot his name out of the book of life*** [I will always keep my word and never change it, as compared to fallen man]. *I will confess his name before my Father and before his angels"* (Rev. 3:5). This verse simply affirms that God's elect cannot lose their salvation, because God does not change the history He ordained in ages past (Isa. 46:10). By saying, "I will never blot his name out of the book of life," God emphasizes that we need never fear that He will change or abrogate His plans and purposes, as fallen man does.

From the following verse, traditional Arminians conclude that God can change His plans: *"'But now, if you will forgive their sin* [of worshipping the golden calf]*—but if not,* ***please blot me*** [Moses] ***out*** *of your book that you have written.' But the LORD said to Moses, '****Whoever has sinned against me, I will blot out of***

my book'" (Ex. 32:32-33). In this verse, Moses laments over the Israelites who, instead of relying on God, made a calf of gold, worshiped it, sacrificed to it, claiming: *"These are your gods, O Israel, who brought you up out of the land of Egypt"* (Ex. 32:8b)! They were not a faithful people, but a crowd of common idolaters. Horrified but loving Moses proposed a "better solution" to God. He asked that God blot him out of the Book of Life instead of the idolatrous Israelites. He was motivated by compassion and love for his people. But if God could accept man's "better" advice, He would cease to be God. No one can advise God! Were God to accept human advice, He would be admitting that His plan was not perfect. Even Abraham could not persuade God to spare Sodom if he could find at least ten righteous men in it—God knew he would not find even one (Gen. 18:23-33).

No one and nothing can cause God to change His eternal decrees, which also applies to the given list of His elect. The Lord dealt with Moses as He deals with us, answering him humanly, intelligibly, in time and space, and correcting his erroneous assumption. Moses was asking the impossible, for a change in the Triune Office, as if God could change and revoke His statutes, decrees, orders. In essence, God responds to Moses—"I will not blot you out, Moses; I will 'blot out' from my book the one who has sinned against me." In fact, in His unchanging yet dynamic mind, God could not have blotted Moses out of His Book, because the Book of Life was established before the foundation of the world (Eph. 1:4). In fact, He would not blot out from the Book of Life the idolatrous Israelites who danced around the golden calf because their names had not been stored in His Book of Life from the foundation of the world (Rev. 17:8). God decided in eternity past who is written in His Book of Life and who is not. From the beginning, He established what will happen in the future, what is unchangeable, and what is guaranteed to happen (Isa. 46:10).

Paul had the same love for Israel that Moses had: ***"For I could wish*** *that I myself were accursed and cut off from Christ for the sake of my brothers, my kinsmen according to the flesh"* (Rom. 9:3). Unlike Moses, Paul understood that God's decree was unchangeable. Therefore, unlike Moses, he did not demand: *"...please blot me out of your book that you have written"* (Ex. 32:32), but he merely sighed in his longing to be accursed for the sake of Israel.

CONCLUSION

18

SUMMARY, TESTIMONY AND PRACTICAL LIFE

CALVINISM IN A NUTSHELL

THE FIVE POINTS IN ROMANS 5:8-11

Together we have penetrated all five points of the Synod of Dort—all five points of Calvinism—which are a direct response to the five points of the Remonstrance:

1. The total spiritual inability, the corruption of man.
2. God's unconditional, sovereign election.
3. Christ's limited, efficacious, purposeful redemption.
4. Irresistible grace, efficacious calling of the Spirit.
5. The perseverance of the saints, the preservation of the saints by God.

We have shown that each of these five points permeates the entire Scriptures. In conclusion, let us return to the verses (Rom. 5:8-11) with which we began[68] and prove that God's saving love and

68 See chapter 1; section: Humanism is Alien to God; heading: Focusing on Man Distorts Scripture

the Cross of Christ do not apply to all people without exception. Moreover, all five points of Calvinism are beautifully summarized in these verses, namely, that God will not share His Glory in salvation with anyone:

- [8] *but God shows his love* ***for us*** [only for us, unconditionally, sovereignly elect—point 2] *in that while* ***we were*** *still sinners* [totally spiritually incapable and depraved—point 1], *Christ died* ***for us*** [Christ efficaciously and purposefully redeemed only us—point 3].
- [9] *Since, therefore,* ***we have*** *now been justified by his blood* [only we have been efficaciously and purposefully justified by the Cross of Christ—Point 3], *much more* ***shall we be*** *saved by him from the wrath of God* [only we will persevere to the end—point 5].
- [10] *For if while* ***we were*** *enemies* [utterly spiritually incapable and corrupt—point 1] ***we were*** *reconciled to God by the death of his Son* [only we have been efficaciously and purposefully reconciled by Christ to God—point 3], *much more, now that* ***we are*** *reconciled,* ***shall we be*** *saved by his life* [only we will be preserved to the end—point 5].
- [11] *More than that,* ***we*** *also rejoice in God through our Lord Jesus Christ* [only we rejoice in the pardon and efficacious calling of the Spirit—point 4], *through whom* ***we have*** *now received reconciliation* [Christ efficaciously and purposefully received only us—Point 3].

LOVE FLOWS THROUGH THE RIVERBED OF TRUTH

Let us repeat what we started with. In order to satisfy the demands of Arminians, Semi-Pelagians, and Pelagians, or anyone else with a man-centered understanding of Scripture, that is, that God loves all people without exception with the same saving love, we would have to rewrite Romans 5:8-11 to the following absurdity:

- [8] but God shows his love for ~~us~~ **all men without exception** in that while we **all men without exception** were still sinners, Christ died for ~~us~~ **all men without exception**.
- [9] Since, therefore, ~~we~~ **all men without exception** have now been justified by his blood, much more shall ~~we~~ **all men without exception** be saved by him from the wrath of God.
- [10] For if while ~~we~~ **all men without exception** were enemies ~~we~~ **all men without exception** were reconciled to God by the death of his Son, much more, now that ~~we~~ **all men without exception** are reconciled, shall ~~we~~ **all men without exception** be saved by his life.
- [11] More than that, ~~we~~ **all men without exception** also rejoice in God through ~~our~~ **all men without exception's** Lord Jesus Christ, through whom ~~we~~ **all men without exception** have now received reconciliation.

TESTIMONIES OF GOD'S MEN

CHARLES H. SPURGEON (1834-1892)

ON CALVINISM AND ARMINIANISM

- *It is no novelty, then, that I am preaching; no new doctrine. I love to proclaim these strong old doctrines, which are called by nickname Calvinism, but which are surely and verily the revealed truth of God as it is in Christ Jesus. (Sermon 41-42; 09/02/1855)*
- *I have my own private opinion that there is no such thing as preaching Christ and Him crucified, unless we preach what*

now-a-days is called Calvinism. (...) It is a nickname to call it Calvinism; Calvinism is the gospel, and nothing else. (Sermon 7-8; 02/11/1855)

- *You have heard a great many Arminian sermons, I dare say; but you never heard an Arminian prayer—for the saints in prayer appear as one in word, and deed and mind. An Arminian on his knees would pray desperately like a Calvinist. He cannot pray about free-will: there is no room for it. (Sermon 52; 12/02/1855)*
- *Whitfield said, "We are all born Arminians." It is grace that turns us into Calvinists. (Sermon 69; 03/02/1856)*
- *The doctrine which is called "Calvinism" did not spring from Calvin. We believe that it sprang from the great Founder of all truth. (Sermon 385-88; 04/11/1861)*
- *I am not a Calvinist by choice, but because I cannot help it. The truths I preach are in me, part and parcel of myself: I do not carry my creed, but my creed carries me. (Sermon 1085)*
- *Calvinism is the gospel, and nothing else. I do not believe we can preach the gospel, if we do not preach justification by faith without works; nor unless we preach the sovereignty of God in his dispensation of grace; nor unless we exalt the electing, unchangeable, eternal, immutable, conquering love of Jehovah; nor, I think, can we preach the gospel, unless we base it upon the peculiar redemption which Christ made for his elect and chosen people; nor can I comprehend a gospel which lets saints fall away after they are called, and suffers the children of God to be burned in the fires of damnation, after having believed. Such a gospel I abhor. The gospel of the Bible is not such a gospel as that. We preach Christ and him crucified in a different fashion, and to all gainsayers we reply, 'We have not so learned*

Christ.' (Spurgeon's Sermons, vol. I [Baker Books, reprinted 2007], 88-89.)

ABOUT FREE WILL

- *Free will carried many a soul to hell, but never a soul to heaven. (Hockney, Mike. Free Will and Will to Power. [s.l.] : Lulu Press, Inc, 2014.)*
- *Free-will doctrine—what does it do? It magnifies man into God. It declares God's purposes a nullity, since they cannot be carried out unless men are willing. It makes God's will a waiting servant to the will of man, and the whole covenant of grace dependent on human action. Denying election on the ground of injustice, it holds God to be a debtor to sinners. (Sermon 502; 03/29/1863)*
- *Free will I have often heard of, but I have never seen it. I have always met with will, and plenty of it, but it has either been led captive by sin or held in the blessed bonds of grace*[69].

GEORGE MÜLLER (1805-1898)

Before this period (1829) *I had been much opposed to the doctrines of election, particular redemption, and final persevering grace; so much so that, a few days after my arrival at Teignmouth, I called election a devilish doctrine. ... I knew nothing about the choice of God's people, and did not believe that the child of God, when once made so, was safe for ever. ... But now I was brought to examine these precious truths by the word of God. ... Being made willing to have no glory of my own in the conversion of sinners, but to consider myself merely as an instru-*

69 *(Spurgeon at His Best: Over 2200 Striking Quotations from the World's Most Exhaustive and Widely-read Sermon Series. S. 218); https://cs.wikiquote.org/wiki/Charles_Spurgeon*

> *ment; and being made willing to receive what the Scriptures said; I went to the Word, reading the New Testament from the beginning, with a particular reference to these truths. To my great astonishment I found that the passages which speak decidedly for election and persevering grace, were about four times as many as those which speak apparently against these truths; and even those few, shortly after, when I had examined and understood them, served to confirm me in the above doctrines. As to the effect which my belief in these doctrines had on me, I am constrained to state, for God's glory, that though I am still exceedingly weak, and by no means so dead to the lusts of the flesh, and the lust of the eyes, and the pride of life, as I might and as I ought to be, yet, by the grace of God, I have walked more closely with Him since that period. My life has not been so variable, and I may say that I have lived much more for God than before. ...*

About forty years later, in 1870, Müller spoke to some young believers about the importance of what had happened to him at Teignmouth. He said that his preaching had been fruitless for four years from 1825 to 1829 in Germany, but then he came to England and was taught the doctrines of grace:

> *In the course of time, I came to this country [England], and it pleased God then to show to me the doctrines of grace in a way in which I had not seen them before. At first, I hated them, "If this were true, I could do nothing at all in the conversion of sinners, as all would depend upon God and the working of His Spirit." But when it pleased God to reveal these truths to me, and my heart was brought to such a state that I could say, "I am not only content simply to be a hammer, an axe, or a saw, in God's hands; but I shall count it an honor to be taken up and used by Him in any way; and if sinners are converted through*

> *my instrumentality, from my inmost soul I will give Him all the glory"; the Lord gave me to see fruit; the Lord gave me to see fruit in abundance; sinners were converted by scores; and ever since God has used me in one way or other in His service*[70].

JONATHAN EDWARDS (1703-1758)

> *Do you know what sparked the Great Awakening? It was a series of sermons Edwards preached in 1734 on 'Justification By Faith' in response to what he considered to be the greatest danger to America. Do you know what he saw as the greatest danger to America? It would ruin the colonies, Edwards said. ARMINIANISM—a plague that would rob God of His glory. It was a plague that would strip the church of the power of God and diminish the worship of God. It was a faulty theology that was centered upon man that brought God down to man's terms. That's what Arminianism is my friends*[71].

PRACTICAL LIFE

PAUL'S DIRECTIVES

Even the born-again Christian, drawn to Christ by the Father—the new inner man, the new creature with a circumcised heart, irrevocably sealed in Christ by the Holy Spirit—remains trapped in the natural body. This is why Paul confesses and gives instructions on how to live the Christian life: *"Every athlete exercises self-control in all things. They do it to receive a perishable wreath, but we an imperishable. So I do not run aimlessly; I do not box as one beating the air.* ***But I discipline my body and keep it under control*** [resist everything that is not of the Spirit of God], *lest after preaching to others I myself should be disqualified"* (1 Cor. 9:25-27). In no

70 *(John Piper 27 Servants of Sovereign Joy)*
71 Steven Lawson

unbeliever is there such a struggle between the law of Christ and the "law" of the members of the flesh. God's people, however, do not need to continually flagellate themselves with this condition. Thanks be to God; His people are delivered to live as Paul exhorts in Romans 8.

The practical Christian life, according to Paul, is a struggle between the new, spiritually born inner man and the outer, old man. Throughout "Salvation and Faith," this struggle is identified with ongoing repentance and sanctification to the end. Who has delivered us from the body of death? Only God! "*...that the creation itself will be set free from its bondage to corruption and obtain the freedom of the glory of the children of God. For we know that the whole creation has been groaning together in the pains of childbirth until now. And not only the creation, but* ***we ourselves, who have the firstfruits of the Spirit, groan inwardly as we wait eagerly for adoption as sons, the redemption of our bodies***" (Rom. 8:21-23). The bodily, second resurrection—the redemption of the body, the receiving of a glorified body—is the final phase of the entire salvation of God's chosen people.[72].

THE COURSE OF A CHRISTIAN

The one who truly believes that Christ has taken his place in punishment, that God has (1) regenerated him for His sake, (2) justified him, (3) gave him power to repent, sanctified him with knowledge, wisdom, and love for God, and (4) will redeem his body on the last day, thus glorifying him. A true believer cannot and will not "nail" the Lord Jesus Christ to the cross again. All of us always want to show love to a loved one, not to torment him. The love of Christ is the born-again person's motivation not to sin. Christ is his lifestyle. The one who truly loves the Lord his God with all his heart, with

72 See chapter 3; section: "Salvation and Faith" According to the Reformation.

all his soul, with all his strength, and his neighbor as himself, who is an integral part of His "salvation and faith," is running toward his Goal. The man of God lives in this world, but is not of the world (John 15:19). He sails on the ocean of the world, but the indwelling Spirit of God seals every crack so that water will not enter his vessel. For the true Christian, sin is not a minor mishap that throws him back into the arms of Christ; it is repentance! This is the only way he can survive and live in a world that is enslaved to evil: *"We know that we are from God* [we are God's children], ***and the whole world lies in the power of the evil one*** [the people of the world are the Devil's children]. *And we know that the Son of God has come and* ***has given us understanding, so that we may know him who is true****; and we are in him who is true, in his Son Jesus Christ. He is the true God and eternal life"* (1 John 5:19-20).

It is not necessary to recall wars, concentration camps, gulags, deliberate famines, genocides, and countless other horrors caused by fallen man in order to describe the evil lifestyle of natural man. It is enough to illustrate it with a tiny but perfectly typical story. It is an "innocent" story that we encounter every day.

I scratched the side of my car in the garage. In the dealership, they suggested that my only option was to replace the door, which they calculated at $2,500 back in 2005. When I raised my eyebrows, the repair person said: "Let us look at it another way. Do you have insurance? What if you parked in front of the supermarket and noticed this scratch when you got back to your car...!?" The temptation was great—$2500 is $2500. I entertained an evil thought for a while, and if God hadn't turned me away from the world to Himself, I would have succumbed. But that would have been my spiritual collapse. I would have had to live with the knowledge of another failure, even if no other living soul knew about it—but nothing is hidden from God. In the end, a private car painter fixed my door perfectly for a quarter of the quoted price.

A CHRISTIAN NO LONGER NEEDS TO SIN

Our inner, invisible sins of thought are so heinous that communication by words alone is a great blessing from God. If we communicated without words, in spirit, by looking directly into the hearts of one another, the whole world would collapse in devastation! Communication from one person to another, even from Christian to Christian, would become impossibly difficult because of how fallen man is!

So how does one defeat inner sin? By constant repentance and turning from evil to God, and by constant prayer. This is sanctification, growth in the knowledge of God. God has equipped His people for this sanctification by creating in us a new inner man. Sin and the Devil no longer have power over God's people as they do over the natural man: *"**Submit yourselves therefore to God**. Resist the devil, and he will flee from you. **Draw near to God**, and he will draw near to you"* (James 4:7-8a). To draw near to God is to seek God through the Scriptures. Without the indwelling Spirit of God, the Scriptures would be an empty letter to us, even though they are God's Word. To know God is to love Him, and he who loves God, who is sealed by the Spirit of God, overcomes temptation. We cannot prevent a bird from sitting on our head, but we can prevent it from building a nest on it.

Joseph should be our example (Gen. 39:1-12). He was tempted day after day by Potiphar's wife, who was certainly attractive because rich and influential rulers choose young beauties to be around them. Joseph was tempted, but he resisted. God and His law were more important to Joseph than Potiphar's beautiful wife. Even when she grabbed him by the robe and urged him on, he did not yield to temptation but slipped away from her (Gen. 39:12), preferring instead to take his heels. Scripture says our practical Christian life should look like this, not giving in to any temptation that is against the law, which for us today is Christ. Every man understands Joseph's situation. But women face temptations as well, perhaps not in the eyes, but in the tongue. We know that sin is fornication, idolatry, adultery, immorality, effeminacy, perversity, self-adulation, theft, covetousness, drunkenness, lying, slander, envy, greed, polytheism, gluttony, strife, hatred (which is unfinished murder in God's sight), selfishness, scheming, self-centeredness, lewdness, etc. etc. The list goes on and on.

God's people, like Paul, hate temptation and sin. Like Paul we know that the law of Christ is good, and for Christ's sake we want to live for the glory of God; like Paul, we groan inwardly (Rom. 8:21-23) and look forward to a new, glorified body in which there will be no more temptation or sin: *"I am hard pressed between the two. My desire is to depart and be with Christ, for that is far better. But to remain in the flesh is more necessary on your account"* (Phil. 1:23-24).

And what if a man of God succumbs to temptation? What happens when in a weak moment sin becomes more attractive than Christ? That's what happened to Peter when he denied his Lord. Then it is no small calamity that brings the man of God to his knees in repentance and prayer. God will not abandon His straying sheep but brings them back to His flock on His shoulders (Luke 15:4-7). God the Son is the Advocate for His children, and no one, not even the Devil, can win them over permanently: *"My little children, I am writing these things to you so that you may not sin. But if anyone does sin, we have an advocate with the Father, Jesus Christ the righteous"* (1 John 2:1).

SUPPLEMENTS

I

EVANGELIZATION IN THE REFORMED CONCEPT

GENERALLY, ABOUT EVANGELIZATION

WHY DO WE EVANGELIZE?

This is the natural reaction of those who encounter the doctrine of predestination and election: "If God has already predestined everything, why should we even bother to evangelize?" A woman sent this to the editorial office of The Battle for Souls, addressed to me: "Since God has already predestined everything, there is no need for a battle for souls." The answer is: "It is precisely because God has predestined everything that evangelization can and must take place." Predestination makes it possible for evangelism to be efficacious. If God had not chosen people from the foundation of the world, if He had left everyone in their natural sinful state, then evangelism would be pointless. There would be no one to evangelize because all would remain in a state of condemnation. All would be outside of God's saving love, outside of His mercy and His purpose to bring His people to Himself in the Kingdom of Heaven. This woman's logic was unsound. She was basically saying, "If God has predestined Mr. Smith to live a hundred years, then Mr. Smith could fold his hands in his lap. He would not have to worry about anything or pay attention to anything—he would not need to eat or drink; he could throw himself in front of trains because nothing will happen to him. God guaranteed him a hundred years." But God not only set the goal, He also ordained all the sub-steps leading to His goal. Everybody has to go through them. God is not only Alpha and Omega, but all the letters—Alpha, Beta, Gamma, Delta ... Upsilon, Phi, Chi, Psi, Omega.

God does not reckon with human self-will and natural "free" will enslaved by the Devil; He reckons with His new creation. Evangelism is always efficacious because though its seeds fall on the wayside, on the rock, among the thorns (Matt. 13:3-7), ultimately, they fall on the good soil (Matt. 13:8). If God had not prepared the good soil, all the seeds would have withered—the efforts of those who preach the Word to a perishing world would be in vain because all the seeds would fall by the wayside, on the rock, or among the thorns. Moreover, if God had not chosen anyone, there would be no one to preach the Word.

Because Calvinists submit fully to God's sovereign power, they evangelize precisely in reliance upon God's election, salvation, and regeneration of sinners. They have confidence that the word they sow will not return empty (Isa. 55:11; 2 Cor. 2:15-16).

Arminians evangelize out of compassion for the lost and desire to save sinners from God's wrath (Heb. 10:31), but they limit God's sovereignty to man's "free" will. Thus, they can only hope that people freely choose Christ rather than reject God's prevenient grace. In short, their hope is man-centered—they rely on man's "free" will and benefit (anthropocentrism), instead of being consumed by God-centered prayer: *"Your kingdom come, your will be done, on earth as it is in heaven"* (Matt. 6:10) and by His purpose, power, and Glory (theocentrism).

SPREADING THE GOSPEL IS A PRIVILEGE

In a sense, physical conception is a physical image of spiritual rebirth. God, out of His providential common grace, created mankind to be able to reproduce physically. Angels have no such privilege. The man sows his seed in the woman's womb, but whether the seed and the womb are capable of physical reproduction is entirely in God's power: *"Then God remembered Rachel, and* ***God listened to her and opened her womb****"* (Gen. 30:22). Likewise, God created a spiritual people out of His saving grace so that they could multiply spiritually. Once again, angels do not have this privilege. The man of God, the evangelist, plants in the heart of his fellow man the seed of the Good News, the powerful Word that testifies of the Son of God who came to save what was lost (Luke 19:10); whether the heart of the recipient is ready to receive the gospel, as preached by Paul in Gal. 1:8-9, whether the heart has been circumcised by God and is capable of bearing spiritual fruit, is determined by the absolute power of God. God is supreme in everything: *"I* [Paul] *planted, Apollos watered* [preached the gospel], ***but God gave the growth*** [circumcised the heart]*"* (1 Cor. 3:6).

The spreading of the gospel is not in vain, for the Lord has His people in many places: *"And the Lord said to Paul one night in a vision, 'Do not be afraid, but* ***go on speaking and do not be silent****, for I am with you, and no one will attack you to harm you,* ***for I have many in this city*** *who are my people.' And he stayed a year and six months, teaching the word of God among them"* (Acts 18:9-11). Such verses about God's Glory and goodness are motivating. God had a chosen people in that land and in those cities who do not yet know that they had been called from their mother's womb (Isa. 49:1; 49:5; Jer. 1:5; Gal. 1:15-16). They did not know that Paul would teach them the Word of God and sow the gospel into their hearts, which God had opened to receive it (Acts 16:14). If we do not sow it, God may create other sowers from stone in our place

(Matt. 3:9). So, who will tell God's people about His praiseworthy works, namely the redemptive Cross of the Lord Jesus Christ? Let us pray that God will not disqualify us from His evangelistic plan because of our sin.

WHAT IS THE GOSPEL? WHO PROCLAIMS IT?

The gospel literally means good news. This is the most concise and succinct definition: *"And Jesus said to him, '**Today salvation has come to this house, since he also is a son of Abraham*** [the promised, chosen one, Zacchaeus]. ***For the Son of Man came to seek and to save the lost**'"* (Luke 19:9-10). All of Adam's descendants are born spiritually dead, separated from God, having fallen into sin; all are born into perdition: ***"For the wages of sin is death*** [physical and spiritual, i.e., eternal separation from God—the lake of fire, hell], ***but the free gift of God is eternal life** in Christ Jesus our Lord* [an eternal, intimate relationship with God]"(Rom. 6:23). Jesus Christ, the Son of Man, was born of a virgin. Like sinful man, He came in the flesh, (Rom. 8:3). He was sacrificed and punished on the Cross for those whom the Father gave Him to redeem from the prison of Satan, where one is spiritually dead, trapped in sin: *"For the law of the Spirit of life has set you free in Christ Jesus from the law of sin and death. For God has done what the law, weakened by the flesh, could not do. By sending his own Son in the likeness of sinful flesh and for sin, he condemned sin in the flesh, in order that the righteous requirement of the law might **be fulfilled in us, who walk not according to the flesh but according to the Spirit**"* (Rom. 8:2-4).

The gospel of Jesus Christ is the most powerful, empowering, supernatural message anyone could ever hear! But only His sheep hear the voice of their Lord (John 10:27) when the gospel is preached: *"For 'everyone who calls on the name of the Lord will be saved'"* (Rom. 10:13). Who preaches the gospel to a perishing world? It is those whom God has already called, called aloud, and commissioned to reign with Him on earth between His two comings (Rev. 20:4b): *"But thanks be to God, who in Christ always leads us in triumphal procession,* ***and through us spreads the fragrance of the knowledge of him everywhere****. For we are the aroma of Christ to God among those who are being saved and among those who are perishing, to one a fragrance from death to death, to the other a fragrance from life to life. Who is sufficient for these things? For we are not, like so many, peddlers of God's word, but as men of sincerity, as commissioned by God, in the sight of God we speak in Christ"* (2 Cor. 2:14-17). We see that true evangelists minister by God's commission because they are His royal priesthood. The qualification for such a mission is to be born-again of the Holy Spirit. However, many church professionals seek a comfortable life in the gospel.

THE CHURCH AGE IS THE AGE OF EVANGELISM

Let us follow Paul's example of evangelism: *"Continue steadfastly in prayer, being watchful in it with thanksgiving. At the same time, pray* [you who are His] *also for us,* ***that God may open to us a door for the word*** [thus that the hearts of God's people may be circumcised], ***to declare the mystery of Christ****, on account of which I am in prison—that I may make it clear, which is how I ought to speak. Walk in wisdom toward outsiders, making the best use of the time. Let your speech always be gracious, seasoned with salt,* ***so that you may know how you ought to answer each person****"* (Col. 4:2-6).

The days between the two comings of Christ are what we call the last days. These are the days of evangelization, the days of the proclamation of Christ, the days of grace, the days of the Church Age, the days of entry into the Kingdom of God. No one enters the Kingdom of God through the "door" opened by St. Peter. Nor does anyone open it themselves. It is opened by the King of kings and Lord of lords, Jesus Christ. When this epoch of the preaching of the gospel comes to an end at the Second Coming of our Lord, the door of entrance will be closed, as it was on Noah's ark. Those who are in Christ will be saved; those who are outside of Christ will be lost, as in the Flood. Then comes the Last Judgment, the Day of the Lord, the New Earth and the New Heaven. The Old Testament prophet Isaiah described the days of grace between the two advents of Christ with wonderful foreshadowing: *"Behold, I am doing* [creating] *a new thing; now it springs forth* [the Church Age], *do you not perceive it?* ***I will make a way*** [Christ is the way; John 14:6] *in the wilderness* [the spiritually dead world] *and rivers* [my elect—the Church] *in the desert"* (Isa. 43:19). *"the people whom I formed for myself* [My royal priesthood; 1 Pet. 2:9] *that they might declare my praise* [they will testify that I have borne their sins and redeemed them from the prison of the Evil One]*"* (Isa. 43:19,21).

The present world is this spiritual desert and wilderness. The people God has created form the Church, the body of Christ. This people who are living in the wilderness of the world will tell of the living water (John 4:10-15), of the way of Christ (John 14:6), of God's praiseworthy deeds, of His saving, unconditional grace which He bestows according to His holy will (Rom. 9:23). Isaiah saw and prophesied about this age of salvation through the Lord Jesus Christ in these words: *"From of old no one has heard or perceived by the ear, no eye has seen a God besides you, who acts for those who wait for him"* (Isa. 64:4). Paul interpreted these words of Isaiah, telling the Corinthian Christians that what eye has not seen and ear has not heard is already here: *"But, as it is written* [in Isaiah], *'What no eye has seen, nor ear heard, nor the heart of man imagined,* ***what God has prepared for those who love him****'"* (1 Cor. 2:9b). What the eye has not seen, the ear has not heard, and the mind has not conceived is the Lord Jesus Christ and the presence of His chosen, newly created people in His kingdom. This is the Glory of God that God's people proclaim to a starving, parched, dying world.

GOD'S PEOPLE EVANGELIZE—REIGN WITH CHRIST

After His ascension, in this last time, the time between His first and second coming, the Lord Jesus Christ rules the earth from His heavenly throne at the right hand of the majesty of God on high (Heb. 1:2-3). With Him reign all "saved and believing," both those in the body and those who have died out of the body whom God has raised spiritually with Christ, bringing them out of spiritual death—this is the first resurrection (Rev. 20:6). He has granted them a privilege such as eye has not seen and ear has not heard (1 Cor. 2:9), so that they may reign with Christ from the heavenly places in this age of the Church: *"...and raised us up with* [the first, spiritual resurrection] ***him and seated us with him in the heavenly places in Christ Jesus*** [it has already happened]*"* (Eph. 2:6).

God's people dwell in a marvelous light because they are in the Lord Jesus Christ: *"But you are a chosen race, a royal priesthood, a holy nation, a people for his own possession,* ***that you may proclaim the excellencies of him*** [that you may evangelize] *who called you out of darkness* [out of Satan] *into his marvelous light* [Christ]*"* (1 Pet. 2:9).

The Church, which is the temple of God, the body of Jesus Christ, the people of God, the Israel of God, the ecclesia, etc., has been raised to eternal life in Christ through the new birth of the Spirit of God. But the Church includes the martyrs who have been persecuted for their witness of Jesus. The Church is also seated in the heavenly places, having been entrusted with judgment. Christ has wrested the Church from the world system and the prince of the power of the air, namely the Devil. She does not wear his mark on her forehead because she does not think in a worldly way; nor does she wear it on her hand because she does not act as the world does: *"Then I saw thrones, and seated on them were those to whom the authority to judge was committed* [the Church, the temple of God, the body of Jesus Christ, the people of God, the Israel of God, the ecclesia, etc.]. *Also I saw the souls of those who had been beheaded for the testimony* [martyrs, witnesses] *of Jesus and for the word of God, and those who had not worshiped the beast or its image and had not received its mark on their foreheads* [they do not think like the world] *or their hands* [they do not act like the world]. *They came to life* [were born-again] ***and reigned with Christ for a thousand years*** [the period of the Church between Christ's two advents]" (Rev. 20:4).

God's people reign with Christ for a long, indefinite period—"a thousand years" (Rev. 20:4) between His two comings. All those in Christ have the keys to the kingdom of God because they are commissioned to proclaim it, and thus to open and close it (2 Cor. 2:15-16)—they have been empowered to proclaim the gospel, the good news.

Those who have been crucified with Christ and are spiritually raised and translated to the heavenly places have become strangers here on earth (1 Pet. 2:11) because they have received heavenly citizenship (Phil. 3:20). Therefore, they are reigning with Christ today, having received power in Him to proclaim the "unlocking and locking" gospel, that is, to tell of the works of God: *"I will give you the keys of the kingdom of heaven, and* ***whatever you bind on earth shall be bound in heaven, and whatever you loose on earth shall be loosed in heaven****"* (Matt. 16:19). In this verse, Christ empowers Peter and all who believe in Christ's Messiahship—the whole people of God—to be ambassadors of their true heavenly homeland. They can make known on earth what has been bound or loosed in heaven, in the name of Christ: *"If you forgive the sins of any, they are forgiven them; if you withhold forgiveness from any, it is withheld"* (John 20:23). As God's ambassadors on earth, they proclaim God's decision, though they do not themselves determine salvation or damnation. What God has bound, rejected, cast off from heaven, His people here on earth proclaim to be bound, rejected, and cast off; this is the fragrance from death to death (2 Cor. 2:16). What God in heaven has released, accepted, and saved, His people here on earth declare to be released, accepted, saved; this is the fragrance from life to life (2 Cor. 2:16). And this is evangelism from on high. God's sovereignty and Glory are absolutely paramount in evangelism. It is not God's people who save, but God Himself. This explains why worldly evangelistic tactics often miss the mark—only God's "tactics" have power in evangelism, as they flow from His decreed, efficacious will.

Just as humans are born bodily by God's sovereign choice, even though humans have physical parents, so all those who are born spiritually are born-again by God's election, even though they also have "spiritual parents—all Christians receive the keys to the Kingdom of God and are therefore authorized to proclaim what is bound and loosed according to heaven. They sow the gospel with the confidence that God will cause it to grow in the hearts of His elect.

A DEEPER ANALYSIS OF EVANGELISM

THE ORDER OF THE MOTIVATION OF EVANGELIZATION

We often see evangelism that is focused on results, numbers, and methods, driven by the desire to see as many people as possible receive Christ and be saved—all without exception. The vast majority of evangelism today focuses primarily on saving people, but reformed evangelism relegates the salvation of our neighbor to a secondary place. If man's salvation is paramount, then the Glory of God is relegated to second place (Isa. 48:11). If man's joy in salvation takes precedence over God's Glory and joy in salvation (Isa. 62:5), then evangelism becomes man-centered. Scripture clearly urges us not to be primarily focused on human needs, but to do everything—including evangelism—for the Glory of God. God wants us to be God-centered in everything we do (1 Cor. 10:31), so the primary objective in evangelism is to proclaim God's Glory and goodness in salvation (Ex. 33:19).

Think about it: If the primary motive of our evangelistic efforts is the Glory of God, and if our efforts are supported by Scripture, our evangelism cannot fail to achieve its God-ordained goals (2 Cor. 2:15-16). But if our motive is to save as many sinners as possible, then our primary focus becomes what will benefit man—and his "free" decision to follow Christ. If God's Glory becomes secondary in His call to evangelize, God's Glory and goodness will be subservient to fallen man's response to choose whatever he wants to do with the crucified Christ. This man-centered approach to evangelism cannot be fully successful since humanistic desire, i.e., the salvation of all mankind without exception, is contrary to God's stated purpose, i.e., the salvation of His own people (Matt. 1:21).

THE GLORY AND GOODNESS OF GOD IS THE CORRECT MOTIVE FOR EVANGELIZATION

We are called to proclaim the glory of God throughout the world. Our primary, God-given motive in evangelism is to proclaim the exaltation of Christ as Creator and Sustainer of all the visible and invisible universe, of which He is both Savior and Judge. We must overflow with Scripture, backed by an unfeigned, fervent enthusiasm for our Lord, who created us both physically and spiritually by His will and for Himself. Such Christ-glorifying enthusiasm is what God delights to transfer to His chosen people through the Spirit's regeneration that draws them to Himself: *"The LORD has established his throne in the heavens, and his kingdom rules over all. Bless the LORD, O you his angels, you mighty ones who do his word, obeying the voice of his word! Bless the LORD, all his hosts, his ministers, who do his will! Bless the LORD, all his works, in all places of his dominion.* ***Bless the LORD, O my soul****"* (Ps. 103:19-22)!

In our zeal for the gospel, such verses should be engraved on our hearts so that our hearts overflow with them: "*...**to keep the commandment unstained and free from reproach until the appearing of our Lord Jesus Christ**, which he will display at the proper time—he who is the blessed and only Sovereign, the King of kings and Lord of lords, who alone has immortality, who dwells in unapproachable light* [outside of space-time], *whom no one has ever seen or can see. **To him be honor and eternal dominion. Amen***" (1 Tim. 6:14-16). When Paul was in idolatrous Athens, he preached the resurrection of Jesus to believing Jews and Gentiles in the inner circle of the synagogue and to unbelievers and philosophers in the marketplace (Acts 17:17-18). His first public evangelistic appearance before a Gentile congregation, however, was on the Areopagus (Acts 17:19-33). He did not begin with the gospel that Christ had come to save the perishing, but he opened his discourse in all godliness. The reason behind Paul's evangelism was the greatness and Glory of God. His primary motive was not to save Gentile Athenians because Paul knew that salvation itself was a consequence of God's Glory and goodness (Ex. 33:18-19). That is why his sermon introduced them to the Most High as a first priority: "*The God who made the world and everything in it, being Lord of heaven and earth, does not live in temples made by man, nor is he served by human hands, as though he needed anything, since he himself gives to all mankind life and breath and everything*" (Acts 17:24-25). In this important evangelistic passage of Scripture (Acts 17:16-33), Paul refrained from mentioning the redeeming Cross of Christ until verse 31 where he mentioned Christ's resurrection, without ever referring to His substitutionary death.

Knowing the Holy One, true understanding of who God is, completely changes a Christian's approach to evangelism. Of course, salvation of the lost is at the heart of evangelism, but the knowledge, exaltation, holiness, and Glory of God precedes the redemptive Cross because the Glory of God culminates in the Cross. The Glory and goodness of God is the cause; the Cross is the effect. A small, finite God could never invent the idea of salvation through the Cross, much less bring it about. The greatness of the salvation of sinners is due to the exaltation of the triune God. The one who hears the Good News must first understand that salvation is through sovereign God who has no limits; otherwise he will understand the Cross in a limited sense, as if it were "only" the man Jesus who saves him through his own personal "decision"—that is, salvation is only in man. The gravity of the Cross is that it was the unlimited Creator of all things who died on it, in the likeness of sinful human flesh, for His divine Glory; this destroys all human evangelistic strategies, man-centered tactics for the benefit of man.

God created His people, the Israel of God, for Himself, and for no one else: *"I, I am he who blots out your transgressions* ***for my own sake****, and I will not remember your sins"* (Isa. 43:25). *"...****the people whom I formed for myself*** *that they might declare my praise"* (Isa. 43:21). God's sovereignty is boundless; it is not limited by anything or anyone, and it is therefore indefinable. Our absolute God creates His own in such a way that we are left in speechless amazement: *"And do not presume to say to yourselves, 'We have Abraham as our father,' for I tell you,* ***God is able from these stones to raise up children for Abraham****"* (Matt. 3:9). This is not an image, but a reality; after all, man was created from the dust of the ground. Let us not think that we can bring someone to faith on our own. God molded us out of clay to make it clear that this immense power given to us is from God and not from us (2 Cor. 4:6-7). He created us anew to sow His glorious salvation to our neighbors, whom we are to love as ourselves (Matt. 22:37-40). It is He who reaps His people from our sowing of the Word; it is He who gives increase.

Our concern in evangelistic efforts should not be whether our neighbor will escape hell through some mechanical exercise of faith in Christ. Our primary concern should be that our neighbor hears from our lips, and especially from our hearts, the immensely glorious majesty of God in the creation of all things visible and invisible, and also in the creation of the new, redeemed, God-approved man. The reason why we evangelize must be rooted first in the Scriptures and second in emotions that flow from the Scriptures. Our primary motive should not be our own man-centered, humanistic desire for all to be saved without exception. Our primary motive must be the holiness and Glory of God, and only then the salvation of man who is evil by nature and deserves only to be separated from the Holy One whom he hates (John 7:7).

A DEADLY SMELL—THE FIRST CONSEQUENCE OF EVANGELIZATION

The first implication of evangelism for the Glory and goodness of God is that the whole of creation, including the angels, testifies that those who were not written in the Book of Life from the beginning are without excuse, because they reject the Savior Jesus Christ and the power of God to save (Rom. 9:22): *"...**to one a fragrance from death to death**"* (2 Cor. 2:16a). These willfully refuse to think, to know, to see, to hear, and to accept the unsearchable presence of God: *"For what can be known about God is plain to them, because God has shown it to them. For his invisible attributes, namely, his eternal power and divine nature, have been clearly perceived, ever since the creation of the world, in the things that have been made. **So, they are without excuse**"* (Rom. 1:19-20). God leaves the reprobate at the mercy of their willfulness, passively hardening them, allowing them to remain blind, and ultimately glorifying His power over them (Rom. 9:22) as He condemns their active, willful unbelief.

Sin is not believing in Christ (John 16:9). Outside of Christ, there is only evil, pride, and selfishness, all of which "glorify" the natural man (Rom. 8:7). Suppression of this evil, the negation of this negative, is a good that glorifies God (Ps. 136:17-18). Heaven exults in God's righteousness and loudly calls for the condemnation of the wicked: *"They* [God's elect in heaven] *cried out with a loud voice, 'O Sovereign Lord, holy and true, how long before you will judge and avenge our blood on those who dwell on the earth?'"* (Rev. 6:10). *"After this I heard what seemed to be the loud voice of a great multitude in heaven, crying out, 'Hallelujah!* ***Salvation and glory and power belong to our God****, for his judgments are true and just; for he has judged the great prostitute who corrupted the earth with her immorality, and has avenged on her the blood of his servants* [His Church, the royal priesthood]'" (Rev. 19:1-2).

In the heart of the natural man is an active antichrist (2 John 1:7) since he denies that Christ, the Son of Man and Son of God, came in the flesh to save His lost people. We direct evangelism to this natural man; when we evangelize, we preach the Word of God, which is always efficacious by God's power, whether it falls on fertile soil or on rock: *"...so shall my word be that goes out from my mouth; it shall not return to me empty, but it shall accomplish that which I purpose, and shall succeed in the thing for which I sent it"* (Isa. 55:11). Evangelism, the proclamation of the Scriptures, softens the hearts of God's elect and hardens the hearts of others: *"What then? Israel failed to obtain what it was seeking. The elect obtained it* [received new hearts], *but the rest were hardened* [God withdraws from them]" (Rom. 11:7).

Luther said something to this effect: "When the sun shines on a lump of wax, it softens, melts, and becomes pliable. When the sun shines on a lump of clay, it hardens and becomes brittle. It is similar when the same gospel shines on the hearts of the elect and the non-elect. One heart becomes more pliable, the other more hardened."

Through His people, God preaches the gospel to all, including those who are not of His flock. In so doing, He convicts them of actively hardening themselves against the life-giving gospel of Christ. There are many Scriptures in which God passively hardens the hearts of unbelievers, leaving them at the mercy of their fallen "free" will. The doctrine of God's rejection is most unpopular in many churches, yet it is clearly the message and truth of the Bible. For example, Joshua describes the kings of Canaan who attacked Israel: *"For it was the LORD's doing to harden* [passively] *their hearts that they should come against Israel in battle, in order that they should be devoted to destruction and should receive no mercy but be destroyed, just as the LORD commanded Moses"* (Josh. 11:20). This hardening of the hearts of the kings of Canaan came from the Lord. God hardened them, withdrew from them, and left them to their "free" will—their willfulness controlled by Satan.

Exactly the same principle applies when reprobate man, left to his own devices, hardens himself against the gospel of Christ and gives himself to his Satan-enslaved "free" will: *"Though he* [Christ] *had done so many signs before them, they still did not believe in him, so that the word spoken by the prophet Isaiah might be fulfilled: 'Lord, who has believed what he heard from us,* ***and to whom has the arm of the Lord been revealed?'*** *Therefore, they could not believe. For again Isaiah said,* ***'He has blinded their eyes and hardened their heart*** [the LORD has withdrawn from them, withholding 'salvation and faith'], ***lest they see with their eyes, and understand with their heart, and turn, and I would heal them.'*** *Isaiah said these things because he saw his glory and spoke of him* [Christ]*"* (John 12:37-41).

As we have just read, the first consequence of evangelizing for the Glory and goodness of God is that we preach even to those whom God has blinded and denied the faith. Isaiah had already proclaimed this truth so difficult to accept (Isa. 6:9-10), precisely because he saw God's Glory, goodness and power in the hardening of their hearts (Ex. 33:19; Rom. 9:22), for he was speaking of none other than Christ. Paul affirms the same principle in a parallel verse: *"What then? Israel failed to obtain what it was seeking. The elect obtained it, but the rest were hardened, as it is written, '**God gave them a spirit of stupor, eyes that would not see and ears that would not hear, down to this very day**'"* (Rom. 11:7-8).

Isaiah, John, and Paul clearly teach in the preceding verses (Isa. 6:9-10; John 12:37-41; Rom. 11:7) that it is God who allows the reprobate to remain in their natural state, where they cannot think, see, or hear. God allows them to reject the gospel and thus to harden themselves progressively under Satan's spirit until the day of judgment. Those who preach the gospel are fragrance from death to death to those whose minds God has dulled (2 Cor. 2:16a). Those who preach the gospel are reigning with Christ between His two comings (Rev. 20:6), so their testimony cannot fail to judge. According to the gospel, they bind what heaven has bound and loose what heaven has loosed (Matt. 18:18).

Scripture is clear, stating in more than one place that no one is seeking God: *"The LORD looks down from heaven on the children of man, to see if there are any who understand, who seek after God. They have all turned aside; together they have become corrupt; **there is none who does good, not even one**"* (Ps. 14:2-3). *"as it is written: 'None is righteous, no, not one; no one understands; **no one seeks for God**'"* (Rom. 3:10-11). Therefore, the gospel of Jesus Christ must be preached to the whole world; all must hear it (Rom. 10:12-17). Even God's elect, in their natural state, are characterized by the ungodly qualities just mentioned.

A LIFE-GIVING FRAGRANCE—THE SECOND CONSEQUENCE OF EVANGELIZATION

The second consequence of evangelism that is for the Glory and goodness of God is that all of creation, including the angels, witnesses God's elect being drawn to Christ through the Spirit of God, by the Father for His Glory: "*...to the other* [we are] ***a fragrance from life to life****. Who is sufficient for these things?*" (2 Cor. 2:16b). God is glorified in His elect through His active mercy, forgiveness, and compassion; this is His Glory, His goodness: "*And when he* [the Lamb] *had taken the scroll, the four living creatures and the twenty-four elders fell down before the Lamb, each holding a harp, and golden bowls full of incense, which are the prayers of the saints. And they sang a new song, saying, 'Worthy are you to take the scroll and to open its seals, for you were slain, and by your blood you ransomed people for God from every tribe and language and people and nation* [Christ did not redeem all without exception, He redeemed all without distinction whom the Father gave Him], ***and you have made them a kingdom and priests to our God****, and they shall reign on the earth* [for a long, figurative period—symbolized as 1,000 years—between the two appearances of Christ; that is, to reign and judge by the gospel (1 Cor. 6:2), and to bind or loose on earth what God has bound or loosed in heaven (Matt. 18:18)]'" (Rev. 5:8-10).

The apostle Paul knew that his evangelistic efforts, which in the positive sense were a life-giving fragrance leading to life, would not be efficacious for all: "***Therefore I endure everything*** [the afflictions of those to whom I am a deadly fragrance] ***for the sake of the elect****, that they* [the elect] *also may obtain the salvation that is in Christ Jesus with eternal glory*" (2 Tim. 2:10).

Like Paul, our mission is to proclaim to all people (without exception) the excellency of God and the substitutionary sacrifice of Christ on the Cross. We proclaim this gospel in the love we have for Christ, not for ourselves. We proclaim it as if all who hear it are elect, for we do not know who belongs to the people of God. We will suffer for our proclamation, and endure afflictions for the sake of the elect, as Paul did. We pray for all who will hear it, with sincere concern and love, knowing that only God the Holy Spirit can save. If we could convince some by our eloquence, they would surely end up in hell.

The Lord Jesus Christ applied His atoning sacrifice only to the elect, declaring: ***"I was sent only to the lost sheep*** [His elect] ***of the house of Israel*** [Israel of God; Gal. 6:16; Eph. 2:12]" (Matt. 15:24b). Immediately after this statement, Jesus healed the demon-possessed daughter of the Canaanite woman. The faith of the woman was great—figuratively speaking (like a dog) she had wanted to feed on the crumbs of bread, the gospel "crumbs" of Christ falling from the table of the children of God, that is, the Israel of God (Matt. 15:25-28). In essence, Jesus was showing that the lost sheep of God's people Israel included this Gentile woman. He came into the world to save His people, and this woman was included.

By Adamic nature, every human being without exception is spiritually dead by birth. However, this does not mean that every person without exception is a lost sheep. The Lord Jesus clearly defined His lost sheep from the Israel of God when He told the Pharisees: *"...but you do not believe* ***because you are not among my sheep****"* (John 10:26). The lost sheep of Jesus, whom the Father draws to Christ through the Holy Spirit, are all the elect for whom He came into the world (Matt. 15:24b). Christ came not only to save elect ethnic Jews, but also to save the elect among the Gentiles. It follows that the lost, perishing sheep for whom Christ was sent, Jew or Gentile without distinction, belong to the House of Israel of God (Gal. 6:16; Eph. 2:12).

Since in the mystery of God we do not know who belongs to His flock, who has been written in the Book of Life from the beginning, we approach all with the gospel of Christ, as if they were written in the Book of Life. Some will never be saved because they are not of Christ's flock; these were never known by God and consequently will never believe. But God circumcises the hearts of some, and opens their eyes and ears, specifically drawing them out of Satan's prison; only these will believe: *"No one can come to me* ***unless the Father who sent me draws him****. And I will raise him up on the last day"* (John 6:44).

11

WILL CHILDREN WHO DIE PREMATURELY BE SAVED?

THE UNIVERSAL SALVATION OF CHILDREN IS NOT MENTIONED IN SCRIPTURE

INTRODUCTION TO THE ISSUE

The question of the salvation of deceased infants, whether in the womb or already born, or of people who are mentally ill from birth is one of the most difficult issues that Christians face. This question is especially concerning for believers who have experienced the trauma of the death of their child. Are these children welcomed into the Kingdom of Heaven? Many theologians, especially those from denominations that baptize children, believe that they are. However, Scripture nowhere explicitly reveals universal salvation for deceased children, or for those who are mentally ill from birth. The belief that they all belong to God is deduced—secondarily derived from the broader context of Scripture and a few verses. We should be thankful that the Holy Spirit did not breathe out Scripture texts that explicitly teach the salvation of prematurely born children as this assurance would have surely been abused by religious zealots, killing them to save them from the pitfalls of a sinful world and assure them of ascending to God in heaven.

Many Christian theologians argue that there is an age of accountability, when the child begins to discern good from evil, Christ from the Devil. They believe that if children die before the age of accountability, they will be saved. However, this kind of argument inherently fits into a Pelagian, Semi-Pelagian, or Arminian theological framework.

My position regarding the salvation of prematurely deceased children or of mentally handicapped persons must therefore be that God's holy nature cannot err, and we must therefore be satisfied with the biblical statement that the hidden thing belongs to God, but the things revealed belong to us (Deut. 29:29). From before the foundation of the world—long before conception—every person either belongs to God or does not belong to God: "*...though they were not yet born and had done nothing either good or bad—**in order that God's purpose of election might continue**, not because of works but because of him who calls—she* [Rebecca] *was told, 'The older will serve the younger.' As it is written, '**Jacob I loved, but Esau I hated**'*" (Rom. 9:11-13). This is the very definition of God's goodness! He has mercy and compassion on whom He pleases (Ex. 33:19). It would not be possible that deceased infants and the mentally handicapped are saved merely because they lack intellectual or spiritual ability. All people, children included, are equal without exception—all are spiritually dead. Intellectual and spiritual abilities do not save us because all are Adam's sinful offspring. I believe that all fallen human being, including deceased infants and the mentally retarded, are saved in the same way—solely and exclusively on the basis of God's sovereign election. We cannot prove on the basis of Scripture whether they are elect, whether

God will forgive their unbelief. Scripture tells us this is necessary for salvation (Mark 16:16)—we should really go no further. Yet all of us (myself included) want to find assurance of their salvation, from a humanistic point of view. Many people (I was one of them) and even theologians find no rest trying to prove what cannot be conclusively proven from Scripture. We will see below the way many wrestle with this issue.

WHAT SCRIPTURE TEACHES ABOUT PEOPLE, AND THEREFORE ABOUT CHILDREN

1. God is in complete control of new life that He creates, as David describes in Psalm 139. God is in control, and He decides every conception, birth, and death. Like everything else, children belong to God; their parents have them "only" temporarily, by God's common grace[73]. The living soul, the whole human being (1 Cor. 15:45), without a doubt, begins at conception: *"Your eyes saw my unformed substance* [yet it was I, David]*; **in your book were written, every one of them, the days that were formed for me**, when as yet there was none of them"* (Ps. 139:16).
2. Children are conceived in sin, not through sin: *"Behold, I was brought forth in iniquity, and **in sin*** [not by sin] ***did my mother conceive me**"* (Ps. 51:5).
3. All people, including children, are descendants of Adam and must therefore die: *"For as **in Adam all die*** [including children], *so also **in Christ shall all be made alive*** [including children]*"* (1 Cor. 15:22). ***"For the wages of sin is death**, but the **free gift of God is eternal life in Christ Jesus our Lord**"* (Rom. 6:23).

73 See chapter 5; section: The Difference Between Prevenient and Common Grace; heading: Common Grace

THE SIN OF SINS

The Bible defines the most basic definition of sin in a succinct but concise way: *"...concerning sin, because* ***they do not believe in me*** [Jesus Christ]*"* (John 16:9). The sin of sins is unbelief—pride, self-centeredness, putting self before God. This pride-motivated sin of striving to be equal with God was first committed by Adam and has subsequently been committed in Adam by each of his fleshly descendants. This original, Adamic sin of sins binds every natural man in unbelief (John 16:9). No natural man can accuse Adam for causing this sin, because his own sin produces in him the same desire for God-equality through pride, and unbelief. Adam longed to be his own god, and every one of his natural descendants has followed in his footsteps: *"I told you that* ***you would die in your sins, for unless you believe*** *that I am he you will die in your sins"* (John 8:24). *"Whoever believes in the Son has eternal life;* ***whoever does not obey the Son shall not see life****, but the wrath of God remains on him"* (John 3:36).

Those who believe in Christ and His cleansing sacrifice on the Cross are forgiven, and only those who are forgiven believe. The one who does not believe has not received God's grace. Unbelievers will not have eternal life—will not live in the company of God (John 17:3)—but will exist in the burning lake in the company of the Devil (Rev. 20:10; 20:15): *"And I saw the dead* [the physically resurrected, but spiritually dead who had not believed in Christ; Dan. 12:2b; Acts 24:15b], *great and small, standing before the throne, and books were opened. Then another book was opened, which is the book of life* [it holds names of those who have believed in Christ and have been pardoned]. *And the dead* [spiritually dead] *were judged by what was written in the books, according to what they had done* [Those who are not partakers of grace will be judged by their deeds]*"* (Rev. 20:12).

DERIVED ARGUMENTS TO PROVE THE SALVATION OF CHILDREN

The argument of those who believe in universal salvation for children is that young children cannot tell the difference between right and wrong, cannot distinguish what it is to believe or not believe in Christ's salvation. Until they reach a certain age of maturity and responsibility, they cannot understand the eternal consequences of unbelief and evil deeds that have accompanied them from birth. They cannot understand "salvation and faith" in the way that a person who "knows good from evil, Christ from the Devil" can (as Pelagianism, Semi-Pelagianism, and Arminianism teach). The child sins, but has no concept of sin; he has no concept of the punishment he deserves. The child has little concept of Jesus Christ, much less of Christ's substitutionary death, which alone can save him, and so on. Until a certain age, a child is not mature enough to be responsible for the sin of sins, that is, for his active, willful unbelief.

According to these arguments, infants who die prematurely and all who are mentally retarded from birth cannot be judged before the judgment seat of Christ on the last day based upon their unbelief in Jesus Christ, which is the sin of sins (John 16:9). Nor can they be judged on the basis of evil deeds they could not "see" or did not commit because of their short lives (Rev. 20:12). Therefore, many Christians believe that prematurely deceased children and the mentally handicapped will yet be saved in the only way possible, which is through the death of Jesus Christ on the Cross. They believe that Jesus Christ paid the price for their sin on the Cross by bearing the wrath of God not only for those who "could" believe, but also for those who "could not" believe due to physical or mental limitations.

Even some Calvinists, who believe that in God's absolute sovereign love, He chose and predestined to salvation all those whom He willed from eternity, before the foundation of the world

(Rom. 9:18), include those who (in their human judgment) could not discern good from evil, Christ from the Devil. Even though it cannot be proven by Scripture, they assert that God from eternity had mercy on all those whom He predestined to die soon after birth or who were mentally handicapped—choosing them and writing them in His Book of Life for the wonderful purpose of displaying His Glory in them. God does not make mistakes, and He has a purpose in everything. And as in this case, everything will glorify God in the end: *"Jesus answered, 'It was not that this man sinned, or his parents,* ***but that the works of God might be displayed in him****'"* (John 9:3).

Let us take look at a remarkable biblical text often cited by those who believe in the universal salvation of prematurely born children, seeking to deduce their argument from Scripture. Interestingly, the preacher in this verse argues that even the soul of an dead fetus is better off than a successful, long-lived person who has not known God: *"If a man fathers a hundred children and lives many years, so that the days of his years are many, but his soul is not satisfied with life's good things* [true good is in Christ alone], *and he also has no burial,* ***I say that a stillborn child is better off than he.****"* (Eccles. 6:3).

We must add that, while deduced arguments like this seem convincing to many, Scripture does not explicitly teach the universal salvation of children.

ARGUMENTS THAT DO NOT PROVE THE SALVATION OF CHILDREN

In the next three headings, I will try to explain why I believe that the verses often cited in Bible literature as proof that prematurely born children are universally redeemed by the blood of Christ are not referring to physical infants, but to spiritual, believing children of God, that is, to adults who are elect, to those who are "saved and believe." In all the verses quoted in this section, verses that refer to children, babes and little ones, nowhere is there a promise of the universal salvation of little children, as many interpret them. The terms children, babes, little ones, and insignificant ones serve only as a type, a physical prefiguration of the spiritual reality, i.e., the born-again, spiritual child who has been reborn of the Spirit and brought into the marvelous light of Christ, and now belongs to God.

A LITTLE CHILD: A TYPE OF THE BELIEVING CHILD OF GOD

Who are these children, babes, little ones, that the Scriptures so often mention? Is Scripture really teaching about literal children who are saved while in a position of immaturity, physical infirmity, and spiritual ignorance? Or is Scripture pointing to children as a type of those who are born-again of the Spirit of God into the kingdom of God, in childlike littleness? *"Now they were bringing even infants to him that he might touch them. And when the disciples saw it, they rebuked them. But Jesus called them to him, saying, 'Let the children come to me, and do not hinder them,* ***for to such belongs the kingdom of God****. Truly, I say to you,* ***whoever does not receive the kingdom of God like a child shall not enter it****'"* (Luke 18:15-17). Jesus is saying here that the kingdom of God belongs to such children who are born-again of the Spirit of God. Fleshly newborn children are being used by Jesus as a type of the spiritual newborn. Jesus was not teaching that adults should receive the kingdom of God in the same way as literal infants or small children, because small children do not understand the nature of the kingdom of God and cannot therefore receive it. On the other hand, an infant is a perfect example of helplessness and trust. The kingdom of God, then, belongs to those who, like little children who are totally dependent on their parents, respond to the Savior in childlike dependence. Just as a carnal child relies on his parents for everything, so the spiritual "child" must rely on his spiritual Father-God. Childlike trust in parents and inability to care for oneself—not childish ignorance—must be the essential characteristic of all born-again, promised, spiritual children of the kingdom of God (Matt. 18:1-4; Mark 9:33-37; Luke 9:46-48): *"At that time the disciples came to Jesus, saying, 'Who is the greatest in the kingdom of heaven?' And calling to him a child, he put him in the midst of them and said, 'Truly, I say to you,* ***unless you turn and become like children, you will never enter the kingdom of heaven.*** *Whoever humbles himself like this child is the greatest in the kingdom of heaven'"* (Matt. 18:1-4). Once again, Jesus uses the image of the little child to describe the personal helplessness, weakness, dependence, humility, and smallness of the Spirit-born, new child of God. The little child is not omniscient, does not exalt himself above his parents, and will not take a step without his parents. Try to take the little one away from his mother. The moment the mother is out of sight, the child will panic, cry, and desperately seek the only security he knows. Who can comfort him? In his helplessness and insignificance, the child trusts his parents in everything, looks to them for security, and shows his feelings and his complete dependence on them.

As desperate as a little child, every Christian should panic when he loses contact with his heavenly Father for any reason. The following verse describes the dependence of God's people on God and has nothing to do with the assurance of salvation of little children: *"Whoever receives you* [whoever believes the gospel which you preach] *receives me* [Jesus Christ], *and whoever receives me receives him* [the Father] *who sent me. The one who receives a prophet because he is a prophet will receive a prophet's reward, and the one who receives a righteous person because he is a righteous person will receive a righteous person's reward.* ***And whoever gives one of these little ones*** [who receives a prophet or a righteous man] ***even a cup of***

***cold water because he is a disciple**, truly, I say to you, he will by no means lose his reward"* (Matt. 10:40-42). When Jesus speaks of little children here, He is not referring to carnal, little children. He is speaking of those who receive Him as Christ, through the testimony of a prophet or a righteous man. He is speaking of those who are blessed because they know in their human spirit that they are little and poor (Matt. 5:3) but they are rich in the Spirit of the Father (James 2:5). It is like when a little child says, "My daddy knows everything." And he who feeds these little ones spiritually, or even physically, will certainly not lose his reward.

*"At that time Jesus declared, 'I thank you, Father, Lord of heaven and earth, that you have hidden these things from the wise and understanding **and revealed them to little children**; yes, Father, for such was your gracious will* [to choose them according to your holy will]'" (Matt. 11:25-26). Thus, the things of the Spirit of God are hidden from the wise and reasonable adults of this world, whether Jewish religious leaders in Jesus' day or educated atheists, agnostics, intellectuals, and liberal preachers and theologians today, who pride themselves on their scholarship and titles. The saving message of the Cross is useless to those who are self-absorbed in their own wisdom and self-identity—all who humanly, anthropocentrically, and independently of God draw wisdom from the world and rely on themselves, all who believe only in what they can do for themselves and in what they have, all who are convinced that they have achieved their success and status by their own efforts, who remain blind and unbelieving. Matt. 11:25-26 makes it clear that only a spiritual newborn can begin to understand and receive the things of the Spirit of God, and such ones are often adult in age.

Luke expands on Matthew's testimony: *"In that same hour he rejoiced in the Holy Spirit and said, 'I thank you, Father, Lord of heaven and earth, **that you have hidden these things from the wise and understanding and revealed them to little children;***

yes, Father, for such was your gracious will. All things have been handed over to me by my Father, and no one knows who the Son is except the Father, or who the Father is except the Son and anyone to whom the Son chooses to reveal him'" (Luke 10:21-22). Notice in this verse that Jesus felt the joyful satisfaction and glorification of the Father in the very fact that the Father chooses His children, His little babes, and leaves the wise and prudent of this world in darkness. In the same way, according to the will of the Father, He—Jesus Christ—reveals His gospel only to those whom He desires (Matt. 11:27; Luke 10:22). Every word here affirms the absolute sovereignty of God and the total dependence of man, even men who never admit it in their love for the world.

SEDUCTION OF GOD'S CHILDREN

Small, defenseless children need special protection. Crimes against children are considered among the most serious crimes, not in the eyes of the general public only, but also in the eyes of criminals. Similarly, one of the most serious spiritual crimes is the atheistic or religious seduction of the "little children" of God: "*...but whoever causes one of these* ***little ones*** *who believe in me to sin* [e.g., through atheistic, evolutionary, or religious philosophies that refute the truth that Christ is the last Adam, who is a life-giving Spirit (1 Cor. 15:45)], ***it would be better for him to have a great millstone fastened around his neck and to be drowned in the depth of the sea****. Woe to the world for temptations to sin! For it is necessary that temptations come, but woe to the one by whom the temptation comes* [especially atheistic and religious scholars] "(Matt. 18:6-7)!

Virtually all humanistic educational and media messages, philosophy, and social "science" based on a materialistic-atheistic worldview—virtually all that emanates from the world's prestigious universities—denigrates Scripture and excludes the Creator God of the Bible. The exclusion of the Cross of Christ of philosophical and pseudo-scientific disciplines is a grandiose effort to seduce God's "little ones." None who seduce God's "little ones" with psychobabble and moral relativism will stand before God, but the worst offenders are those who seek to lead God's "little ones" away from Christ with another "gospel" (Gal. 1:8-10), that is, by associating the Cross of Christ with the realm of satanic religious systems. Do we fully realize the disastrous end that will come to the world system with its worldly and religious self-sufficiency and wisdom (Rev. 18:4-10)? *"For the word of* ***the cross is folly to those who are perishing, but to us who are being saved it is the power of God****. For it is written, 'I will destroy the wisdom of the wise, and the discernment of the discerning I will thwart.' ... but we preach Christ crucified, a stumbling block to Jews and folly to Gentiles* [perishing, educated and uneducated Jews and Gentiles throughout the whole world]*"*(1 Cor. 1:18-19,23).

ALL GOD'S CHILDREN ARE SAVED

The Scriptures are not speaking of physical babies, but of little children of God whom the gates of hell can never overcome because they are saturated in the Spirit with the coherent, biblical Word of God, those who break bread and drink the fruit of the vine in remembrance of Him. In themselves, these "little ones" are helpless and poor in spirit (Matt. 5:3), but in Christ they are invincible, rich in the Spirit of God (James 2:5). They sit in the heavenly places and reign with Christ[74]. They are protected from the seductions of the Evil One and can stand as a bulwark against the doctrines of the Devil and all the ministers of evil: ***"Out of the mouth of babies and infants*** [the mouth of all who are in Christ], *you have established strength because of your foes, to still the enemy and*

74 See SUPPLEMENTS; I. EVANGELISM IN THE REFORMED CONCEPT; section: Generally About Evangelism; heading: God's People Evangelize—Reigning with Christ.

the avenger [the Devil]" (Ps. 8:2). And it is to this Davidic verse that Jesus points the Jewish chief priests and scribes, referring to the chosen remnant, the children of God, the children of Israel, when they recognize Christ as the Son of David in the temple: *"But when the chief priests and the scribes saw the wonderful things that he* [Jesus] *did,* ***and the children crying out in the temple, 'Hosanna to the Son of David!'*** [God's elect children, as they recognize Christ] *They were indignant, and they said to him, 'Do you hear what these are saying?' And Jesus said to them, 'Yes; have you never read* [what David wrote in Ps. 8:3], ***'Out of the mouth of infants and nursing babies you have prepared praise'"'*** (Matt. 21:15-16)?

Who today tells of God's glorious, praiseworthy act of salvation? Certainly not little ones who are merely physically small! It is the little ones who are poor in the spirit of the world and rich in the Spirit of God, who rely on the Spirit of God alone. From whom does the world (which these little ones once belonged to) learn of the mighty and saving Cross of Christ? It is from the mouths of "babes and little children" who are now nourished by the gospel of Christ.

Even the Lord Jesus called His disciples little children, yet we know from the context of Scripture that He was not referring to the physical size of His followers, for they were grown men: *"And the disciples were amazed at his words. But Jesus said to them again,* ***'Children****, how difficult it is to enter the kingdom of God'"* (Mark 10:24)! *"****Little children****, yet a little while I am with you. You will seek me, and just as I said to the Jews, so now I also say to you, 'Where I am going you cannot come'"* (John 13:33).

III

HOW TO EXPLAIN THE CAUSE OF ADAM'S FALL?

INTRODUCTION TO THE ISSUE

How do theologians try to explain the connections regarding the causes of both Satan's and Adam's Fall? I hate to bring up this difficult subject; I have always avoided it because it raises more questions than it answers. But dodging the question, "What role did the decision of the Absolute Ruler of the universe play in Adam's Fall?" will not make it go away. It is impossible to derive these causes directly, satisfactorily, and unambiguously from Scripture. I agree with monergism—it is inconceivable that anything, including the fall of Satan and Adam, happened behind God's back. Adam's Fall did not blindside God, forcing Him to come up with Plan B. God superimposed one of His eternal purposes over Adam's Fall: The salvation of His people through the Son of God, in accordance with sovereign will. This occurred in unapproachable light (1 Tim. 6:16) in eternity, "before" it took place in space-time history, as evidenced, for example, by the following verse about the eternal election of God's people: "*...even as he* ***chose us in him*** [in Christ]

before the foundation of the world [In eternity, in the inaccessible light, in the third heaven], *that we should be holy and blameless before him. In love"* (Eph.1:4).

God's eternal purpose to save His people through the crucifixion of His Son is further evidenced by the following verse concerning the election of the Savior before the ages, before the creation of the universe, outside of space-time: *"He* [Christ] *was foreknown before the foundation of the world, and* ***came for your sake*** [for the sake of the elect in Christ, not for the sake of all without exception] *at the end of time* [the Church Age between the two advents of Christ]*"* (1 Pet. 1:20).

Everything that happens in the created world, visible and invisible, is part of God's unique, timeless plan. English has a play on words: History is His story. The following verse confirms this: *"In this last time* [the Church Age] *He has spoken to us in His Son* [Jesus Christ], *whom He appointed heir of all things,* ***through whom also He created the ages*** [epochs, history]*"* (Heb. 1:2). If anything had happened without His knowledge, God would cease to be God. I could stop at this point—stop researching, stop philosophizing, and settle for this: *"As the heavens are higher than the earth,* ***so are my ways higher than your ways****, and my purposes than your purposes"* (Isa. 55:9).

Nevertheless, I can understand why theologians try to unravel the mystery of the Fall. Everything, even the most insignificant, basic, indivisible spiritual or physical particle, is controlled by God, and this includes the fall of Satan and Adam—otherwise God is not God. Everything happens in His "space;" God transcends everything; He is transcendent so He cannot not be present. If we believed He was not involved, we would be deists. We can safely say that God created ages and history, so that He would be most glorified. All the history of the visible and invisible universe has been created by God for Himself, for His sake and for His Glory. God always glorifies Himself in every event, whether good or evil.

Thus, Adam had such a degree of freedom that the choices he made were within the preordained, determined context of the Garden of Eden and God's prohibition against eating of the tree of the knowledge of good and evil (Gen. 2:17), without that freedom being limited in any way by other persons or institutions. Satan tempted, influenced, but could neither limit nor determine Adam's choice. God did nothing to tempt, influence, limit, or determine Adam's choice. Yet Adam's decision was in harmony with God's eternal plan to save His elect through the crucifixion of the Son of God, the Son of Man. Similarly—though not identical to Adam's choice—fallen men make voluntary choices, yet the circumstances leading to those choices are ordained by God. God glorifies Himself through choices for which sinners bear full responsibility, fulfilling His eternal plan (Acts 2:23; 4:27-28)[75].

Believers accept God's ways and permissions as revealed to them through the Scriptures. At times, God creates passively by withdrawing His presence, allowing darkness (1 Sam. 16:14) or evil (Isa. 45:7)[76], to manifest—even though there is not the slightest darkness or evil in Him (1 John 1:5). He shows His power to those who fall into His wrath and are destined for destruction; He shows the riches of His Glory to those on whom He has mercy (Rom. 9:21-24). Let us zoom in on a few "ifs" regarding the Glory of God:

1. If God had not allowed Adam to fall, man would have remained sinless and immortal, for the wages of sin is death (Rom. 6:23). Had Adam and Eve withstood the test and not sinned, glory would have fallen on man; the glorious salvation of God in Jesus Christ, would not have taken place and would

75 See chapter 9; section: Man is Responsible—Compatibilism.

76 See chapter 6.

have been meaningless. God would have had to share the glory with His creation.

2. If God had applied only justice and left all to condemnation, which would have been just, His manifold glory would not have been made manifest. He would have only displayed His glory by suppressing all evil.
3. If God had wanted to exercise only saving grace and save all, He might have prevented Adam's Fall or never subjected him to the test of obedience at all. Then no one would have been chosen, and the Cross of Christ would have been unnecessary. God would have displayed His glory without manifesting His mercy, goodness and justice.
4. One last option remains: God allowed Adam's voluntary Fall. Furthermore, He exercised both His justice—even His power in condemnation—and His saving grace, mercy, and compassion by granting "salvation and faith." In this way, God glorified Himself to the utmost, in manifesting His wrath and power over those destined for destruction because of sin and also in manifesting the riches of His Glory over those on whom He had mercy and compassion through the blood of His Son (Rom. 9:21-24; Ex. 33:19).

Again, if it were up to me, I would end up here with the potter (Rom. 9:21-24). Scripture reveals nothing beyond this statement. However, since theologians do not rest but ask virtually unanswerable questions, let us now look at some of their open-ended tongue twisters.

LAPSARIANISM

DEFINITION OF THE TERM

Lapsus (Latin for "lapse, slip, fall, error"). We recognize the root of the word in the term *collapse*. Lapsarianism is thus a theological term that refers to the doctrine of man's fall and salvation. It refers to five irrefutable decrees of God, decrees that are affirmed in Scripture:

- Chosen or left in condemnation.
- The call to salvation.
- The redemption by Christ.
- Allowing to fall.
- Creation of the world and people.

These decisions were made by God's decretive will[77] in eternity, in inaccessible light, in the third heaven, outside of created space-time. Therefore, lapsarianism does not deal with the chronological, temporal sequences of these five decisions, as if they took place one after the other in time. Lapsarianism is concerned with the logical, timeless interrelationships of the superiority and inferiority of these five eternals, parallel, collateral, simultaneous divine decisions.

TERMINOLOGY

First, let us explain the two prefixes. (1) "Infra" means "inferior" or "after," in the logical sense, not in the temporal or spatial sense. (2) "Supra" means "superior" or "before," again in the logical sense, not in the temporal or spatial sense.

Lapsarianism is therefore concerned with this question: "Is God's decision to save His chosen, eternally beloved people inferior (infra) or superior (supra) to God's decision to allow Adam's spiritual and physical fall (collapse)?"

1. INFRALAPSARIANISM—SALVATION "AFTER" THE FALL

God's decision to save is subordinate to the decision to allow Adam's Fall. More clearly, as if "in time," God decided to save

77 See chapter 10; section: God's Will; heading: Degrees of Will.

"after" the Fall. Infralapsarians conclude that God's decision to save must logically be subordinate to God's decision to allow Adam's Fall. According to infralapsarians, God must have called His people to salvation "after" Adam's Fall. If He called His people "before" Adam's Fall, as supralapsarians claim, then we could accuse God of injustice and attribute authorship of sin to Him.

2. SUPRALAPSARIANISM—SALVATION "BEFORE" THE FALL

God's decision to save is superior to the decision to allow Adam's Fall. To put it more clearly, as if "in time," God chose to save "before" the Fall. Supralapsarians conclude that it is necessary for God's decision to save to be logically superior to God's decision to allow Adam's Fall. God's eternal purpose to save some and condemn others necessarily requires the Fall. This fact, however, in no way makes God guilty[78]. God cannot be accused of anything simply from the standpoint of His immensity, indefinability, and the consequent non-judgmentable nature of all His purposes and decisions. Moreover, salvation "before" the Fall fits better with Scripture's description of God's sovereign prerogative to use evil to accomplish His purpose—to glorify Himself in creation and salvation history. God's sovereignty, power, Glory, and goodness in both the destruction of His enemies (which all of us are in Adam) and the salvation of His children (which all in Christ are) require the Fall and sin in order for God to triumph over them, both through the powerful condemnation of God's rejected enemies and through God's sovereign, saving grace and love toward His people. If God's ultimate purpose is to display His Glory in the person and work of the Lord Jesus Christ, and if God's Glory and power include, among many other things, righteous wrath toward sinners, then God's eternal purpose to save His people includes the Fall of Adam. The

78 See chapter 9; section: Man is Responsible—Compatibilism.

physical and spiritual collapse of mankind did not happen behind God's back. God actively foreknew it and passively accomplished it through Adam and Satan. If Adam's Fall had occurred "outside" God's plan, then God would have had to react in surprise to Adam's Fall and had to take some remedial action after the fact.

CONTEMPORARY SUPRALAPSARIANISM

Modern theologians concerned with lapsarianism argue that neither infra- nor supralapsarian traditional schemes follow the logical sequence that governs the realization of any intention. The procedure we use in every intention is as follows:

1. We determine the ultimate goal we wish to achieve.
2. We plan all the necessary steps that are necessary to achieve our ultimate goal, from the most superior to the most inferior.

Let us look at an example of a logical sequence of simultaneous decisions, from most superior to most inferior. We follow this process in making dozens of decisions every day, with variations that depend upon the immediate context in which we find ourselves. This type of process in decision making cannot be avoided:

1. I want to visit Australia. (i.e. the primary, most superior, overriding intention).
2. I want to fly there.
3. I need to buy a ticket.
4. I need money for a ticket.
5. I have to work to earn and save money for the ticket.

The process of these five decisions seems to occur simultaneously, with the collateral steps in sync with the primary steps, but their order, from the most superior to the most inferior, seems logically fixed and unchangeable at the end of the decision. However, in fact, in chronological time and space, in the way history unfolds, my seemingly "concurrent" logical decisions proceed in exactly the reverse order, from most inferior to most superior:

1. I work, earn, and save money for airfare.
2. I have money for airfare.
3. I purchase a ticket.
4. I fly to Australia.
5. I am in Australia. (i.e. the primary, most superior, overriding intention is the last to be fulfilled in time and space.)

From this example, we see that the logical, primary, supreme purpose is the last to be fulfilled in space-time history. But what if God's primary, supreme purpose was to show His wrath and reveal His power? What if God also wanted to show His love and the riches of His Glory to those on whom He has mercy, those whom He had prepared for glory beforehand? *"What if God, desiring to show his wrath and to make known* ***his power****, has endured with much patience vessels of wrath prepared for destruction, in order to make known the riches of* ***his glory*** *for vessels of mercy, which he has prepared beforehand for glory"* (Rom. 9:22-23). Thus, the existence of sinners becomes necessary in God's ultimate purpose; the fall of all men in Adam is essential. And thus, we arrive at supralapsarian, the logical—not chronological—sequence of God's decisions, again from most superior to most inferior:

1. God's purpose: to reveal to all creation His Glory in the salvation of the elect and His power in the righteous wrath and condemnation of the reprobate (Rom. 9:22-23)—His primary, most superior, overriding purpose.
2. God's election: to give the saving grace of Christ to elect sinners.

3. God's decision: to redeem elect sinners through Christ's suffering on the Cross.
4. God's choice: to allow the Fall of all in Adam.
5. God's choice: to create a perfect world and perfect man.

Note well that below, in the spatial-temporal history of the world, in what seems to be God's "simultaneous," and "concurrent" logical purpose, His election, decisions and choices unfold in reverse order, from the most inferior to the most superior—just as our ordinary life choices do:

1. God choice: creating a perfect world and man.
2. God choice: allowing the Fall of man in Adam.
3. God decision: redeeming the elect sinners through Christ's suffering on the Cross.
4. God election: giving the saving grace of Christ to elect sinners.
5. God purpose: ultimately revealing His Glory to all creation in the salvation of the elect and His power in the righteous wrath and condemnation of the reprobate (Rom. 9:22-23)—His primary, most superior, overriding purpose will be the last to be fulfilled in time and space.

AN OVERVIEW OF THE FIVE LAPSARIAN VIEWS

I will conclude with the five major lapsarian views in a clear, tabular format. Each viewpoint is identified by a Roman numeral and its name in columns. The degree of superiority and inferiority of each of God's eternal decisions is indicated by the Arabic numeral in the rows[79]:

79 Modified from www.monergism.com and https://www.thegospelcoalition.org/essay/lapsarian-views/

	FIVE VIEWS ON THE FIVE ETERNAL DECISIONS OF GOD FROM MOST SUPERIOR TO MOST INFERIOR				
	I. Current SUPRA-LAPSARIANISM (Reformed)	**II.** Traditional SUPRA-LAPSARIANISM (Reformed)	**III.** Traditional INFRA-LAPSARIANISM (Reformed)	**IV.** AMYRALDISM "four-point" Calvinism	**V.** ARMINIANISM
1.	God's decree of election and condemnation of sinners, so that God may glorify Himself in the elect and show His power in the reprobate (Rom. 9:22-23).	God's decree to predestine the elect to eternal life, with Christ as their head, and to predestine the reprobate to damnation for their sins, all to the praise of His glory.	God's decree to create the world for His glory.	God's decree to create the world and (all) men.	God's decree to create the world.
2.	God's calling the elect to salvation	God's decree to create the world.	God's decree to permit the Fall.	God's decree that (all) men would fall.	God's foreknowledge of the Fall.
3.	God's decree to redeem the elect through the work of Christ on the Cross.	God's decree to permit the fall of mankind.	God's decree to elect certain fallen people to salvation by grace in Christ and reprobate others to just condemnation.	God's decree to redeem (all) men by the Cross work of Christ.	God's decree to send His Son as Savior for those who repent, believe, and persevere.
4.	God's decree to permit the Fall.	God's decree to send His Son and Spirit to save the elect.	Redemption of the elect through Christ	God's election of some fallen men to salvation (and the reprobation of the others).	God's decree to provide means to enable repentance and faith.
5.	God's decree to create the world.			God's decree to apply Christ's redemptive benefits to the elect.	God's foreknowledge of which individuals will repent and believe.
6.					God's decree to save those who believe, do good works, and persevere, and to condemn those who do not.

We must still keep in mind that these are only theological, lapsarian systems. The Holy Spirit is silent in Scripture on this point. If I had to choose, Column I—contemporary supralapsarianism—is certainly the most defensible. God is a rational Being, and that throughout history He has carried out His purposes from the most inferior decisions—the creation of the world, the earth, and humans—to the most superior one—glorifying Himself in salvation and manifesting His power in reprobation (Rom. 9:22-23). Similarly, He also created this principle in all men who are made in His image. Column I, contemporary supralapsarianism, fits this principle seamlessly as it unfolds in reverse sequence throughout history, as we are witnessing today:

1. Creation of the world and human beings.
2. Allowing the Fall.
3. The redemption of the elect through Christ.
4. The calling of the saved to salvation.
5. The election and reprobation of sinners, so that God may be glorified in the elect and His power displayed in the reprobate.

On the other hand, Column V—Arminianism does not satisfy this assumption at all, for it reverses the sequence of God's eternal, parallel, simultaneous, collateral decrees from that of contemporary supralapsarianism. This is because Arminianism relies on the free will of sinners to make decisions that involve God's Spirit. It is as if events are unfolding behind God's back—as though He were constrained, obligated to respect the decisions of sinners, and required to adjust His plan accordingly.

In conclusion, I must say that in this world I do not know and will never know why and how God allowed the Fall of Satan and Adam, how He made His sovereign decision to allow evil. For His sake. He has not told us much about this in Scripture—the world in which we live is His domain, His field of operation, and thus beyond our comprehension. God has not granted us clear understanding of this issue. The only thing I can be sure of is that God has created the history that will most glorify Him. I trust Him completely, and I know that we have gained infinitely more in Christ's salvation than we lost in Adam's Fall.

ABBREVIATIONS

BIBLICAL

ESV—English Standard Version
KJV—King James Version
GNV—New Geneva Study Bible
WEB—World English Bible
YLT—Young's Literal Translation

TEXT

Square brackets [ ]—text or commentary inserted by the author

LITERATURE USED

- *Catechism of the Catholic Church*
- *MacArthur John: New Testament, Verse by Verse Commentary*
- *Mathison: Dispensationalism Rightly Dividing People of God*
- *Owen John: Life by His Death*
- *Schaff Phillip: The Creeds of Christendom, Volume 3, Baker Books, Grand Rapids, 1996, pp 545ff.*
- *Sproul R. C.: Willing to Believe*
- *Sproul R. C.: Chosen by God*
- *Sproul R. C.: Grace Unknown*
- *Steele D. N.: Thomas, C. C., The Five Points of Calvinism*
- *Stevenson: Systematic Theology*
- *Webster's Dictionary*

Printed in the United States
by Baker & Taylor Publisher Services